Quick Hits for Teaching with Technology

Quick Hits for Teaching with Technology

SUCCESSFUL STRATEGIES BY AWARD-WINNING TEACHERS

Edited by

ROBIN K. MORGAN and **KIMBERLY T. OLIVARES**

Contributing Editors

MARCIA D. DIXSON, ANDREW D. GAVRIN, MICHAEL C. MORRONE, JOAN ESTERLINE LAFUZE, and **ANASTASIA S. MORRONE**

Foreword by

MICHAEL A. MCROBBIE

INDIANA UNIVERSITY PRESS
Bloomington and Indianapolis

This book is a publication of

Indiana University Press
601 North Morton Street
Bloomington, Indiana 47404-3797 USA

iupress.indiana.edu

Telephone orders   800-842-6796
Fax orders   812-855-7931

♾ The paper used in this publication meets the minimum requirements of
the American National Standard for Information Sciences—Permanence of
Paper for Printed Library Materials, ANSI Z39.48-1992.

Manufactured in the United States of America

Cataloging information is available from the Library of Congress

1 2 3 4 5 17 16 15 14 13 12

CONTENTS

3 Enhancing Evaluation   63

4 Becoming More Efficient   87

FOREWORD

I am delighted to welcome you to *Quick Hits for Teaching with Technology*, a publication of Indiana University's Faculty Colloquium on Excellence in Teaching (FACET). The current volume, like its predecessors, offers an accessible and user-friendly collection of approaches, strategies, and tactics for effective instruction, developed by master teachers both within Indiana University and across the nation. The volume explores both the advantages and potential pitfalls of using technology in the classroom.

The importance of technology to the teaching and research missions of IU cannot be overstated. As the Principles of Excellence explain, IU is committed both to adopting "innovative modes of teaching and learning that improve the educational attainments of students," and to ensuring that "information technology is pervasively deployed at IU by leveraging and continuing the support of the university's long-standing and internationally recognized excellence in information technology services and infrastructure." Excellence in the use of technology in instruction is therefore a natural subject for an IU publication on excellence in teaching.

This volume is particularly timely because information technology, both inside and outside of the classroom, is a rapidly moving target. Current and future faculty will be expected to adapt to this fluid environment in order to maximize their effectiveness when using technology as a teaching tool. The current generation of students, reared on information technology and often more comfortable with it than their instructors, increasingly expect a technologically sophisticated academic environment.

One challenge facing university faculty will be to ensure that injecting technology into the classroom doesn't merely represent the latest "bells and whistles," but that such innovations prove their worth pedagogically. In this volume of *Quick Hits*, seasoned instructors, representing a multitude of academic disciplines, describe their innovative efforts to use various technologies to achieve effective, course-specific learning objectives.

The use of technology in education inevitably demands that we return to fundamental questions about pedagogy — always a healthy undertaking. Virtually all aspects of course development and delivery can be altered by the technology available to faculty today. As discussed by the authors of this volume's entries, the adoption of technology by faculty will require careful planning, identification of educational goals, anticipation of possible unintended consequences, and ongoing assessment of student learning. These are familiar issues, but the use of new technologies gives them added urgency. *How and how much technology should I bring into the course or the classroom? Should I teach an online course or a hybrid? Will distance learning lead to the same outcomes as face-to-face teaching? Should I test online, and if I do, how do I ensure the integrity of the students' work? Do online chat rooms and discussion forums afford the same kind of active learning as in-class group work?* And these are but a sample of the appropriate and unavoidable concerns that instructors confront as technology becomes an expected part of the educational experience. The purpose of this volume is to equip instructors to identify and answer these questions as they relate to the technologies of today and tomorrow.

The speed with which new technologies emerge means that the prospects for large-scale, systematic research on best practices are limited. The fast moving target that is technology, especially in the educational setting, may not stand still long enough to support such in-depth efficacy research, and absolutely will not if we are to be innovators in adoption of these techniques. Thus, the faculty member who chooses to embrace new technology might best think of the classroom as a laboratory, with each topic, assignment and class period an opportunity to learn what works and what does not. Ongoing assessment of student learning outcomes in response to technology related changes in pedagogy is likely to become increasingly important.

In this environment, the advice of colleagues will be particularly valuable in expanding the range of an individual instructor's effective experience with new techniques and technologies. Seeking out colleagues who have adopted similar strategies may prove similarly enlightening. This volume of Quick Hits, authored by award-winning teachers, provides just such counsel. It serves as a jumping off point for exploring the perils and promises of technology in the classroom, and I enthusiastically recommend it to you.

Michael A. McRobbie
President, Indiana University

WELCOME TO
QUICK HITS FOR TEACHING WITH TECHNOLOGY

Twitter, Facebook, smart phones, GPS, Wii, "Angry Birds" ... Students entering the university today are comfortable using technology to communicate with their friends, navigate the world, and as a form of entertainment. Faculty, too, have bridged the seeming 'digital divide' between themselves and students by increasingly adopting technology in their personal lives and to streamline their faculty roles. Few faculty could function without email, course management systems, and word processing programs.

Due partly to this familiarity with technology, faculty have progressively added technology into their courses. The variety of technology being used is simply astounding. However, no matter how much we enjoy the technological tool being used, the addition of specific technological tools in the classroom must focus on the goal of enhanced student learning.

In essence, the individual faculty member is left with quite the tall order. The addition of a technological tool into a course is fraught with obstacles. First, the faculty member must learn how to use the technological tool. Learning a course management system, how to create a podcast, how to use clickers involves a time commitment. Once the technological tool is learned, the faculty member must decide how to utilize that tool in a particular course, changing the course structure, and leading, most likely, to modifications in course assignments. Finally, faculty are being asked to assess that the addition of this technological tool enhances student learning. Of course, all of this must be done in the context of the many other responsibilities – demands for scholarship, service, other classes – confronting the faculty member.

The *Quick Hits* series of books was designed to lessen the burden on the faculty member by providing a concise description of tested teaching experiences. The phrase, 'Quick Hits,' arose during the 1991 Indiana University Faculty Colloquium on Excellence of Teaching (FACET) retreat when several members offered engaging but quick strategies for involving students in learning. These ideas led to the publication of the first volume, *Quick Hits: Successful Strategies by Award Winning Teachers*. Over the years, four additional *Quick Hits* volumes have been published, each addressing contemporary challenges of teaching and learning. The early volumes were authored by members of FACET; subsequent volumes have been authored by a wider range of contributors and have become peer reviewed publications.

The current volume of *Quick Hits for Teaching with Technology* addresses the use of technological tools in the classroom. As in prior volumes of *Quick Hits*, the focus of each submission is describing strategies that have been shown to be successful. The strategies in this volume are organized into four chapters: promoting engagement, providing access, enhancing evaluation, and becoming more efficient. For the first time, this volume of Quick Hits is being published concurrently with the launch of a Quick Hits website (www.quickhitstech.com). This site will allow for a continuing conversation about 'teaching with technology.' Submissions not included in the book will be found on the site, a forum will allow for conversations to continue, and a submission and peer review process will lead to additional Quick Hits relating to teaching with technology. Technology changes quickly; this website provides a forum for innovations in teaching with technology and an outlet for dissemination ideas.

It is our expectation that you will find some of the Quick Hits in this volume to be more applicable to your own teaching efforts than other submissions. Consider which strategies work best with your own teaching style, your level of comfort with technology, and the amount of time you have to devote to modifying your class. Please consider sharing your results on our website or submitting your own Quick Hits for peer review on the website.

Kimberly T. Olivares
FACET Administrative Manager

David J. Malik
Former University Director, Faculty Colloquium on Excellence in Teaching, Indiana University
Chancellor's Professor of Chemistry, Indiana University Purdue University Indianapolis
Executive Vice Chancellor of Academic Affairs, Indiana University Northwest

Robin K. Morgan
University Director, Faculty Colloquium on Excellence in Teaching, Indiana University
Professor of Psychology, Indiana University Southeast

About FACET

The Faculty Colloquium on Excellence in Teaching (FACET) was established as an Indiana University Presidential Initiative in 1989 to promote and sustain teaching excellence. Today, FACET involves over 500 full-time faculty members, nominated and selected through an annual campus and statewide peer review process.

FACET is a community of faculty dedicated to and recognized for excellence in teaching and learning. FACET advocates pedagogical innovation, inspires growth and reflection, cultivates the Scholarship of Teaching and Learning and fosters personal renewal in the commitment to student learning.

INTRODUCTION
STUDENT SUCCESS IS OUR MISSION

David J. Malik
Former University Director, Faculty Colloquium on Excellence in Teaching, Indiana University
Chancellor's Professor of Chemistry, Indiana University Purdue University Indianapolis
Executive Vice Chancellor of Academic Affairs, Indiana University Northwest

Higher education today has been challenged to improve student outcomes and to ensure that our graduates will successfully adapt to an ever-changing workplace. The demand for graduates who possess strengths in both their fields and in their use of technological advancements is increasing. In addition, the accountability movement addresses the demonstration of these talents in our graduates. Our stakeholders have been vocal in the need to establish our claims of talented students on firmer metrics than mere anecdotal stories of our selected, illustrious alumni.

Over the last several decades, university student populations have come to reflect a very different demographic profile. What once was perceived, and likely had been, an elite education available to those with resources and the proper educational background is now replaced with a breadth of diversity that is nearly inspirational. Larger numbers of high school graduates, and returning adults have recognized the potential economic, intellectual, and sociocultural benefits of higher education. Progress in higher education is in transition toward methods of education that are more efficacious and that encompass strategies to enhance the bottom line: student success.

Although the expectation that our students should be learning demonstrable content and skills necessary for lifelong learning is not new, the accountability to a wider range of stakeholders is new. While the specific metrics and tools associated with this assessment are still in debate, we as faculty have great impact on student success. Of course there are institutional policies and practices that affect the rate of change and the level of success achieved, but faculty still have great latitude to make choices and judgments that significantly impact student learning. Higher education can and will adapt to these new expectations. The rate of change is no doubt either hampered or advanced by our institutional environment, but those environments can change. Will all faculty embrace the necessary steps to improve student success? What is apparent is that most faculty *will* identify ways that they can best participate in this transformation. Together, faculty and their institutions will advance to form a more effective structure.

Student learning outcomes can be enhanced or improved through the judicious use of technology. However, technology *per se* is not a panacea for all learning challenges. It is imperative that we correctly exploit the advantages of technology. Technology can facilitate delivery, speed up communication, allow pedagogical variations and methodologies that enhance learning, provide more radical changes for time on task, and enliven and broaden reflection and introspection of concepts and principles among larger groups of students. The faculty role will determine how a technology can be effectively used to advance in-depth understanding. Faculty can connect students to applications to both inspire and motivate, and provide exposure to visual and auditory content not readily available through traditional pedagogies.

What engages faculty to achieve effective teaching?
Chickering and colleagues (1987; 1991; 1996) have developed concepts of good educational practice. Chickering and Gamson (1987) noted these initially, and Chickering and Ehrmann (1996) re-stated them in the context of technology. The latter restated the "Good Practices" as follows:

- Good Practice Encourages Contacts Between Students and Faculty
- Good Practice Develops Reciprocity and Cooperation Among Students
- Good Practice Uses Active Learning Techniques
- Good Practice Gives Prompt Feedback
- Good Practice Emphasizes Time on Task

- Good Practice Communicates High Expectations
- Good Practice Respects Diverse Talents and Ways of Learning

Most faculty did not receive extensive pedagogical training as graduate students. While many new programs have emerged in recent years, such as "Preparing Future Faculty" programs, exposure to and training on specific pedagogies has been pursued inconsistently. Many professional societies now have meeting components that address teaching, but then faculty must choose between attending disciplinary content presentations vs. pedagogical content presentations. Faculty need accessible ideas, or a toolbox of potential strategies, to explore how their courses can be changed and improved with resulting greater student success. In addition, faculty need to anticipate how an innovation might impact their work loads and style of teaching. Faculty need to understand what support exists in their departments, schools, and universities to sustain an innovation long enough to ensure its adequate implementation.

Faculty need time to adapt and adopt some of the newer practices. Department chairs and deans need to accommodate newer practices. Arguments need to be advanced for particular initiatives to gain acceptance, not only by administrators, but by potentially skeptical peers.

Finally, faculty time on these initiatives must be balanced by the value and worth that is extracted from these activities. How do these successes impact faculty roles and rewards? There needs to be well conceived pathways to peer review, dissemination, disciplinary recognition, and impact on others. These attributes define scholarship and are part of the currency of the realm. Faculty incentivization is key to promoting change on the largest scale. When improvements in pedagogy lead to greater student learning and these outcomes can be documented, faculty have identified a link to their own success.

What engages students in the context of technology?
Students learn best when they are engaged, interested, and motivated. Given the extraordinary and imaginative media to which students are regularly exposed, it will be difficult to achieve a comparable level of engagement. The challenge for faculty will be to determine how we can best use those tools to capture their attention. It may not be that it is anything more than a few limited examples of attention-getting activity that can do the trick, but what are those examples?

As a member of the chemistry discipline, I am reminded of those demonstrations done decades ago in my introductory chemistry classes that kept students in rapt attention with any unanticipated outcome. These fostered my own interest in doing similar displays in my courses. I even incorporated some media that would demonstrate similar reactions or explosions for the course.

Motivating students will take a course structure that demonstrates the value of the learning and knowledge, and will need to provide "relevance" to the content. Here, some fields will find this easier than others, but this does not mean there are not real connections. Pragmatism plays a role in this context as well: Is success in the course a vehicle to a specific end? Admission to graduate school? Employment at a special business? Job security? Or is it a vehicle to a more abstract goal? Civic engagement? Personal fulfillment? Improved personal relationships?

Courses that demonstrate a variety of modalities impact the students in unanticipated ways. Given the breadth of student backgrounds, customizing pedagogical devices for different constituencies may be relevant. Since research has demonstrated that all of the senses play a role in retention, faculty and students would be best served by incorporating sight, sound, smell and touch to reinforce particular ideas or concepts. Additionally, special visitors in the classroom can occur by exploiting communications protocols, such as Skype, or FaceTime, or even a custom video.

Blended curricula offer a combination of face-to-face opportunities in concert with online resources, but the online tools can make content more accessible, allow for replay or practice, and can offer more diversity in content delivery. Research has indicated that integration of online innovations or activities do not sacrifice content mastery in students.

Keep in mind that students today have wide disparities in their knowledge and comfort with technology. Especially in adult learners, the time required to adapt to these newer modalities may take practice and persistence. Traditional aged students, raised in a multi-media world, may lack the ability to meaningfully utilize technology for non-entertainment purposes. The variation in age, ethnicity, educational background, and external social pressures may all need to be considered in optimizing the student-teacher interface. Social networking often relieves the stress associated with these differences.

What is valued by our institutions and by future employers?

The individual faculty member today must be in a position to defend his/her approach to student learning. Technology can be used to facilitate some of these new approaches to better learning. We do not need to independently invent the best, new pedagogies; we can gain from the experiences of others. Sharing the techniques used by innovative teachers for improved success is no different from the research model for disseminating discovery. Aligning our educational interests with the institution's obligation to demonstrate efficacy and stewardship of funding is a visible statement of support of the learning mission. This does not require any drift away from our commitments to our disciplines as up to date scholars in our field. If anything, our efforts to improve our ability to better inform the next generation of educated citizens and prepare them for lifelong learning, will support our disciplines.

Realities of student learning: Current thinking in effective pedagogies

There is a sizable repository of literature on student learning, certainly too vast to describe in detail here. However, there are three dimensions of effective pedagogies that play to distinctive role. First, the development of learning offered by Vygotsky and his Zone of Proximal Development (1978) creates an overall paradigm for the progress of learning. Second, collaborative learning, and other active learning strategies, enhance the quality of time on task. Lastly, contemporary neuroscience, as represented in the work by John Medina, can help inform pedagogically sound practice.

Vygotsky introduced the concept of the *Zone of proximal development* (ZPD) which roughly describes a threshold where a student can work independently, through an upper limit of understanding facilitated by a content expert, or other person skilled more technically in collaborative learning strategies. ZPD describes a range of understanding where deeper understanding can be facilitated, or optimized. For optimized learning, the interaction by the assisting person can be moderated to transition the student to higher levels of understanding. The facilitation can occur also with technological intervention, perhaps software that is challenging the student, or active-learning connections that move the understanding to a higher level. To optimize the dialog and reflection by the student, social networking and idea exchange can also assist. The target reality is to move the ZPD to a higher level at the conclusion of a learning session. The ZPD is the focal point of an active or collaborative learning session.

Collaborative and active learning strategies are emerging on multiple fronts of education within a myriad of disciplines and fields. Those in the field of education know that the benefits of collaborative learning have been known for decades, yet seem not to have substantive impact in other fields. In science, these strategies appeared to a large extent in the 1990s but have been relatively slow to be widely embraced, though the science-specific evidence of learning has been reported widely.

Why have the rates of acceptance been so slow? In part, collaborative learning de-emphasizes the role of the faculty member by transferring learning responsibility more toward the student. The actual process or paradigm for active learning involves preparing instructional materials that are suitable for students, placing an increased or new burden on faculty. Most collaborative learning paradigms also have higher instructional costs due to use of student facilitators who have training in collaborative learning strategies.

The effectiveness of collaborative learning may be due to several factors, among them:
- Reflective explorations that approach more in-depth problem solving and concepts
- Students only reinforce non-threatening environment and peer support
- Mutual reinforcement of ideas, concepts, and approaches
- Communication interactions kept dynamic either *in situ* or mediated through technology
- Potential for access at unconventional times that can be mediated by technology

Finally, a recent publication, *Brain Rules* by John Medina (2008), offers a collection of ideas relevant to how we think about brain function impacting education, to wit:
- "Students do not pay attention to boring things": How can we introduce course features that attend to increasing the level of interest in what we do?
- "Strategies to maintain attention bring about better brain coding resulting in better retention, accuracy, and clarity of thought": The Ten Minute Rule suggests a "change up" in the stream in the classroom flow, perhaps using a video clip, change in perspective, or other activity to reinforce thinking and sustain attention.

■ Introduce novel stimuli in the conduct of the course to further engage students. These interventions can include new media, clickers, demonstrations, activities adding sounds and sights, etc. [arousal = attention, orienting network = locating, executive network = response to stimulus]

■ Students benefit from structured organization with the holistic view first (few details), and then progressive details as topics are expanded

Keeping the perspective on scholarship

As we consider all of the possibilities to improve student learning, we should keep in mind faculty advancement and what that means in your own environment. The success and impact of what you do drives your students' success, but also affords the opportunity to advance your own career in your local context. So you need to ask the fundamental question: Can I improve student success and bring a measure of value to my career advancement? In order to answer that, you must ensure you are speaking the same language as your colleagues and institutional administration. What follows are some general statements about ensuring that there is impact on a larger scale that can at least provide some degree of sway with your colleagues.

Most of us would consider the work we do to improve student success impacts our work in the area of "teaching." This usually means not only the routine and innovative components of our teaching portfolio, but also what scholarship supports our work. Simply, a contribution would be considered scholarship if it were an innovative work; has impact on the field, discipline, or the academy; was peer evaluated or reviewed; was disseminated; and could be transferred to other contexts and applications. Appropriate journals or other vehicles for dissemination should be identified, keeping in mind that the actual journal will be assessed by peers. These questions are the same ones applicable for discovery research and many faculty would expect the same type of review. The quality of the peer review is often governed by the publication and who is charged with the review.

Dissemination also occurs through presentations at meetings, special events, or other universities. The discussions and reflections that occur in these public occasions can play an important role in understanding what the weaknesses and strengths of your contribution might be, but also serve to give you new insights into improvements or variations. Know the population that is most impacted by your intervention. If your approach solves an institutional challenge, you may be able to transfer it to other disciplines there.

It is important we not lose sight of the role of peer review. When our work is recognized by others, this recognition serves to advance our reputation, that of our department or school, and bring attention to our institution.

Overall comments: Merging technology with effective pedagogies

As you read *Quick Hits for Teaching with Technology*, think of the innovations that you can institutionalize in your courses and roles. Not all approaches work for all faculty, but the greatest impact on student success follows from those strategies that have your commitment and interest.

Technology can improve learning and sustain engagement, but you do not want the learning to be overwhelmed by the "device" or gadget. Some devices have large overhead in set-up, marginal reliability, and dubious educational value. It is important we not be distracted by fad technology, but understand how a device may favorably impact learning. Technology is most valuable that allows us to more effectively challenge and guide student thinking, contextualize an idea in ways not so accessible by oral communication alone, and to explore predictions or other possibilities.

Technology and simulation can put information readily at hand that would not be available in a static environment: clickers allow us to explore the progress of learning and plot new directions *in situ*, simulation can afford us opportunity to investigate what if scenarios, the new "hypertext" would allow us to explore to greater depth and dimension within our own slides and presentations.

In this volume of *Quick Hits*, the submissions have been organized into four chapters: Promoting Engagement, Providing Access, Enhancing Evaluation and Becoming More Efficient

Promoting Engagement

Research on active learning has solidified the importance of student engagement. Simply put, students who are engaged retain more information and are able to utilize that information in more sophisticated ways. In this section, you will find submissions that focus on how technology – in face-to-face, distributed, hybrid or online classes – can assist in promoting student engagement. These submissions focus on increasing student-to-student as well as faculty-student communication, increasing student effort, enhancing student motivation, and stimulating student interest via new ways of learning.

Providing Access

Technology provides an opportunity to increase access to higher education. For some, coming to a university campus or taking part in traditional university experiences may not be economically feasible. For others, specific learning or physical limitations may make the traditional classroom challenging. In this section, the submissions illustrate the range of technological possibilities that can be utilized to reduce these challenges.

Enhancing Evaluation

Increasingly over the past decade, faculty have confronted the necessity of developing student learning objectives and evaluation measures that specifically address such objectives. Such evaluation measures provide faculty with the ability to determine if students are learning the assigned material as well as suggesting whether the teaching methods being utilized are effective. As the use of technology has spread, faculty must develop methods of evaluation that are effective as well as efficient. The authors of the submissions in this section share their own successes and failures in creating effective methods of evaluation.

Becoming More Efficient

A consistent complaint of university faculty is that they are continually being asked to do more with less. Developing efficient methods for developing effective courses and grading student work is a necessity. The authors of the submissions in this section demonstrate how technology may allow us to become more efficient in our classrooms.

References

Chickering, A. W., & Ehrmann, S. C. (1996). Implementing the seven principles: Technology as lever. *AAHE Bulletin, 49*(2), 3-6.

Chickering, A. W., & Gamson, Z. (1987). Seven principles for good practice in undergraduate education. *AAHE Bulletin, 40*(7), 3-7.

Chickering, A.W., & Gamson, Z.F. (1991). Applying the seven principles for good practice in undergraduate education. *New Directions for Teaching and Learning, Volume 47*, San Francisco: Jossey-Bass Inc.

Medina, J. (2008). *Brain Rules: 12 Principles for Surviving and Thriving at Home, Work, and School*. Seattle, WA: Pear Press.

Vygotsky, L. S. (1978). *Mind in Society: The Development of Higher Psychological Processes*. Cambridge, MA: Harvard University Press.

PROMOTING ENGAGEMENT 1

TECHNOLOGY TRANSFORMING LEARNING

GREGOR NOVAK
PROFESSOR EMERITUS, DEPARTMENT OF PHYSICS
INDIANA UNIVERSITY PURDUE UNIVERSITY INDIANAPOLIS

> *Learning technologies should be designed to increase,*
> *and not to reduce, the amount of personal contact between students and faculty on intellectual issues.*
> *(Study Group on the Conditions of Excellence in American Higher Education, 1984)*

In the May 13, 2011 issue of Science, Louis Deslauriers and colleagues report the results of an interesting experiment conducted at University of British Columbia (Deslauriers, Schelew, & Wieman, 2011). In the words of the authors:

> "We compared the amounts of learning achieved using two different instructional approaches under controlled conditions. We measured the learning of a specific set of topics and objectives when taught by 3 hours of traditional lecture given by an experienced highly rated instructor and 3 hours of instruction given by a trained but inexperienced instructor using instruction based on research in cognitive psychology and physics education. The comparison was made between two large sections ($N = 267$ and $N = 271$) of an introductory undergraduate physics course. We found increased student attendance, higher engagement, and more than twice the learning in the section taught using research-based instruction."

"The instructional approach used in the experimental section included elements promoted by CWSEI and its partner initiative at the University of Colorado: pre-class reading assignments, pre-class reading quizzes, in-class clicker questions with student-student discussion (CQ), small-group active learning tasks (GT), and targeted in-class instructor feedback (IF). Before each of the three 50-min classes, students were assigned a three- or four-page reading, and they completed a short true false online quiz on the reading."

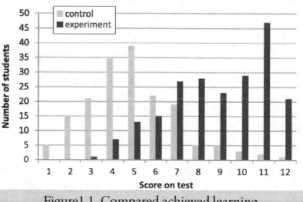

Figure1.1. Compared achieved learning.

The rather striking results of this experiment highlight two important trends that research into teaching and learning has spawned during the past three decades (Bransford, Brown, & Cocking, 2000). The first is the realization that replacing passive environments, even if presided over by charismatic, knowledgeable and engaging presenters, with active student-centered pedagogies leads to superior learning outcomes.

The second trend, without which the first would be much less effective, is the growing use of technology, inside and outside of the classroom.

The key features of the Deslauriers experiment are: pre-class reading assignments, pre-class reading quizzes, in-class clicker questions with student-student discussion, small-group active learning tasks, and targeted in-class instructor feedback. All of these parts carefully aligned with one another and all of it informed by education research. The students were actively involved in carefully planned activities at all times. Technology, supporting the experience in and out-of-class, was brought in as needed by the pedagogy involved. An experiment similar to the one above, but more narrowly focused, was recently conducted at North Georgia College & State University (Formica, Easley, & Spraker, 2010).

Student centered activity-based lessons and the use of information technologies in teaching and learning are work in progress, but the evidence from the classroom indicates that we are on the right track.

The two critical theoretical underpinning of these efforts are constructivism and cognitivism. To learn means to construct meaning rather than memorize facts. Student-instructor, student-student and student-content interactions, facilitated by the use of technology, drive the effort. These interactions encourage students to assume some ownership of and control over their learning, provide realistic and relevant contexts and encourage the exploration of multiple perspectives and metacognition. Cognitive science research into how the human brain processes and stores information provides the theoretical basis for lesson designs. Learning tasks are constructed to engage the learner in the learning process, to scaffold the learning as needed to foster the development of understanding, and to provide timely and meaningful feedback.

Technical tools have been assisting learning since the cave paintings. Arguably, serious large-scale use of the technology in teaching and learning can be traced to the educational films developed for the large number of servicemen returning from WWII. Media-based presentations of educational materials are still with us with Power Point and streaming video and audio. The fifties saw the emergence of two major designs, programmed instruction and mastery approach. In programmed instruction the material to be learned is broken up into small units, incorporating frequent feedback and correction. Mastery approach is based on Bloom's taxonomy of intellectual development.

These forms of instruction have evolved into CAI, computer-based and computer-assisted instruction, still with us today. During the 1980s and 1990s computer environments were developed where learners can build, explore, and immerse themselves in micro-worlds and simulations. Another major step was taken when the world-wide-web was made public in the mid-nineties, paving the way for computer-mediated-communication, CMC, which creates an always-open communication path for student-instructor, student-student and student-content interaction. CMC also provides tools for the maintenance of learning communities and for course and curriculum management. The internet has made possible the creation of distance learning, courses fully online, as well as hybrid designs, such as Just-in-Time Teaching, blending on-line work and in-class activities with live teachers. The next advance is likely to come when the mobile technologies of today are harnessed in the service of teaching and learning (Sharples, Milrad, Arnedillo Sánchez, & Vavoula, 2009). The audience for this is the next generation of students, growing up with these tools (Schachter, 2009). An astounding number of very young children are users of mobile technologies (Gutnick, Robb, Takeuchi, & Kotler, 2010). Seventy-five percent of 5 - 9 yr-olds use cell phones.

There is not much doubt that student-centered instruction, facilitated by available technology, is here to stay in one form or another. The question debated in the educational research community is: how does one optimize the many benefits of the new paradigm: easy access to course materials, improved student motivation and participation (Kulik & Kulik, 1991), differential instruction serving different learning styles, etc. Resource availability and cost issues aside, and there are many, the intellectual challenge is to find the proper balance between technology tools and live human interactions. The pedagogical strategies must follow from evidence-based science of learning or instruction. The past several decades have seen the emergence of discipline-based education research such as PER in physics and a deeper understanding of the learning process through cognitive science research (Bransford, Brown, & Cocking, 2000).

For learning to be effective, the learning activities must be designed to work in harmony with the human cognitive system. Cognitive science can help optimize the delivery of information to the learner by determining what is critical, what is salient and most directly valuable to the cognitive system (Dror, 2008). Cognitive science studies, combined with discipline-based pedagogical research, can help us choose technologies appropriate for the task. Technology can emphasize the relevant with correct use of color and animation for example. Technology can be the servant of the pedagogy or can become the tyrant. Misuse of technology in teaching and learning is not uncommon and hard to guard against (Tufte, 2003; Norvig, 2003). Technology is frequently employed to process larger numbers of students with fewer live instructors. But even in the absence of mercenary motives and with the best intentions, technology can be misapplied. It is tempting to take advantage of technology to let the student loose with the content in the name of ownership and control over the learning process. But research has shown that guided and structured exploration is more effective than free-for-all constructivism. "Minimally guided instruction is less effective and less efficient than instructional approaches that place a strong emphasis on guidance of the student learning process. The advantage of guidance begins to recede only when learners have sufficiently high prior knowledge to provide 'internal' guidance" (Kirschner, Sweller, & Clark, 2006).

How does one go about appropriately incorporating technology into ones teaching? A good start is getting familiar with educational research results, including cognitive science research, of the last three decades. The "How People Learn" book is a good start. The second step would be a good look at the pedagogical research literature in one's discipline so that one would supplement the content knowledge required of an expert with the pedagogical content knowledge required of a teacher (Shulman, 1986). The third step would be a look at the literature, describing currently accepted best practices in the use of technology in teaching. This would include a general reference such as technology for teaching (Norton & Sprague, 2001) as well as technique and tool specific information: simulations (Adams, et. al., 2008), clickers (Caldwell, 2007) or JiTT (Simkins & Maier, 2009). Lastly, one would examine one's personal teaching style and subject matter idiosyncrasies and choose the time and place where to include appropriate technology to best serve the intended learner. These are fun times with major developments taking place in the world of teaching and learning with something to fit every teaching and learning style.

Reference

Adams, W.K., Reid, S., LeMaster, R., McKagan, S.B., Perkins, K.K., Dubson, M., & Wieman, C.E. (2008). A study of educational simulations part I —Engagement and learning. *Journal of Interactive Learning Research*, 19(3), 397-419.

Bransford, J. D., Brown, A. L., & Cocking, R. R. (2000). *How people learn: Brain, mind, experience, and school*. Washington, D.C.: National Research Council, National Academy Press.

Caldwell, J. E. (2007). Clickers in the large classroom: Current research and best-practice tips, *CBE Life Sci Educ*, 6(1), 9-20.

Deslauriers, L., Schelew, E. & Wieman, C. (2011). Improved learning in a large-enrollment physics class, *Science*, 332, 862-864.

Dror, I. E. (2008). Technology enhanced learning: The good, the bad, and the ugly. *Pragmatics & Cognition*, 16(2), 215–223.

Formica, S.P., Easley, J.L. & Spraker, M.C. (2010). Transforming common-sense beliefs into Newtonian thinking through Just-in-Time Teaching. Physical Review Special Topics - *Physics Education Research, 6* .

Gutnick, A.L., Robb, M., Takeuchi, L., & Kotler, J. (2010). *Always connected: The new digital media habits of young children*. New York: The Joan Ganz Cooney Center at Sesame Workshop. Retrieved on July 14, 2011: http://www.joanganzcooneycenter.org/upload_kits/jgcc_alwaysconnected.pdf

Kirschner, P.A., Sweller, J., & Clark, R.E. (2006). Why minimal guidance during instruction does not work: An analysis of the failure of constructivist, discovery, problem-based, experiential, and inquiry-based teaching. *Educational Psychologist*, 41(2), 75–86.

Kulik, C. C., & Kulik, J. A. (1991). Effectiveness of computer-based instruction: An updated analysis. *Computers in Human Behavior*, 7, 75-94.

Norton, P., & Sprague, D. (2001). *Technology for teaching*. Boston: Allyn and Bacon.

Norvig, P. (2003). *The Gettysburg PowerPoint presentation*. Retrieved on July 14, 2011: http://norvig.com/Gettysburg/

Schachter, R. (2009). *Mobile devices in the classroom: Phones, netbooks and iPods are finding a place in the curriculum and expanding student access to technology*. Retrieved on July 14, 2011: http://www.districtadministration.com/viewarticle.aspx?articleid=2198

Sharples, M., Milrad, M., Arnedillo Sánchez, I., & Vavoula, G. (2009). Mobile learning: Small devices, big issues. In N. Balacheff, S. Ludvigsen, T. De Jong, A. Lazonder, & S. Barnes (Eds). *Technology Enhanced Learning: Principles and Products*. Heidelberg: Springer.

Shulman, L. (1986). Those who understand: Knowledge growth in teaching. *Educational Researcher*, 15(2), 4-14. Retrieved on July 14, 2011: http://www.leeshulman.net/domains-pedagogical-content-knowledge.html

Simkins, S., & Maier, M. (Eds). (2009). *Just-in-Time Teaching across the Disciplines and across the Academy*. Sterling, VA: Stylus Publishing.

Tufte, E. (2003). PowerPoint Is Evil. Retrieved on July 14, 2011: http://www.wired.com/wired/archive/11.09/ppt2.html

PROMOTING ENGAGEMENT IN AN ONLINE COURSE: IT CAN BE DONE, BUT WISELY!

RANDALL E. OSBORNE
TEXAS STATE UNIVERSITY-SAN MARCOS

PAUL KRIESE
INDIANA UNIVERSITY EAST

Keywords: critical thinking, engagement

Framework

Colleagues often complain about online courses suggesting: (1) you cannot promote critical thinking in an online platform, (2) you cannot teach sensitive topic courses that way, and (3) you really cannot have open and honest dialogue in an online environment. As we designed our team-taught course on the Politics and Psychology of Hatred, we set out to create an online course and course environment that would prove each of these comments to be false.

Kuhn (1999) makes the basic assumption that critical thinking is a process of learning and demonstrating cognitive competencies that he defined as "meta-knowing." Rather than first-order knowing skills that involve an awareness of the facts and opinions that one holds, meta-knowing (which Kuhn defined as involving "second-order" skills) involves an awareness of "how" one knows, NOT "what" one knows. We made a concerted effort in the development of our course to promote student practice with demonstrating not just what they know but how they know it.

Making it Work

The following information (developed from the literature briefly cited above), is provided to our students in the syllabus:

A Model for Critical Thinking
We expect students to demonstrate a significant amount of critical thinking in this course. Specifically, we believe that critical thinkers demonstrate the ability to address issues at each of the following levels:
1. **Recitation** – state known facts or opinions. A critical component of this step is to acknowledge what aspect(s) of what is being stated is factual and what is based on opinion.
2. **Exploration** – analyze the roots of those opinions or facts. This step requires digging below the surface of what is believed or known and working to discover the elements that have combined to result in that fact or that opinion. This is an initial analysis without an attempt to comprehend the impact of those facts or opinions.
3. **Understanding** – involves an awareness of other views and a comprehension of the difference(s) between one's own opinion (and the facts or other opinions upon which that opinion is based) and the opinions of others.

To truly "understand" our own opinion in relationship to others, we must initiate an active dialogue with the other person about his or her opinions and the roots of those opinions. In other words, once we become aware of the roots of our own opinions, we must understand the roots of the opinions of others.

4. **Appreciation** – means a full awareness of the differences between our views and opinions and those of others. To truly appreciate differences, we must be aware of the nature of those differences. The active dialogue undertaken in the third step (understanding) should lead to an analysis of the opinion as recited by the other. The result should be a complete awareness of the similarities and differences between our own opinions (and the roots of those opinions) and those of the "other." Although we may still be aware that our opinions differ, we are now in a position to truly appreciate and value those differences.

The goal is not to get everyone to agree; the goal is to get people to truly explore and understand how and why opinions differ. To understand means to realize the circumstances and motivations that lead to difference and to realize that those differences are meaningful. To raise the issue without using the elements of critical thinking and exploration we have outlined above may simply reinforce prejudices by giving them voice without question.

promote student practice with demonstrating not just what they know but how they know it.
•••••••••••

Future Implications

Feedback from students has been very positive. Not only do they know that we want them to critically evaluate their ideas, we provide the framework by which they can assess their own efforts at doing so. Students have suggested on course evaluations that the model is a critical element of promoting engagement in the course because they know what is expected and have a method for making that effort.

The second and third concerns of faculty, that you cannot approach sensitive topics in online courses – we believe it is because faculty perceive that they would have less "control" in an online environment – and that an online platform does not promote open and honest dialogue, were harder to address. MacKnight (2000) states that faculty must provide a framework that encourages critical thinking but do so in a way that promotes respect. Specifically, students must know what the expectations are for the dialogue and the assignments and the course structure must encourage them to:

- ask the right questions,
- listen to each other,
- take turns and share work,
- help each other learn,
- respect each other's ideas,
- build on each other's ideas,
- construct their own understanding, and
- think in new ways. (MacKnight, 2000, p. 39)

Students are provided with course etiquette built from this literature and are told that we will follow this etiquette in all course postings. Students have commented on course evaluations and in unsolicited letters and emails that this etiquette helped to quell their concerns over speaking their mind and also gave them a method they could use to know how to express themselves but to do so in ways that invite communication instead of confrontation. When "tempers" flare in course postings, we can easily calm things down again by reminding students to follow the course etiquette and to, "ask questions instead of making statements."

References

Kuhn, D. (1999). A developmental model of critical thinking. *Educational Researcher*, 28, 16-26, 46.

MacKnight, C.B. (2000). Teaching critical thinking through online discussions. *Educause Quarterly*, 4, 38-41.

Course Etiquette and Participating in an Internet Course:

This is an Internet course. As such, the success of the course relies on active participation by each class member throughout the entire semester.

Even though we are the professors for the course, it is designed as a seminar course, meaning active participation from students is essential.

Although face-to-face interactions will not occur because of our use of the Internet, we do expect continual communication between members of the class and the course faculty. We expect students to use the same etiquette that would be used in a classroom during face-to-face interactions. This etiquette includes:

1. respect for others (their viewpoints, their values, their beliefs),

2. the right to disagree (but requires sensitivity to the viewpoints of others),

3. taking responsibility for being involved in developing the issues and topics relevant to this course,

4. active participation in all elements of the course,

5. continual feedback to the instructors about the course, course assignments, and individual viewpoints,

6. a commitment to the mutual exchange of ideas. This means we will not isolate definitive "answers" to the issues we raise but we will actively explore and respect the multiple sides to those issues, and

7. a responsibility to "police" ourselves. We are attempting to develop a community and this requires trust. In order to develop trust, we must know that we can share our ideas and not be "attacked." This also requires that we allow other class members the same trust and freedom we expect.

Figure 1.2. Course etiquette and participating in an internet course.

INTRODUCTORY POEM FOR ONLINE COURSE

SUZI SHAPIRO
INDIANA UNIVERSITY EAST

Keywords: community, ice breaker, discussion forum

Framework

Building a community of learners can be an important part of an online course. Rather than having students write a traditional introduction to their classmates, I ask them to post a poem to the discussion forum. I not only post the original poem that was the source of the assignment, but I post a poem that I have written about myself as another example and a way for them to get to know me better. The poem is an activity I heard about at a conference years ago and it has worked well in many different types of online courses.

This activity works well in many different types of courses and is enjoyed by younger traditional students as well as more mature students. I have used it in a variety of Psychology courses dealing with topics such as Lifespan Development, Neuroscience, Sensation and Perception, and Organizational Behavior. Even people who tell me they don't know how to write a poem can usually come up with something reasonable by following this format.

Making it Work

1. Tools: Basic text editing in the online discussion forum
2. Implementation: The instructions can be posted to the discussion forum or emailed to students. The discussion forum works well as it automatically makes all poems available for classmates to read. The poems could also be posted to student blogs, a course wiki, or other interactive space.
3. The assignment is posted as follows:

Write a poem about yourself following the format given. A poem written by George Ella Lyons titled Where I'm From has become the starting point for a lot of self reflective poetry.

Where I'm From
by George Ella Lyons

I am from clothespins,
from Clorox and carbon-tetrachloride.
I am from the dirt under the black porch.
(Black, glistening
it tasted like beets.)
I am from the forsythia bush,
the Dutch elm
whose long gone limbs I remember

as if they were my own.
I'm from fudge and eyeglasses,
from Imogene and Alafair.
I'm from the know-it-alls
and the pass-it-ons,
from perk up and pipe down.
I'm from He restoreth my soul
with a cottonball lamb
and ten verses I can say myself.
I'm from Artemus and Billie's Branch,
fried corn and strong coffee.
From the finger my grandfather lost
to the auger
the eye my father shut to keep his sight.
Under my bed was a dress box
spilling old pictures,
a sift of lost faces
to drift beneath my dreams.
I am from those moments-
snapped before I budded-
leaf-fall from the family tree.

"Where I'm From" appears in George Ella Lyon's *Where I'm From, Where Poems Come From,* a poetry workshop-book for teachers and students, illustrated with photographs by Robert Hoskins and published by Absey & Co, Spring, Texas, 1999.

Format for Your Poem: Where I'm from
Now, it's your turn. Create your own "Where I'm from" poem by following these guidelines:
1. The first section should describe things you did when you were young or the place where you lived.
2. The second section should describe your favorite foods or things you remember eating, tasting, or smelling.
3. The third section should describe the people who are important in your life
4. The fourth section should describe the things that you do frequently

Future Implications

Students receive credit for any level of completion. Student comments have been positive with several students mentioning on how pleased they were with their final products. Many report sharing the poem with family and friends. Students are often surprised to find that they are not alone in having a particular belief or experience. This provides some sense of connection to their classmates

In some courses where the content of the poems is relevant to course content, such as Developmental Psychology, I ask students to draw conclusions from the collection of poems during the second week of course discussion. Possible analysis questions might include:

    a.   Are there any themes or topics that are common to many of the poems?

    b.   How might some of the experiences mentioned change what someone would like or dislike today?

    c.   How do the items mentioned in the poems reflect the culture that your classmates grew up in?

The poems become a source of data for analysis by the class as well as a personal activity.

USING e-REWARDS TO PROMOTE ENGAGEMENT AND RE-ENGAGEMENT IN THE ONLINE CLASSROOM

JOHANNAH CASEY-DOECKE
INDIANA UNIVERSITY PURDUE UNIVERSITY INDIANAPOLIS

Keywords: e-Rewards, classroom engagement and re-engagement

Framework

When was the last time you rewarded a college student's work with more than an 'at-a-boy' (or girl) remark in your "Instructor's Comments?" Research has always indicated that students invest more effort in their classwork when they are stimulated by the opportunity to gain a reward for their efforts. Students in my H363 Personal Health–Distance Learning class at IUPUI not only look forward to their e-Rewards, they suggest new e-Rewards that can be given to future classes. So what's an e-Reward?

Making it Work

An e-Reward is a URL, jpeg, or web link that opens a pleasant experience related to the material studied.

Here are some of my favorite e-Rewards for H363: Personal Health.

Moose in the Sprinkler (Sometimes beauty finds you. Take the time to enjoy it.)
http://www.wimp.com/babymoose

Lying to your Death Clock (You could be in control of your life.)

Most Death Clock directions tell the person to accurately answer health questions in order to compute the hour and date of their death. So negative! It's more fun to lie because you get a better death date and you start to realize that you have some control over the length of your life.

Death Clock
http://www.deathclock.cc/

Ballroom Doggie (Dancing for fun, fitness, and wellness) How did he teach his dog to do this?
http://www.youtube.com/watch?v=Nc9xq-TVyHI&feature=player_embedded

Teaching Your Mind to Be Calm (Taking charge of your emotional health)

The students are given three pictures of common figures that appear to be still until they stare at them. The figures move until breathing is controlled and emotions are calm.
http://petm.iupui.edu/doecke/Mind_Games_1.GIF
http://petm.iupui.edu/doecke/Mind_Games_2.bmp
http://petm.iupui.edu/doecke/Mind_Games_3.GIF

Heart Attack Grill: "A Meal to Die For" (We are what we eat.) Would you eat here? Lots of Food for Thought!

"A Meal to Die For"
http://www.youtube.com/watch?v=zbKRSYAuSNg

Thanksgiving Reward (Have a Healthy Holiday)
http://petm.iupui.edu/doecke/CaseyDoecke_E-Rewards_PT2_Thanksgiving_Rewards.docx

Future Implications

Start collecting e-Rewards as they arrive in your regular e-mail. Friends send "cute" websites to friends and other people send the links to more friends. Encourage your students to send in website addresses and class related cartoons for extra credit. In no time, you will have a free file of e-Rewards for your students and better comments on your student evaluations. My favorite student comment is, "Dr. D really takes the time to give us motivations to learn. I love this class."

YouTube reviews

Jacqueline K. Owens
Ashland University

Keywords: YouTube, review, media clip

Framework

How to find an intriguing method to engage students with online course content? This Quick Hit describes a YouTube (2011) Review assignment used to present content related to leading causes of morbidity and mortality (i.e., disability and /or death) in a wellness course.

Making it Work

The purpose of this assignment is to familiarize students with information about a variety of leading causes of morbidity and/or mortality (e.g., hypertension, suicide, asthma). To cover a reasonable number of causes, this activity is most appropriate for a web-based class size greater than fifteen. Faculty and students require access to a learning management system, the internet, and a word processing program.

Students previously selected one cause of morbidity or mortality and presented a 10-minute talk with a one-page handout for classmates. Most students concentrated on their topic and paid little attention to presentations on other topics. The YouTube (2011) Review now entices students to find a media clip to enlighten classmates about their cause. They search for a clip that has scholarly merit and evaluate the worthiness of all potential clips to select the one they feel best addresses their topic. While searching, students repeatedly think about and reflect on the specifics of the topic. An instructor-created review sheet encourages them to share knowledge they have learned about this topic and requires them to select three classmates' topics for additional review.

The YouTube (2011) Review activities timeline is three weeks when assigned concurrently with other course activities. Steps for this assignment are:

1. **Week 1:** Students select and research one leading cause of morbidity and/or mortality from an instructor-created list of approximately thirty choices. They access YouTube at http://www.youtube.com/ and utilize the site-provided search feature to explore clips about their cause. Students copy the URL from the YouTube clip about their topic and post it to a dedicated course discussion thread (prompt below) for others to access and view. The subject line of their post is the topic they selected, so everyone can see all topics. Once someone posts a link about a cause, it is considered "taken" and latecomers must pick something different. This encourages students to enter the course early to benefit from a large selection of possible topics.

2. **Weeks 2 and 3:** Students review topics posted by classmates and select three of interest for additional review. This time is allotted for independent review of these three clips and completion of the review form.

3. **End of week 3:** Students submit completed review form for grading to a dedicated drop box.

Sample Discussion Forum Prompt (used with ANGEL learning management system): Post your YouTube clip here. First, create a new post. Put your name and the topic you have chosen in the heading. To post a link, you need to click on the Insert Web Link button on the toolbar above. A pop up box will come up - there is a space to paste the URL you copied from your YouTube clip. Once you do this, it should provide a live link for others to view the clip from the link in your posting. If you absolutely cannot do this - paste the URL directly into your post and we can copy and paste it to our browser.

Future Implications

Students often report anecdotally that they became extremely engaged with their topic in the search for what they felt was the very best clip to share, thus suggesting the repeated engagement that supports learning. One thread of this course is evaluation of online health information, so students have been exposed to better and lesser quality content to help them make this evaluation. Their clip selection should reflect knowledge of this previous content. Posting a quality clip (e.g., posted by someone who provides verifiable credentials, seal of a university or respected healthcare facility, cites searchable literature support) is worth 40% of the overall score. A thorough and thoughtful review sheet (example below) is worth the remaining 60%. Points are deducted for inadequate or incomplete reviews or posting a topic previously selected by another student.

They became extremely engaged with their topic in the search for what they felt was the very best clip to share

EXAMPLE: YouTube Review Sheet: Leading Causes of Morbidity/Mortality

Section 1: Your Topic
- The topic I chose for this review is:
- I selected this topic because:
- Tell me 2 facts about the topic you have chosen (such as definition of topic, major risk factors, who is at risk/why, possible treatments/preventive measures:

Section 2: Review of Other Topics
Please review any 3 other students' YouTube clips of your choice (use links from discussion forum postings — if they did not include a live link, copy and paste the URL in the post to your browser). Provide the following information.
List topic and title of clip 1:
- List 3 things you learned from the clip about this topic:
- What dimension of wellness (from the 7 we discuss in this course — e.g., physical, emotional, social) do you feel this topic most impacts and why?
(Repeat for clips 2 and 3)

The topic list has continued to grow. Students may find clips or have interest about additional topics and inquire as to whether or not a topic not yet listed is appropriate; these requests expand the choices for future groups.

This activity could be implemented with a smaller class if each student considered more than one topic. The assignment, as described, is utilized with mostly freshman and sophomore level students, but could easily adapt to upper level students by increasing the rigor of the review sheet. It could be done as an online activity for a hybrid course, or with a face to face assisted search for those newer to technology and/or search strategies, followed by an independent review.

In sum, YouTube (2011) Reviews require a low level of technological expertise from faculty and students. This type of assignment can stimulate prolonged engagement with a topic in an environment increasingly familiar and enjoyable to many.

Reference

YouTube, LLC. *Broadcast yourself.* (2011). Available: http://www.youtube.com/

Promoting online courses' student engagement and group cohesion through the use of chat-rooms

Julien Simon
Indiana University East

Keywords: engagement, literature course, online chat

Framework

Many scholars have emphasized the need to find ways to engage students in the online environment (see for example, Diaz & Bontenbal, 2001; Lim, 2004; Angelino, Williams, & Natvig, 2007). In a large, fully online literature class (Introduction to Spanish Golden Age Literature in Translation), the chat tool was used to promote student interaction and bonding among classmates in order to impact classroom retention and student learning (Angelino, Williams, & Natvig, 2007). This approach to discussing in a virtual environment assigned readings and other course materials could also be useful in smaller classes as well as hybrid classes.

Making it Work

The first day of the semester, students receive via email a list of options for a 2-hour long chat session, to which they must respond within three days to indicate their first, second, and third choices. In the rare occasions where they cannot make any of the available sessions, they are asked to provide the instructor with their availabilities. The number of chat sessions is dependent upon class enrollment. Group size should be between four and seven students. Each group has its own chat-room.

Online discussions take place every week and on week #2 they begin. The first time, instructors should make sure to be available at the beginning of each session to walk students through the process. After that, chat sessions can run without the presence of the instructor. At the first session, no reading assignments are discussed and the purpose of that session is to engage in a conversation about what will be covered in the class, to assess students' prior knowledge of the subject, and to help them reflect on what they will learn.

The chat sessions are accompanied by a discussion guide consisting of 15 to 20 questions which follow up on students' reading responses submitted the week before. These questions can be of different kinds:

1. **Questions written by the instructor.** For example:
   The intervention of a deus ex machina is a frequent feature of Lope's comedias (see Introduction, p. vii). Below is a definition of deus ex machina:
   "Stage device in Greek and Roman drama in which a god appeared in the sky by means of a crane (Greek, mechane) to resolve the plot of a play. Plays by Sophocles and particularly Euripides sometimes require the device. The term now denotes something that appears suddenly and unexpectedly and provides an artificial solution to an apparently insoluble difficulty." (Britannica Concise Encyclopedia)
   Who serves the role of the deus ex machina in "Fuente Ovejuna?" Explain.

2. **Unidentified quotes taken from students' responses.** For example:
   A student wrote: "It is a poem, but also a meditation to get closer to God."
   Do you think this is a "good" summary of what Teresa of Ávila meant to write? Whether you agree, partly agree or disagree with this statement, please cite passages of the text to support your argumentation.

3. **Questions written by students (as part of their reading responses, students have to write two questions that they wish to ask their peers).** For example:
   In the two stories seen, the main character cuts her hair and disguises herself as a man. How are these disguises used differently?

Future Implications

The online discussion fosters student learning in a variety of ways: It draws students' attention to overlooked aspects, it provides them with additional background information to appreciate more the literary works, and it leads them to gain a deeper and richer understanding of the texts read.

By using students' questions and comments (which they undoubtedly recognize), we can create a more inclusive learning environment in which they are more willing to participate and learn. The discussions are in general very lively. The real-timeness of the chat-room, just like its offline counterpart (the physical classroom), facilitates bonding among students and thus heightens the class's sense of cohesion. While waiting for the session to begin and upon finishing the session, students often engage in conversations about what is happening in their life or ask questions about the course and the upcoming assignments. At the end, some of

them will also thank their groupmates and say that they look forward to meeting them the following week.

Furthermore, chat-room discussions present some advantages over classroom discussions. For instance, since students must write regularly in the chat to be 'present,' they cannot be passive participants. Moreover, the online format encourages participation from all students, even the ones who tend to be shy in front of a live audience. Finally, students are more accountable due to the fact that the chat histories are archived and can be viewed later; something that also helps at a pedagogical level when they want to review for the final exam. Moreover, these archived chat histories also make assessment of class participation easier and less subjective as it is completed a *posteriori* and *not in media res.*

online discussion fosters student learning it leads them to gain a deeper and richer understanding

. . . .

Modifications can be implemented to further increase class cohesion and the sense of group togetherness. For example, a virtual presentation or a peer-reviewed assignment could be added (e.g., students can each be assigned a novel to study and write a review that can subsequently be evaluated by classmates). In addition, to enhance student learning and group cohesion, higher performing students (identified as such based on the first reading responses) could become peer-assistants and be paired with those in the class who experience difficulties completing their work.

References

Angelino, L. M., Williams, F. K., & Natvig, D. (2007). Strategies to engage online students and reduce attrition rates. *The Journal of Educators Online*, 4 (2), 1-14.

Diaz, D. P., & Bontenbal, K. F. (2001). Learner preferences: Developing a learner-centered environment in the online or mediated classroom. *Education at a Distance*, 15 (8). Retrieved July 26, 2011: http://home.earthlink.net/~davidpdiaz/LTS/html_docs/lrnprefs.htm.

Lim, C. P. (2004). Engaging learners in online learning environments. *TechTrends*, 48 (4). 16-23.

The real-timeness of the chat-room, just like its offline counterpart (the physical classroom), facilitates bonding among students and thus heightens the class's sense of cohesion.

USING TEAM-BASED LEARNING TO ENGAGE STUDENTS IN ONLINE COURSES

MARCIA D. DIXSON
INDIANA UNIVERSITY PURDUE UNIVERSITY FORT WAYNE

Keywords: team-based learning, online teaching, student engagement

Framework

One of the consistent findings in online education research is the risk of student isolation (Lewis & Abdul-Hamid, 2006; Ortiz-Rodriguez, et. al, 2005). Students in online courses are more likely than other students to feel disconnected from content, other students and the instructor. Therefore, researchers (Chickering & Ehrmann, 1996; Gaytan & McEwen, 2007) encourage instructors to provide opportunities for student-student interaction as well as student-teacher interaction. However, simply assigning students to "post replies to five people's posts" does not help students develop connections and may feel like busy work. The challenge is to create meaningful interaction that also engages them with the content of the course. One solution is team-based learning.

Team-based learning, created by Larry Michaelsen, is somewhat formulaic. However, more than ten years of using this strategy has taught me that the closer assignments follow Michaelsen's steps and checklists (see Michaelsen, Knight, & Fink, 2002), the better the learning outcomes for students. The method can be used with any content reflecting information, principles, or skills students need to learn and a way for them to "practice" the information by applying it to some kind of group project, case study, or problem.
Making it Work

Michaelsen's team-based learning consists of three types of work: individual preparation, small group interaction, and whole class comparison. Below I list these steps and provide examples from my current online course, COM 212 Interpersonal Communication.

1. **Individual Preparation:**
   a. **Reading/watching a lecture video:** I give them a set of concepts from the textbook to study. I find this more effective than telling them to read a set of pages/chapters.
   b. **Quiz/assignment:** (the first two steps are called the readiness assurance process – more specifics are available from Michaelsen, Knight, and Fink, 2002): an online quiz over the concepts preparing them for group work.
   c. **Individual posting of initial answer to group problem/case study/project:** students are asked to answer the question "What should X do next?" about a case study concerning an interpersonal interaction, conflict situation etc. Their answer

can only be a phrase or a sentence. However, they then must provide support, citing specific ideas/concepts (with page numbers) from the text. Students post their individual answers by the opening day of the discussion. This assures that some students do not get credit for coasting along and agreeing with the work other students are doing and also that the discussion gets off to a strong start.

2. **Small Group Work:** Discussion forum to reach decision about case study/problem: Students discuss the case study and must reach consensus about the specific action to be taken by X. Again, the answer can only be a phrase or sentence, so they can not just incorporate everyone's original ideas, they must discuss!
Effective group projects use the three S's:
   a. **Same problem:** all groups work on the same issue so they can compare answers later in a meaningful way;
   b. **Specific choice (word, phrase, or sentence):** when students must reach a specific decision (i.e., yes/no, the two best solutions are, the person should do this), they cannot easily split up the work but must talk through the application of the concepts and reach a decision; their work must be focused; and groups will be able to easily identify differences in their answers during the whole class discussion;
   c. **Simultaneous reporting to the class:** groups can not "change their mind" after seeing another group's answer (Michaelsen, Knight & Fink, 2002, p. 61).

3. **Class Work:** Discussion forum to compare group answers: I move the final answers from the group to a "debate" forum where students are encouraged to question the answers of other groups. They look for errors and omissions or they comment on perspectives they had not considered. I award extra credit for the debate "winners"(those who best defend their answers). Even after dealing with a case study individually and in small groups, students still have more to say and learn in the whole class discussion forum. In the Spring 2010 semester, the debate forums had another 70 - 90 posts (from about 20 active students) during the three days of the debate in each unit.

Using this process assures that each student works with the content in five ways: individually in reading/listening to the material, taking a quiz, and applying it to the analysis of the case study/problem, in a small group to talk the problem through with their peers, and, finally, as an entire class to see how other groups applied the concepts to the assignment. Besides this multi-step learning process, team-based learning has several other benefits: 1) it requires meaningful interaction with other students to reach a decision; 2) it has both individual and group accountability; and 3) it offers the opportunity for interaction with the instructor.

Future Implications

Depending on the content and the students, instructors can be very active in the process or maintain a facilitator-when-needed role. Fairly early in the group discussion, the instructor should give each group feedback about how their conversation is progressing, whether they are misunderstanding a key idea, etc. Of course, the instructor provides a grade and comments for each of the groups' final answers. Since instructors grade just the group answers, there is time to provide meaningful comments. Individual grades for group discussion are based on having the initial post up on time and participating meaningfully in the conversation (i.e., five content posts —something more than "I agree").

Team-based learning accomplishes the goals of learning and helping students feel engaged with the course, the instructor and their peers. Students in my Fall 2010 COM 212 course reported an average 4.3/5.0 when asked about applying the concepts in the discussion and a 4.75/5.0 for instructor presence in the course, with comments like, "I liked the group discussions and being able to see things through my peers perspective. " and "got a lot of great views on interesting topics." Team-based learning is a very useful tool for both learning and student engagement in the online course environment.

References

Chickering, A.W. & Ehrmann, S.C. (1996, October). Implementing the seven principles: Technology as a Lever. *AAHE Bulletin*, 3-6. Retrieved October 7, 2007 from Teaching, Learning and Technology Group Website: http://www.tltgroup.org/programs/seven.html.

Gayton, J. & McEwen, B.C. (2007). Effective online instructional and assessment strategies. *The American Journal of Distance Education*, 21(3), 117-132.

Lewis, C.C. & Abdul-Hamid, H. (2006). Implementing Effective Online Teaching Practices: Voices of Exemplary Faculty. *Innovative Higher Education*, 31, 2, 83-98.

Michaelsen, L.K, Bauman Knight. A. & Fink, L.D. (Eds). (2002). *Team -based learning: A transformative use of small groups in college teaching*. Sterling, VA: Stylus.

Ortiz-Rodríguez, M., Telg, R. W., Irani, T., Roberts, T. G. & Rhoades, E. (2005). College students' perceptions of quality in distance education: The importance of communication. *Quarterly Review of Distance Education*, 6, 97-105.

||||||||||||||||||||||||||||||||||||||||||||||||||||||||||||||||||||||||||||||||||||||||||||||||||||||||||||||||||||||||||||||||||||

THAT'S WHY THEY CALL IT YOU-TUBE

DEDE WOHLFARTH, DAVE MORGAN, AND NATE MITCHELL
SPALDING UNIVERSITY

Keywords: engaging students, active learning, video clips

Framework

How do we convince our multi-tasking students to tear themselves away from Facebook, twitter, and cell phones, and actually read our (often dry) textbooks? To make learning relevant, we hunt for cool YouTube clips and internet resources that demonstrate key lecture points. In adopting more active-learning, student-centered paradigms, we realize that *seeing* Piaget's conservation task, for example, is much more memorable than *telling* about it.

Making it Work

But here's a solution to get students to read for class: **have students read ahead for the next assignment and scour the internet for an awesome video clip to demonstrate what they learned** by sending the hyperlink via email. Students can add a two sentence email explaining why they think their video clip fits conceptually with the reading, providing informal feedback about a student's text understanding. Although some texts offer video resources, students are rarely motivated to preview these websites, fearing they will be as boring as our texts.

One may choose to offer extra credit points for students' efforts, with bonus points going to the juiciest video, but students will often work without extra points because they're excited when "their" video clip is shown in class. They feel a sense of ownership and control, consistent with the expectations of learner-centered ideology. (Important tip: preview the clips!). An additional benefit of this activity is that overwhelmed professors who know we "should" be making our lectures more visually appealing can do so while shifting the work (which is often a synonym for "learning") to students. Additionally, students often find more culturally relevant clips than we do, despite our efforts to stay "hip."

We also recommend using YouTube clips as presentation requirements for students. Have students assume responsibility for not only finding the video, but introducing it to the class, describing how the clip relates to course content, and discussing its theoretical and real world implications. Offer additional class points if students identify and describe content or theoretical errors in the clip itself. In a YouTube video I once showed to my learning class, college students had staged a Pavlovian conditioning demonstration. Although the video was entertaining, the video actors actually confused conditional and unconditional stimuli in their demonstration description. Instructing students to find such errors enhances their critical thinking with regard to the subject matter.

Future Implications

Audience
This technique works for all class sizes, academic levels, and course disciplines. To modify the activity with larger class sizes, request video clips from only 5-10 members in the class at a time.

Tools
Access to a "smart" classroom with internet access and the technology to show web-based video clips.

Implementation
Implementation time requires reading a few emails from students and clicking on a few links to watch clips, which is far more time efficient than looking them up ourselves.

Outcomes/Assessment
We have not formally assessed the use of this technique, but students report that this activity directly contributed to their learning in course evaluation feedback.

Modifications
In an on-line or hybrid class, this activity should work equally well.

(Thanks to Todd Zakrajsek at UNC for the initial idea for this tip).

||||||||||||||||||||||||||||||||||||||||||||||||||||||||||||||||||||||||||||||||||||||||||||||||||||||||||||||||||||||||||||||||||||||||||||||||||||||||||||

"Reading in Context" for networked engagement with course readings

Daniel T. Hickey
Indiana University Bloomington

Keywords: reading, online assignments, discussion forums

Framework

"Reading in Context" is a networked instructional activity. I have been using it to help graduate students efficiently learn to (a) locate, interpret, and critique personally relevant articles, (b) uncover the ultimate meaning of those articles and assigned core articles as they have been taken up in the literature more broadly, and (c) learn the subtle nuances of scholarly referencing. These proficiencies are crucial for graduate students but difficult to foster in classroom contexts. They require extensive individualized guidance from someone with deep knowledge of the relevant literature. Some graduate students never really appreciate how the broadening meaning of a specific article ultimately resides in the way it is taken up and interpreted in the broader literature (Rose, 1996); this challenge is heighted within digitally networked scholarship (Ingraham, 2000). As such, many students don't appreciate the broader meaning of core readings, or even see how they came to be "core" in the first place (Diezmann, 2005). Many don't tackle the nuances of referencing (such as the appropriate use of e.g., i.e., and c.f.) in their own writing until they get to their thesis or dissertation (Cafarella & Barnett, 2000). This is laborious for advisors and aggravating for committee members. Worse still, some graduate complete their studies with culminating papers that knowledgeable editors or search committee members dismiss outright because of sloppy referencing.

Making it Work

This activity uses tools that are free (Google Scholar), open-source (the Zotero referencing plugin for the Firefox browser), and available in most course management platforms online teaching resources (e.g. wikis and discussion forums). Students first locate and critique personally-relevant articles that reference a core article. Students then use networking tools to collaboratively identify which of the articles are "more appropriate" and "less appropriate" references to the core article. By searching for references that are relevant to their specific interests, students see how the core article has been being taken up by others, and expand their knowledge of the relevant research literature. Critiquing the range of references naturally reveals subtle nuances of this crucial scholarly practice.

I developed and refined this activity in the context of two courses in Cognition and Instruction in a graduate school of education. I use a more modest version in an online introductory course. Students use Google Scholar to locate professionally-relevant articles that reference a widely-cited core article. They then examine how the core article was referenced, as well as the broader arguments in the referencing article. The specific assignment has them locate at least one "more appropriate" reference and at least one "less appropriate" reference. Students then post their references and their observations to their wikifolio for that week for discussion (Figure 1.3). I provide feedback and support discussion with classmates via public comments posted directly to the wikifolios (Figure 1.4). A discussion forum is used to identify the "most appropriate" and the "least appropriate" reference. Students complete the activity by reflecting on three types of engagement (*consequential, critical,* and *collaborative*). Points are awarded based on evidence of learning in the reflections; the actual content of the assignment is not formally graded. The activity is quite ambitious for MEd students in an introductory course. Nonetheless, every student was able to complete it successfully in the most recent course. The reflections showed convincing evidence of disciplinary engagement with the core article and referencing articles, and a developing appreciation of the nuances and pitfalls of scholarly referencing.

In the more advanced hybrid course, I had students complete the activity with each of the core articles that comprise the course reading. Students are shown how to use Zotero and a shared Zotero database that was set up for the course (Figure 1.5). For each of the core articles, students locate and cite referring articles that are themselves widely cited and relevant to their specific sub-interest. They then save PDF's of the articles in which they comment on whether or not the authors have referred to the core article appropriately, and then discuss those comments (Figure 1.6). Students are specifically encouraged to search for articles that (a) misrepresent the point of the core article, (b) use the core article to warrant arguments that the core article does not actually support, and (c) use inappropriate referencing abbreviations. When the class meets, the culminating activity is identifying the most appropriate and least appropriate reference to the core article. Compared to previous classes with similar students, literature review papers completed for the most recent course showed referencing that was more ambitious and more precise. Compared to previous classes, the instructor feedback and individual discussions of papers were able to delve more immediately into the substantive issues in the paper, without having to also identify and explain referencing errors.

Reading in Context Wiki

Least Appropriate Reference

After reviewing the following article called An Investigation on Experienced Teachers' Knowledge and Perceptions of Instructional Theories and Practices by Leping Liu, I feel that the author did not correctly inform the audience of Brown and Adler's view on learning. In the article listed above, the author states different instructional strategies used by teachers. For Brown and Adler the author stated "open education" as an instructional strategy used. I do not feel this use of terminology really portrays the fact that Brown and Adler view that students learn best by learning and collaborating with each other through various forms of discourse: in person, blogs, wikis, facebook, etc. In fact, when I looked up what "open education" means it said that there are no admission requirements for higher education and should not be confused with open educational resources. This is far from what Brown and Adler wrote about in their article, which in fact talked about open educational resources. Lastly, the article talks about Web 2.0 and integrating the use of technology into the classroom as a means of learning, and doesn't even site Brown and Adler. Therefore, the article doesn't portray Brown and Adler to their fullest beliefs and ideas about educating students of today.

Here is the link to the article (access on campus): http://pdfserve.informaworld.com/338405_731200576_919333832.pdf

More Appropriate Reference

After viewing a few different articles, one of the articles that I felt referenced Brown and Adler most accurately was an article written by Rick Kopak called Open Access and the Open Journal Systems: Making Sense All Over. This article did a great job of explaining how many individuals are learning through Open Educational Resources, such as journals, which was highly stressed throughout Brown and Adler's article. Brown and Adler made note that due to the vast amount of career changes this mode of learning is ultimately needed because there is not enough time to return to school for every new experience. Thus, the article stressed the importance of making more journals available via the internet to further this growth. Another important component that this article stated that relates to Brown and Adler's beliefs is that there is a growing need for "demand-pull" rather than supply-push". By making more articles available via the internet, students could access information and collaborate with others who are interested in the same ideas. Kopak even used a specific quote from Brown and Adler's article to support his claim.

Here is the link to the article (access on campus): http://asselindoiron.pbworks.com/f/14_2kopak.pdf

Conclusion:

After reviewing a few articles, it seems like articles related to higher education tend to incorporate the ideas of Brown and Adler more accurately; whereas, articles written related to elementary education do not seem to have a good understanding of Brown and Adler's view point. Therefore, it is important that elementary educators and researchers get on board with the important ideas presented by Brown and Adler because younger students can learn as well through social interaction with their peers and the teacher.

Figure 1.3. Example of "Less Appropriate" and "More Appropriate" references to core article (i.e., Brown and Adler's 2007 Minds on Fire).

Future Implications

So far, I have learned that shared public and persistent discourse allows struggling students to learn from the posting and discussions of their classmates, while substantially reducing instructor workload. Providing detailed feedback on early posts allows the instructor to simply reference those examples when providing feedback to others. The focus on personally relevant articles and the grading of reflections seem to have eliminated the risk of plagiarism. All of the students in the introductory course engaged with articles and referencing practices that were heretofore only attempted in the advanced course. And all of the students in the advanced course developed referencing skills that previously had required intensive review of course papers and one-on-one feedback.

A near term goal for both of these courses is the incorporation of social bookmarking tools (e.g., Digg). Another near term goal for both courses is creating a challenging set of items for the course exam that will efficiently provide valid evidence of the understanding that each student takes away from the activity. These items will support the long term goal of iteratively refining the feature of the activity each year, documenting the consequences of those refinements, and convincing more instructors to attempt it.

References

Caffarella, R. S., & Barnett, B. G. (2000). Teaching doctoral students to become scholarly writers: The importance of giving and receiving critiques. *Studies in Higher Education, 25*(1), 39-52.

Diezmann, C. M. (2005). Supervision and scholarly writing: Writing to learn—learning to write. *Reflective Practice, 6*(4), 443-457.

Ingraham, B. (2000). Scholarly rhetoric in digital media. *Journal of Interactive Media in Education.*

Rose, S. (1996). What's love got to do with it? Scholarly citation practices as courtship rituals. *Journal of Language and Learning across the Disciplines, 1*(3), 36-47.

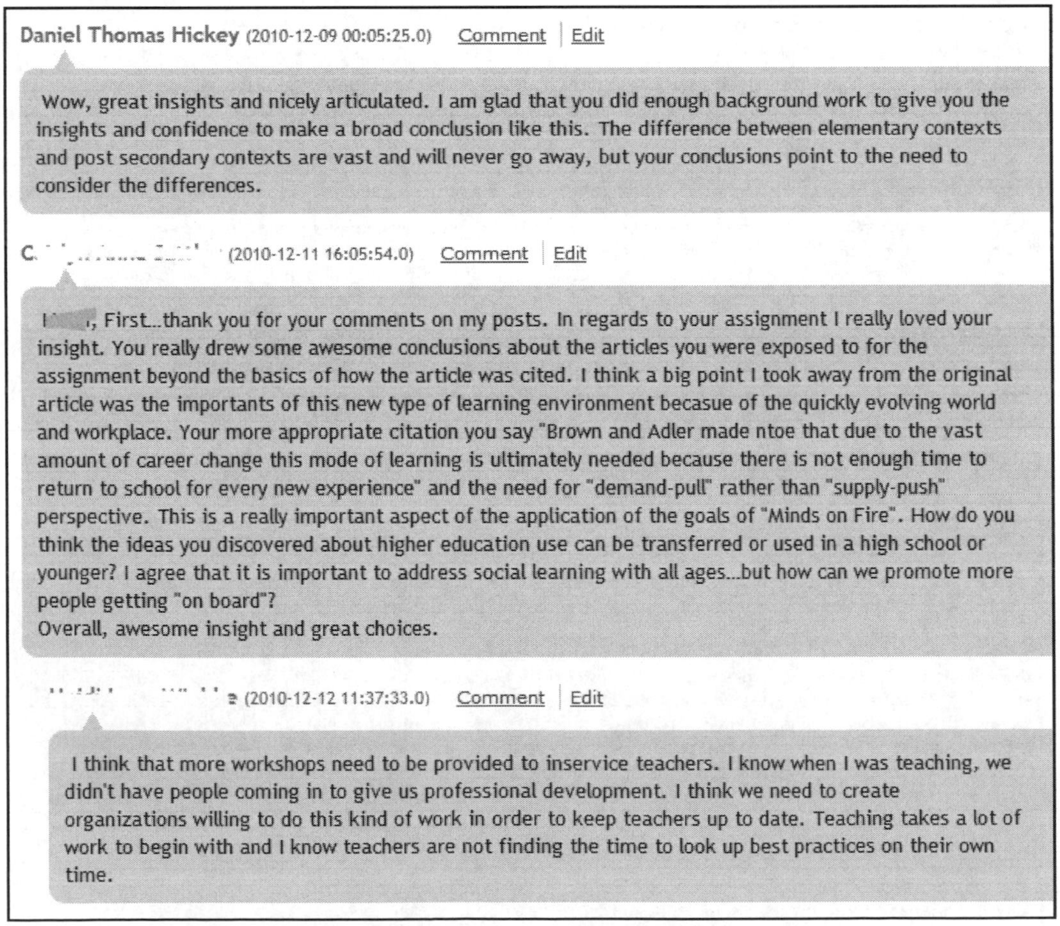

Figure 1.4. Example of instructor and peer commenting on post.

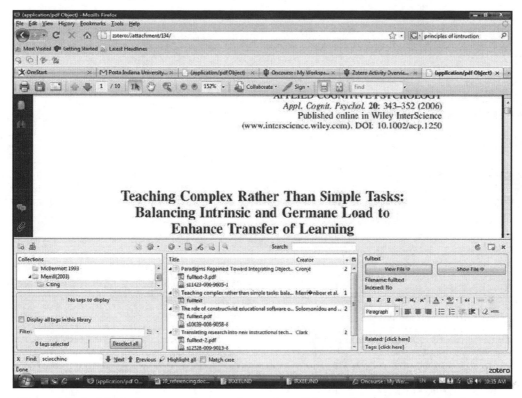

Figure 1.5. Articles referencing core articles in shared Zotero database in advanced course.

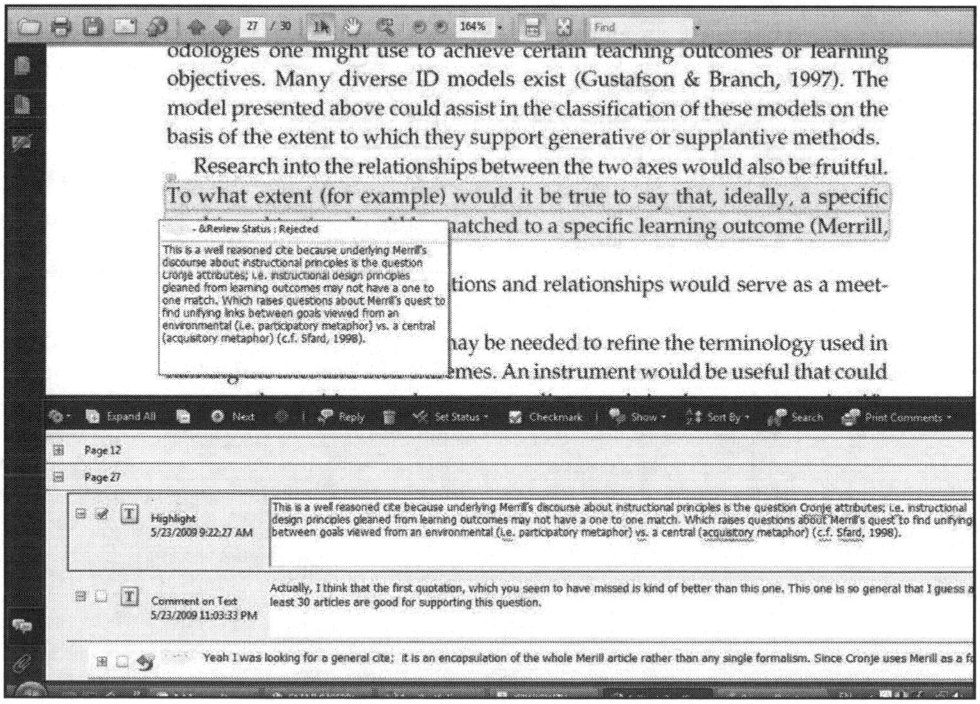

Figure 1.6. Embedded discussion of references to core articles in advanced course.

Scavenger hunt

Joan Lafuze
Indiana University East

Keywords: online instruction, course management systems

Framework

There are a number of students who register for my online courses from colleges and universities outside Indiana University. Because students from other campuses may not be aware of the specifics of the Indiana University course management system or because we may have to establish library or other access connections, I designed the course with a preliminary "scavenger hunt" assignment.

Making it Work

The scavenger hunt assignment is composed of a series of tasks that document student knowledge of the IU system and ensure that students have access to necessary course materials. First, all students are asked to find their group assignments and use the messaging system contained within the campus course management system to send me their group membership identification and to send a message to their group members. This not only helps them learn to navigate the messaging system appropriately, but also lets me know that I have not missed assigning a student to a group or that I have mistakenly assigned a student to more than one group. Second, students are asked to post a special assignment using the assignments tool of our system; this assignment requires them to introduce themselves in a separate discussion forum and to respond to the posting of at least one other student in the same discussion forum. Third, students must download a file and answer questions requiring the use of different media depending upon the course. For example, students may be asked to use an Adobe file or Microsoft PowerPoint. Fourth, there is a link to a course created special library that they will use to read a peer-reviewed article. Finally, students complete a quiz over the introduction section of the text in the test and survey portion of our management system. This way, I can determine that they have both acquired the text and that they can use the test tool. I award points for each activity. This

pleases the student, and I am rewarded by knowing we will not have surprise discoveries throughout the course that might keep any student from being able to participate fully in the course.

Future Implications

Audience: This activity was designed for an online course but could be used in any course requiring the use of technology. Similarly, the size of the class and the content being taught would not matter.

Tools: This activity utilizes the campus course management system. All students have access to this system from a campus computer even if they do not own their own computer. As such, there should be no additional costs for students or the university.

Implementation: Developing course-specific scavenger hunt activities can only be completed once the course syllabus is completed so that you know which computer technologies your students will be utilizing. Each scavenger hunt activity can be developed within two to three hours.

Outcomes/Assessment: Assessment is built into this activity as each sub-activity within the scavenger hunt has a 'product' that was developed specifically to assess whether students had met the learning outcome, that is, if the student can successfully utilize the technology.

Future Directions/Modifications/Hybrid Contexts: This activity is endlessly modifiable by simply changing the sub-activities of the scavenger hunt. A possible modification might be to develop a sub-activity that requires students to interact with one another by going on a virtual scavenger hunt to find an answer to a question in cyberspace.

The scavenger hunt assignment is composed of a series of tasks that document student knowledge of the IU system and ensure that students have access to necessary course materials.

JUST-IN-TIME TEACHING: USING THE WEB TO ENGAGE STUDENTS IN THE CLASSROOM

ANDY GAVRIN
INDIANA UNIVERSITY PURDUE UNIVERSITY INDIANAPOLIS

Keywords: educational technology, active learning

Framework

Just-in-Time Teaching (JiTT for short) is a pedagogical method that promotes engagement by leveraging homework time to promote interactive learning in the classroom. My collaborators and I use the WWW to create a feedback loop between a new class of online homework assignments and the classroom experience. By using the results of this new homework in class, we make the classroom more effective in addressing students' needs. The results include

- Improved learning
- Better student attitudes
- Opportunities to cover material in greater depth.

JiTT was developed in the late 1990's by the author and collaborators in the physics departments at IUPUI and the US Air Force Academy (Novak, Patterson, Gavrin, & Christian, 1999). JiTT is now used in introductory, advanced, and graduate level courses across the university curriculum; it is used in community colleges and research universities (Simkins & Maier, 2009). JiTT can improve results in classes large and small, but it has the biggest impact in medium to large lecture settings.

Most campuses already have the necessary technology for JiTT. All that is needed is a means to ask students questions online, and for faculty to collect their answers. Most course management systems are more than adequate to the task. An enterprising instructor (or one with a little help from IT) can create all of the necessary technology using just a web server and a few simple scripts to handle the interactions. The time to implement JiTT is primarily in the time to prepare and post good questions for the semester—probably an hour or two per week.

Making it Work

The centerpiece of the JiTT method is the new category of homework that we term "Warm up exercises." The "warmups" (for short) are web-based assignments that students complete before the class period in which the relevant material is to be discussed. Students complete these assignments based on assigned pre-class reading. Think of the warmups as online, pre-class, reading quizzes. Like reading quizzes, students have an increased incentive to prepare before class. There are several additional benefits, though, that distinguish JiTT from a reading quiz.

- The warmup is online, so no class time is used.

- Students must think about the material rather than simply read it uncritically.
- The instructor can evaluate the results before class.

This last point is critical. Based on her students' performance, the instructor makes adjustments to her plans for the class time. She may change the emphasis, add or drop topics, etc. We also find it useful to bring examples of students' responses to class and use these as talking points during the class discussion.

The JiTT instructional process consists of five steps.
1. Students read the material in a textbook or other source.
2. Students complete the warmup, which is due a few hours before class.
3. The instructor reviews the warmup responses and makes "just-in-time" adjustments to her plans for the class period.
4. The instructor brings excerpts from the students' responses to class, and incorporates them in the discussion.
5. The instructor prepares or adjusts the subsequent warmup to match the needs of the class.

Faculty have considerable flexibility in implementing JiTT. The gap between the time the warmup is due and the class period may vary from hours to days. The frequency of warmups each week, the length of the assignments, how credit is determined, etc., may all be adjusted to local needs. Even the names of the assignments vary: faculty at the US Air Force Academy use the term "Pre-flight check."

What makes a good warmup? A few questions that are open-ended enough to draw students out, and that produce answers that will be good "discussion starters" in the classroom. We often construct questions by asking "In your own words, explain what <new idea> means."

How can the warmup responses be incorporated in the discussion (step four, above)? We prefer to use anonymous excerpts from students' work as "talking points" in class. For instance, an instructor may project an example of student work on the screen and ask students to respond to it. Is it correct? Is it complete? Is it based on the concepts being introduced in class? A faculty member may post two responses to the same question, and ask students to discuss the relative merits with their neighbors before polling the class on which one is best. Faculty may post exemplary answers, praise them, then ask under what other circumstances these answers will remain valid or require modification. Each instructor will find ways that suit him or her. Our only caution is never to deride answers in front of the class.

Future Implications

The benefits of interaction among faculty and students are widely recognized (Hake, 1998; McKeachie, Pintrich, Lin, & Smith, 1986). Alexander Astin (1997) identified student-student and student-faculty interactions as the most important factors contributing to student success (along with time-on-task). Using JiTT, these interactions can be dramatically enhanced. JiTT also clearly promotes increased time-on-task by promoting timely completion of assigned reading. Grounding the classroom discussion in warmup responses also makes the class explicitly learner-centered, and encourages students to participate (McCombs & Whistler, 1997).

student-student and student-faculty interactions as the most important factors contributing to student success

We have evaluated the effects of JiTT on both student attitudes and measures of learning, and found positive results in both cases. For instance, we have used pre-test/post-test methods and shown that students' gains on items related to warmup exercises are significantly greater than on items associated with additional traditional homework problems (Marrs, Blake, & Gavrin, 2003).

References

Astin, A. (1997). *What matters in college? Four critical years revisited*: Jossey-Bass, San Fransisco.

Hake, R. R. (1998). Interactive-engagement versus traditional methods: a six-thousand-student survey of mechanics test data for introductory physics courses. *Am. J. Physics* 66(1), 64-74.

Marrs, K. A., Blake, R. E., & Gavrin, A. (2003). Use of internet-based warm up exercises to determine students' prior knowledge and misconceptions in biology, chemistry, and physics. *J. Coll. Science Teaching*, 33(1), 42.

McCombs, B. & Whistler, J. S (1997). *The learner-centered classroom and school: Strategies for increasing student motivation and achievement*. San Francisco: Josey-Bass.

McKeachie, W. J., Pintrich, P. R. Lin, Y.-G. & Smith, D. A. (1986). *Teaching and learning in the college classroom: A review of the research literature*. Ann Arbor, MI: University of Michigan.

Novak, G. M, Patterson, E. T., Gavrin, A. & Christian, W. (1999). *Just-in-time teaching: Blending active learning with web technology*. Upper Saddle River, NJ: Prentice-Hall.

Simkins, S., & Maier, M. (Eds). (2009). *Just-in-time teaching across the disciplines and across the academy*. Sterling, VA: Stylus Publishing

THE SIMPLE VISUAL MAPPING TOOL FOR THINKING ALOUD

JU WON PARK
INDIANA UNIVERSITY NORTHWEST

Keywords: visual mapping, brain storming, and student engagement

Framework

Visual mapping is an effective activity that enables students to clearly and critically think about their concepts/ideas/perspectives (Bitter & Legacy, 2008). This activity is also known as concept mapping. When visual mapping is put into action, an instructor has the ability to challenge students' spontaneous thinking and help them develop critical-thinking skills. Because students can visualize their concepts/ideas/perspectives, visual mapping enhances their understanding and perception of each topic (O'Bannon & Puckett, 2010). Among dozens of visual mapping tools, "Inspiration" is one of the widely used products. However, installing Inspiration requires a purchase fee for individual students' acquisition. As a result, instructors were in need of an alternative tool.

Making it Work

In my courses, I have used "Bubble Mapping" (www.bubbl.us), which is easy to use and free of charge (see Figure 1.7.). In the classroom, an instructor can demonstrate how to use this tool; in the computer lab, an instructor can allow students to create on their own, after viewing a demonstration; even in an online course, students can easily learn how to use, due to the interactive user guide. Although this bubble mapping tool is not as functional as Inspiration, it can generate a hands-on experience for such activities as concept mapping and brain storming. Simply, as long as instructors and students have Internet access, they can utilize bubble mapping, due to this web browser-based application.

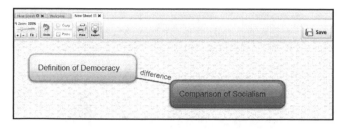

Figure 1.7. Example of Bubble Mapping.

I have implemented this tool for college students in my computer classrooms and this tool can also be used in traditional classrooms, as long as these classrooms have Internet access with a projector/projection screen. Because this tool was used for concept mapping and brain storming, I consider the activities within this tool to be very useful, for virtually any kind of major fields. During the implementation process, I needed Internet accessible computers with a projector/projection screen.

I used this bubble mapping tool when students were introduced to complicated concepts and needed to compare different facts/perspectives on the same theme/topic. In my courses, students needed to (a) have concepts/ideas/opinions/facts for visualization, (b) see an instructor's demonstration, (c) practice with the Bubble Mapping application before formal activity, and (d) create bubbling sheets.

Future Implications

Since I have used this tool for class activities with both undergraduate and graduate students, I have received

positive reactions about this tool from a majority of them. Their qualitative comments are the following: (a) It allows the teacher and student to work interchangeably with their projects; (b) I think that this will help students organize their thoughts in writing and reading; (c) the feature that turns visual maps or flow charts into outlines would be especially helpful for them as they begin to write papers; (d) this program gives the students an opportunity to make their thoughts more clear and organized; and (e) it could encourage students to be more creative, to organize ideas, and to plan and structure their thoughts through a process of brainstorming.

As the Bubble Mapping Company continues to develop new features and offer more diverse functions, I believe students will benefit more from the newer version. When instructors utilize this tool for an active learning module, it is anticipated that college students are more engaged in their class activities, promoting strong learning motivation and effective cognitive comprehension. In addition, since bubble sheets can be made as photo files, it can be used for college students' electronic portfolio.

References

Bitter, G., & Legacy, J. (2008). *Using technology in the classroom.* Needham Heights, NJ: Allyn and Bacon.

O'Bannon, B., & Puckett, K. (2010). *Preparing to use technology: A practical guide to curriculum integration.* Boston: Pearson.

COMBINING LEARNING COMMUNITIES WITH ELECTRONIC SELF AND PEER ASSESSMENTS TO INCREASE STUDENT ENGAGEMENT IN DISCUSSION-BASED COURSES

SHARRON D. HUNTER-RAINEY
NORTH CAROLINA CENTRAL UNIVERSITY

Keywords: assessment, engagement, learning

Framework

Discussion based teaching improves student learning relative to outcomes achieved using lectures exclusively (Barnes, Christensen, & Hansen, 1994). Student preparation before and outside class increases engagement with and learning of content (Maier & Simkins, 2009). Self and peer assessment (SPA) assignments require student preparation outside class allowing instructors to monitor completed submissions before class, then integrate student responses into classroom discussions. Combining discussion teaching and SPA assignments in learning communities increases learning and ultimately retention of key concepts without

the lag time typically involved in instructor administered assessments such as exams.

Instructors teaching a variety of subjects seek to increase student engagement. Maximizing engagement in strategic management is important because its principles will eventually be used during advanced stages of management professionals' careers, yet students learn this content in capstone courses completed shortly before starting their careers. Therefore, instructors must use course design and teaching tactics enabling students to learn critical concepts in ways to retain knowledge useful at appropriate times in their careers.

A restructured strategic management course holds students accountable for understanding concepts such as definition of strategy, five generic strategies, plus characteristics of environments external to and internal to the organization. The redesigned course relies upon three elements: learning communities, discussion based teaching, plus SPA assignments. Together these elements increase short-term learning and long-term retention of content.

SPA assignments allow students to practice applying new concepts to context-rich scenarios

• • • • • • • • • • • •

Learning communities support rigorous analysis and collaboration in an environment characterized by mutual respect (Barnes et al., 1994). In this context, classrooms become safe spaces for students to share even nascent ideas, without fear of ridicule. Discussion-based teaching creates partnership between students and instructors promoting critical thinking and problem solving. Students and instructors share power, accountability, and tasks (Barnes et al.). SPA assignments allow students to practice applying new concepts to context-rich scenarios. The electronic submissions also reveal which concepts and/or applications are well understood, plus areas requiring further explanation.

Making it Work

SPA assignments involve: (1) reading textbooks, (2) responding to prompts, (3) scoring assignments electronically, (4) clarifying questions about concepts or applications, and (5) explaining course concepts. Before class, students read textbook chapters providing foundation for planned discussions using a detailed schedule specifying learning objectives with submission deadlines for each. After reading, students write one-page responses to open-ended prompts requiring them to apply textbook concepts. Students submit written assignments electronically using Blackboard's SPA module before class. After class, a detailed rubric, prepared by the instructor, becomes available electronically and students use it to maintain scoring consistency, for their own work plus that of two classmates, where identities of all parties are known. After each evaluation period ends, the instructor transfers average scores into the electronic gradebook providing real-time perspective about the quality of their submissions relative to the class average.

During class, the instructor summarizes elements of well-written SPA responses and answers students' clarifying questions to ensure they have made appropriate connections between textbook concepts and context-rich assignments. These discussions create opportunities to clarify any misunderstandings about application of course concepts in general and SPA assignments in particular. Reviewing electronic submissions enables the instructor to incorporate examples into the interactive discussions reinforcing answers to clarifying questions to promote retention of accurate understanding of basic concepts.

Each assignment is worth ten points. The two lowest scores of twelve SPA assignments are omitted. The remaining ten SPA assignments comprise eleven percent of points available in the course, creating an incentive for students to participate. Omitting the two lowest scores may discourage full participation.

Future Implications

During the first semester after SPA assignments were piloted, student participation reached a high of 100 percent and low of 69.4 percent in two sections including 32 students each. Of those who completed the assignments, mean scores ranged from 6.48 to 8.57 with standard deviations ranging from 1.33 to 2.02 across 24 SPA assignments. These data suggest students use a reasonable range of partial credit in scoring SPA assignments. The first academic year SPA assignments were implemented, no failing grades were assigned for the first time in the instructor's four academic years teaching strategic management.

Benefits

SPA assignments can be implemented within a semester. They promote proactive time management encouraging students to prepare for class in advance, leaving time for reflective review of content. SPA assignments also increase awareness of concept mastery, or lack thereof, for students and instructors providing opportunities for students to seek instructors' input as needed to clarify misunderstandings about concepts presented in textbooks and application of these concepts in context rich situations. Completing SPA assignments improves students' understanding of concepts leading to long-term retention of principles for future application. The electronic process also allows instructors to archive student submissions.

Costs

SPA assignments can be implemented without students incurring software or hardware costs if a course management system, such as Blackboard or Moodle is available. Students invest incremental time required to prepare, submit, and score three electronic assignments weekly. Instructors invest time to create electronic assignments, prepare rubrics, transfer data electronically, and review assignments. Time invested by students and instructors makes teaching and learning more efficient and effective than either process is without SPA assignments.

Conclusions

SPA assignments can very likely be used in teaching areas other than strategic management where students and instructors seek to share responsibility for learning outcomes. Implementing SPA transfers accountability for learning outcomes by encouraging advance preparation and use of clarifying questions. Using SPA assignments in learning communities creates space for students to practice concepts without feeling compelled to understand them perfectly before testing their ideas publicly. Students value SPA assignments when instructors show explicit connections between readings, SPA assignments, and other class activities designed to reinforce concepts.

References

Barnes, L.B., Christensen, C. R., & Hansen, A. J. (1994). *Teaching with the case method (3rd ed.)* Boston: Harvard Business School Press.

Maier, M. H., &.Simkins, S. P. (2009). Just-in-time teaching in combination with other pedagogical innovations. In S. P. Simkins & M. H. Maier (Eds.), *Just-in-Time Teaching: Across the Disciplines, Across the Academy* (pp. 129-151). Sterling, VA: Stylus.

A SOURCE FOR LECTURE LAUNCHERS: MINING PUBLIC MEDIA FOR ACCESSIBLE ILLUSTRATIONS

KEVIN L. McELMURRY
INDIANA UNIVERSITY NORTHWEST

Keywords: public media, discussion, lecture illustration

Framework

Many classrooms now include multimedia equipment and internet connectivity. In addition to allowing for the use of traditional recorded media, this technology makes it possible to easily stream a wide variety of audio and visual content into the classroom from the World Wide Web. As is often the case, spread of this new technology presents itself as somewhat of a double-edged sword for classroom instructors. On the one hand, we have access to an unprecedented wealth of content. On the other hand, we are presented with the problem of how to first identify, and then integrate, this content in such as way that does not overwhelm our lesson plans. Presented below is a source for very brief pieces of content that can launch classroom lectures and discussions. My goal in using this material is to make memorable the key concepts, theories, or research findings that make up a typical day's lesson plan by tying these to readily available discussions of world events, cultural criticism, or even "news of the weird."

Making it Work

Consider National Public Radio (NPR). The network's website www.NPR.org archives 88 programs currently in production. All of these programs are produced at least weekly. And many, such as "Morning Edition," "Fresh Air," "Talk of the Nation," and "All Things Considered" are produced daily. Some productions are half an hour or even a full hour discussion focused on one topic. However, many are composed of several shorter topical segments linked together by brief introduction or musical interlude. For example, just one of these daily productions, "All Things Considered," averaged 16 discrete stories on a wide range of topics per day over the past year. Each of these 3–5 minute stories that make up a program is individually archived on the NPR's website. Summaries and transcripts for these stories currently exist for broadcast dating back to January 1st of 1995 and streaming audio is available to January 1st, 1996. This is true for almost every program broadcast on NPR. This is a wealth of high-quality, topically focused, publically available content, and now each of these archived stories is keyword searchable.

Searches on broad topical areas like "Gender," "Cloning," or "Cell Phones" returned many hundreds of stories. Of course not all of these will be directly on point or particularly relevant. However, searches can be further narrowed by date, program, and using NPR's own topical categorization. Like many search engines, Boolean operators such as AND, OR, and quotation marks can be included to narrow searches as well. Just for fun, I tried more specific keywords that may be of interest across campuses. "Tocqueville" returned 44 stories, "Sartre" 41, and even "Bayesian" returned a story on the application of an algorithm for sorting and categorizing great works of literature.

Once a story has been identified, it is relatively easy to copy and paste the permanent link for the audio into

Combining a personal and relatable narrative with images and illustrations has proved a powerful way to form abstract disciplinary ideas in students' minds

PowerPoint slides, lecture notes, or any electronic communication with students. For example, I regularly teach an introductory sociology course. One of the early and fundamental points that students often struggle with is the power of everyday social interaction. Illustrating "the social" as an empirical domain separate from, yet integral to, individual experience is often a first step in inviting students to exercise their sociological imaginations. In searching the materials outlined above, I found a story about a college student living with autism. While we do not focus on autism per se, this student's personal account of her struggles to understand normative interactions on her campus helps my students to develop perspective on an often taken-for-granted aspect of any society. Often, as is the case here, these stories are accompanied by pictures or other graphics. Continuing with this example, I include these pictures along with some animations and, particularly noteworthy, quotes in a Power Point presentation that I display as the audio plays. Combining a personal and relatable narrative with images and illustrations has proved a powerful way to form abstract disciplinary ideas in students' minds.

Future Implications

I have found that using these short reports and stories is a good way to introduce and focus students' attention on a particular topic or idea at the beginning of class. Then I can make reference to these stories throughout our discussion of course material. It provides a "hook" upon which students can hang the day's lesson. This has been effective in both large and small classroom settings. The only equipment required is a computer with internet connectivity and a small audio system. Lecture launchers like these can be implemented very quickly and have proven to stimulate recall and comprehension as demonstrated on quizzes, exams, and in essays.

"HEARING EVERY VOICE:" PROMOTING ENGAGEMENT THROUGH ELECTRONIC DISCUSSION

PATRICK J. ASHTON
INDIANA UNIVERSITY PURDUE UNIVERSITY FORT WAYNE

Keywords: threaded discussions, electronic participation, diversity, engagement, large classes

Framework

Conscientious college teachers are always concerned about student participation. In a large class —typically anything over two dozen students — the challenge can be particularly daunting. No matter how interesting the topic or animated the instructor, students will differentially participate in the discussion. While instructors can proactively encourage reticent students, there is no way to guarantee relatively equal participation. One way around this difficulty is to use an electronic discussion board. This can take the form of either a threaded discussion or a blog. Many academic campuses subscribe to course management software like Blackboard or OnCourse that makes it easy to implement this feature. If your campus does not provide a system, you can download free discussion software from the web.

Making it Work

You, as the instructor, can get the discussion rolling by posting an open-ended question, much like you would do live in the classroom. If you come up with questions for each major topic in your class, then you will have a series of threaded discussions. Then, if you require students to post at least one substantive response to each topic, you will guarantee that each student's voice is heard at least once on each topic. I tell students that a substantive response is one that is at least a paragraph long and adds information, opinion, analysis, or argumentation to the discussion. Short comments such as "I agree." or "That's so true." (or text-like responses of OMG or LOL) are not substantive, though students should be encouraged to post such comments as a way of building and reinforcing a sense of community. The instructor just needs to make it clear that only substantive comments count toward the requirement. For me, substantive comments can be replies to the instructor or to another student. Because students have an opportunity to reflect on the postings and edit their own response before posting it, the quality of their responses is, in my experience, more thoughtful. The instructor can also join the discussion by posting probes to draw students out and to encourage more critical thinking. Course management software makes it easy to grade a student's response and give immediate feedback, if you wish. I prefer not to grade individual responses, as I have found that it inhibits the discussion. I simply count the number of total topics to which students posted a substantive comment and give a percentage grade. I count electronic participation as 15–25% of a student's final grade, depending on the course.

It is important to emphasize norms of civility and mutual respect in these discussions. Here is the statement I provide on my syllabus and on the electronic bulletin board: "Each person in this course has unique prior experiences and a unique viewpoint to share. This offers a great opportunity for us to learn from each other. Though disagreement and even conflict may occur, I expect your cooperation in maintaining an atmosphere of mutual respect. When participating in discussions, it is perfectly acceptable to have strong opinions — in fact I encourage you to do so. I also encourage you to discuss your own personal experience and relate it to that of others. In the process, however, I expect you to respect the basic intelligence and humanity of each of the other participants in the discussion. Disagreement is not necessarily a bad thing, as long as there is a commitment to mutual respect. Hateful and demeaning speech will not be tolerated. When using the web, please use appropriate Netiquette." I post a guide to netiquette on the electronic board (it is available on my website – see below).

Future Implications

On the course evaluation each term, I ask students to comment on the extent to which participating in the online discussions contributed to, or failed to contribute to, their understanding of the course material. Positive comments far outweigh the negative. Students say things like "I liked the online discussions because we got to see how each person felt about all of the topics." "I felt as though we are all in a conversation." "[You] get to express personal feelings through personal experiences and interacting with others." "Enabled me to express my opinion in a stronger or more thorough way than I would have in class." "It let me see my peer standpoints and helped learn things I didn't [know] before." "[They] really helped to apply what we were learning in class to real life situations – they really made people think." "Helped me see different perspectives." "They allowed us to voice our learning and hear other views." Negative comments are rare, but they tend to express that the student did not find the discussions personally helpful: "Not very helpful, but interesting." "They didn't apply much from the class that I learned." "They were tedious."

An additional benefit of an asynchronous electronic discussion board is that it can empower students with certain disabilities to be equal participants. Recently I had a student who had been severely disabled by an auto accident. While his mind was sharp, difficulties with his expressive speech made it impossible for him to express his opinion in real time. I was concerned about what other students in the class might think of him. This student's comments on the discussion board — dictated very slowly to an assistant or family member — showed him to be intelligent, insightful, and witty. They changed the dynamic of how students reacted to him in the classroom. (See also Marsh, n.d.)

In the future, I would like to pair my students up with students in another country or another part of this country taking the same or a similar course. The students would share a common electronic discussion board, and would be held to the same requirement to make at least one substantive posting to each topic. This would introduce an added dimension of diversity into the course, but would also allow students to explore commonalities with people they may initially perceive as very different.

References

Blackboard Higher Ed. Retrieved from http://www.blackboard.com/

Indiana University Oncourse Collaboration and Learning, Retrieved from https://oncourse.iu.edu/portal

Marsh, D. (n.d.) Online learning for students with disabilities: Great option for access. Retrieved from http://www.disaboom.com/online-learning/online-learning-for-students-with-disabilities

Netiquette Home Page. Retrieved from http://www.albion.com/netiquette/

Patrick Ashton website. Retrieved from http://users.ipfw.edu/ashton

CREATING WITH INTENTIONALITY: USING A PERSONAL MULTIMEDIA NARRATIVE TO EMPHASIZE WRITING PROCESS

RONALD KATES
MIDDLE TENNESSEE STATE UNIVERSITY

Keywords: writing process, technology, composition

Framework

In an effort to both model and teach my students how to "show, don't tell," I implement the "Who I am Without Words" assignment in my computer assisted instruction (CAI)-based first-year writing course, asking students to create five to seven minute electronic, visual representations of who they "are" without verbally explaining

details. Students develop a fully encapsulated presentation they show without commentary in a format that requires them to step aside and let the presentation do the talking. I suggest to them that carefully-chosen songs can impact an audience, as does a well-planned presentation, and that the best presentations have a sense of intentionality about them. While some students choose slideshow formats like PowerPoint, increasingly students opt to make movies, use Prezi, or create hybrid presentations that combine formats, in the process discovering creative ways to express their thoughts.

Making it Work

I generally assign this project early in a semester and allow class members six to eight weeks to accumulate images and devise project plans. At five to seven minutes each, allotting time also for uploading material, I set aside three hour-long class periods for this project for a twenty person class. Teaching my writing classes in a CAI environment enables students to show their presentations on the projection screen, but more importantly to collaborate with one another during the project development stage, thus limiting my need to impart technological know-how. I conclude the project by explaining that, while learning about one another enhances the classroom community, the process of creating and organizing the presentations also has specific pedagogical values. I ask them how long the assignment took to assemble, how they decided to order their presentations, what they chose to leave in or out, whether they intentionally wove a theme throughout the assignment, whether audience considerations influenced what images or songs to include/exclude, and, finally, whether they had pride in their work. In each class, the students admit to

approaching "Who I am Without Words" with an intentionality largely lacking in their other work, leading me to ask the obvious question: If you can approach this assignment with audience awareness, an organizational plan, an eye towards continuity, a general theme (or thesis) that pervades through the presentation, and a sense of pride ... why not approach every assignment in this course in the same fashion? This crucial "teaching" aspect of the assignment provides students a process base I can refer to in my comments throughout the semester by connecting more current work to the "Who I am Without Words" assignment.

Future Implications

I have also used this assignment in 4000-level writing courses with similar results. Additionally, a colleague recently implemented this assignment into her FYE University Seminar as a means of sparking discussion over the high school-to-college transition process, and several former students have discussed how they might implement "Who I am Without Words" in a secondary Language Arts classroom. I could foresee adapting "Who I am Without Words" to fit classes in various disciplines including history, political science, art, psychology, and organizational communication.

DESIGNING AUTHENTIC CROSS-CLASS COLLABORATION BY FOCUSING ON ACTIVITY

JOSHUA A. DANISH
INDIANA UNIVERSITY BLOOMINGTON

Keywords: online learning, collaboration, authentic problems

Framework

Increasingly, students are enrolling in wholly online courses, or are being asked to participate in substantive online components as part of residential classes (Allen et al., 2007). With this shift, new questions arise about how to effectively support student interaction in online spaces. In this paper I propose an approach grounded in Activity Theory (Engeström, 1999, 1990; Wertsch, 1981), which provides a principled process for designing and integrating online instruction in a manner that encourages robust, authentic activity. I illustrate this approach with a description of the Cross-Class Collaboration Project (CCCP). In the CCCP, students from two different graduate level courses, one residential and one online, challenged each other to synthesize and apply their course materials to solve real-world problems.

Designing Through Activity Theory
Activity Theory (Engeström, 1999, 1990; Wertsch, 1981) emphasizes a need to focus not only upon individuals, but

upon joint, collective activity as the site at which learning occurs, a relationship expressed in an expanded mediational triangle (see Figure 1.8). The activity triangle depicts the relationship between the individual subjects (students), the object of their activity, available tools, and the rules and division of labor that shape interactions with the local community. In my classroom design activities, I find that the triangle is an effective heuristic to help me systematically account for these six elements as well as the relationship between them.

Activity is defined by the shared object of the participants within an activity (Wertsch, 1981), and I therefore approach the design of learning activities by determining the object of students' activity. In the case of the CCCP, I was working with students in two different graduate level courses. Students in P540: Cognition and Learning surveyed major theories of learning in an online distance-education setting. The second face-to-face class, P574: Computational Technologies in Educational Ecosystems, surveyed many of the theoretical and practical innovations related to implementing technology in learning contexts.

The students in both courses, therefore, shared a general interest in learning and education.

Making it Work

The shared object that I identified for these students was, however, one that may apply to many disciplines and courses: how to answer messy, real-world questions in their area of interest. In particular, they wanted to see how they might apply course content to the practical questions that they would encounter in their current and future careers. Furthermore, this kind of authentic activity has been shown to increase the likelihood that students will be able to apply what they have learned once they leave class (Brown, Collins, & Duguid, 1989). My identification of the object stemmed from repeated observation and conversation with the students. In other situations, however, it might have been necessary to either poll students to solicit a shared object, or engage the students in activities designed to inspire a shared object. For example, I have often found that once students are presented with a sufficiently interesting and yet unanswered question, they will adopt the answering of that question as a goal for their immediate activity.

Given this goal, and a general concern that students in online courses often feel isolated from their peers, I decided to ask the students to answer authentic questions that were driven by the needs and interests of the very community they might one day work with — their peers in the other course. All that remained, then, was to determine the tools, rules, and division of labor that might effectively support the students' attainment of their goal of applying the course theories to answering their peers' questions. For this step of the design process, I find it makes more sense to begin with whichever mediator comes to mind first and then to use the activity triangle as a heuristic to ensure not only that the mediators are all addressed, but that they are complementary. In this case, my students were already using Oncourse (the IU implementation of the Sakai Learning Management System) and so a shared forum made sense as a location where the students might meet.

Finally, I determined the rules and division of labor that I believed would best support students in engaging in a forum discussion aimed at applying their theories to real-world problems. The assignment therefore had two tasks: first, post a question for the students in the other course. Students in P540 asked the P574 students questions how they might implement technology in their learning environments while the P574 students asked how learning theory might influence their technology designs. Then, to ensure substantive and diverse answers, I required students to answer at least 3 questions with a minimum length of 2-3 paragraphs. The end result was a lively set of discussions in which students struggled, in the most productive sense of the term, with how to adapt the "clean" theories they had been learning to the "messy" realities of their peers' real-world contexts.

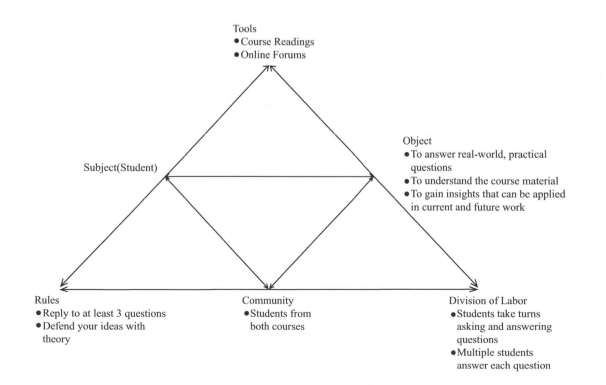

Figure 1.8. The Cross-Class Collaboration Project Activity System
Adapted from Engestrom, 1987. See also Cole, 1996 for a more in-depth discussion of activity theory.

Future Implications

From my standpoint, the exercise was a success. The majority of student answers were longer than required, and showed a depth and insight into the course theories that was largely absent from more traditional essay tasks. Furthermore, when surveyed upon their experiences, the students consistently responded that they found the exercise to be challenging, but also realistic, interesting, and rewarding. For example, one student wrote, "A project like this has forced (in a positive way) me to think critically on the readings, and how they apply in practice. [...] With a project like this I have to examine the needs of another and find the fitting theory. Here's a bonus, I really enjoyed it."

As an illustration of how the Activity Triangle provides a systematic way to design learning activities, the CCCP shows the potential of leveraging shared online forums to engage students in different but related classes in a rich, meaningful manner. Asking students to respond to their peers in this way, in lieu of traditional essays, has the added benefit of providing authentic, messy problems that are akin to those that students will face when they leave our classes.

References

Allen, I. E., & Seaman, J. (2006). *Making the grade: Online education in the United States, 2006*. Needham, MA: The Sloan Consortium and Babson Survey Research Group.

Brown, J. S., Collins, A., & Duguid, P. (1989). Situated cognition and the culture of learning. *Educational Researcher, 18*(1), 32-42.

Cole, M. (1996). *Cultural psychology: A once and future discipline*. Boston, MA: First Harvard University Press.

Engeström, Y. (1999). Activity theory and individual and social transformation. In Y. Engeström, R. Miettinen, & R-L. Punamäki (Eds.). *Perspectives on Activity Theory*. Cambridge, UK: Cambridge University Press.

Engeström, Y. (Ed.). (1990). *Learning, working and imagining: Twelve studies in activity theory*. Helsinki: Orienta-Konsultit Oy.

Engeström, Y. (1987). *Learning by expanding*. Helsinki: Orienta-Konsultit Oy.

Wertsch, J. V. (1981). The concept of activity in Soviet psychology: An introduction. In J. V. Wertsch (Ed.), *The Concept of Activity in Soviet Psychology* (pp. 3-36). Armonk, N.Y.: M.E. Sharpe.

Using a business strategy simulation

Charles Scott and Jeremy Schwartz
Loyola University Maryland

Keywords: simulations, economics, management

Framework

We use a business strategy simulation (BSS) as a valuable classroom tool to reinforce the major topics we cover in Managerial Economics. A BSS is an on-line application that students purchase and participate in on-line. We have used both Business Strategy Game (http://www.bsg-online.com) and Capstone (http://www.capsim.com) ($38.95 and $44.99 per student), each requiring only Internet access. Students make a variety of decisions in order to run a virtual business in competition with others in the class. The BSS enhances courses that have a primary objective of applying theory to business decision making, such as a business, economics, business

Since much of the simulation work is done outside of class, simulations work well in on-line and hybrid contexts.

• • • • • • • • • • •

ethics, globalization or strategy course. The simulation provides an ideal laboratory for either graduate or undergraduate students in classes below 40 students, to apply the concepts and statistical tools of these courses and personally experience the results of their use.

Making it Work

To ensure a successful course, we
1. create teams that distribute students' skills evenly to ensure no one team falls far behind and loses interest,
2. determine and publish due dates for each business decision and written forecast and annual reports,
3. develop a grading scheme that creates incentives to take the simulation seriously (typically around 30%–40% of total grade),
4. adjust topic coverage order to address the most relevant topics to the simulation as early as possible, and
5. educate students on the BSS through a practice simulation run on the first day of class to generate excitement in the course, allow students to see the value of the simulation as a laboratory, and teach the technical aspects of navigating the BSS.

We expect teams to meet regularly to apply course tools in developing their firm's strategy and meet the deadlines for entering on-line decisions. In addition, throughout the course we use the simulation as a learning tool by incorporating it into our lectures, class exercises and projects.

For example:
1. When covering market structure, students recognize they are operating in an oligopoly and how this affects their market and their firm's choices.
2. Students calculate the price sensitivity of their product interpreting its implications during class.
3. Students use their company's data to develop their own sales forecast.
4. Instructors can also adjust specific variables, such as exchange or interest rates, to emphasize particular concepts.

Future Implications

We assess our students on the performance of their companies and out of class exercises related to the BSS. With the proper incentives students are vested in the performance of their team, which results in: (1) greater student interest in the course, (2) more effective student-faculty interaction, and (3) greater motivation to learn the why and how of course tools for running a business. The practical management and teamwork experiences also prepare students for interviews, internships, and their future careers.

Contexts

Since much of the simulation work is done outside of class, simulations work well in on-line and hybrid contexts. Mentoring for the BSS can be done in person, via e-mail, or via on-line interaction or through simulation-provided support.

ENGAGING STUDENTS THROUGH A VIRTUAL CHILD SIMULATION

GWENDOLYN METTETAL, CAROLYN A. SCHULT, LAURA TALCOTT, AND KATHY RITCHIE
INDIANA UNIVERSITY SOUTH BEND

Keywords: simulation, engagement

Framework

We have used the My Virtual Child simulation in our developmental psychology classes for several years, with excellent results. This web-based simulation (developed by psychologist Frank Manis) allows students to raise a child from birth to age 18, making parenting decisions that influence the child's outcomes. Students can purchase access online for $25 at myvirtualchild.com, or access codes can be bundled free with Pearson psychology textbooks as part of the MyDevelopmentLab supplement.

Making it Work

Students sign in from any computer, complete questionnaires about their personality and aptitudes (to provide input on genetics), and are told that they (or their partner) have given birth. The text-based program provides information about the child's development (doctor's reports, meetings with teachers) and life events (divorce, accidents, a sibling's birth). There are also short videos that illustrate key concepts, such as secure attachment. "Parents" are asked to make many decisions, given in a multiple-choice format. These decisions include nutrition, activities, education, and reactions to child misbehaviors. The decisions and life events directly influence how the child develops. Successfully parented children get into good colleges, while neglected children may end up in rehab. It takes approximately eight hours to complete the program;

however, students may stop and resume as many times as they wish. (As in real parenting, there are no "do overs." Students cannot change a parenting decision that has already been made.) Instructors can set up a class code, so that they can see how their students are progressing. The program periodically provides students questions relating their experience to course concepts that students may answer and submit to their professor, although instructors can easily provide different questions, on a different timetable, in their syllabus. A comprehensive instructor's manual gives a complete listing of the decision points, the questions for students, and many ideas for implementation. Although best suited for a chronologically-organized child development course, we have successfully adapted the program for lifespan development, topically-organized child development, and parenting courses. We have asked students to "raise" their child at the beginning, end, or throughout the course, with papers due throughout or at the end.

Future Implications

Several years ago, we surveyed students from four classes about their experience in raising the Virtual Child. They indicated that the simulation helped them learn important foundational concepts and applied issues. They reported strong engagement with the program, and preferred it to research papers, group projects or even observations of real children. Anecdotally, we have been impressed with the enthusiasm shown by students, particularly the young males (who are sometimes less excited about the course content). We were concerned that students who were parents would find the simulation irrelevant, but that has not been the case. In fact, several students have made changes in their real-life parenting style, because they saw the likely outcomes if they continued their current practices. Even those who are grandparents have enjoyed the opportunity to try a different parenting style.

As the simulation is refined, we have new options. For example, instructors can now "re-set" a student's virtual child back to birth. This allows students to try raising the child in two very different ways, to see the different consequences.

Social engagement

Lisa Fiedor
North Carolina State University

Keywords: social presence, online engagement, learning management systems, web conferencing systems, distance education

Framework

By using a welcome video, biography assignments, "Introduce Yourself" forums, and customizable profiles in a Learning Management System (LMS), Web conferencing system, or other platform used by all of the students in your course or curriculum, you can help establish social presence and engagement in not only Distance Education (DE) courses, but also help to establish rapport in blended courses. When it comes to distance education, few things help students (and attrition rates) more than knowing there are actual people on the other end of the computer to whom they are responsible. This is especially true when students are assigned group work (Richardson & Swan, 2003). If they can see the pictures of and know where the instructor and other students are coming from, this can increase the richness of their work.

Participant profiles in an LMS such as Moodle (http://moodle.org), or Web conferencing systems such as Elluminate (http://elluminate.com), allow for uploading an image, which could be a picture of the student or other avatar, as well as city and state information, and a place to list interests. Using these platforms can often be a better, more private way of connecting than using a social networking system like Facebook. If you have access to a Web conferencing system, but don't plan to use it to fully deliver your course, you could conduct one session where you use a webcam to introduce yourself, and encourage the other students to do the same, or at least offer an audio or chat message to the group. This can give each person a real face or voice presence, and help the students identify with your and each other.

Making it Work

Faculty can encourage social presence and engagement between the students by assigning students to engage in an "Introduce Yourself" forum, requiring them to provide some basic information about who they are and why they are taking the course. A simple starting sentence such as,

> *"Please take a moment to share with your classmates any pertinent professional or academic information you would like to provide, as well as your reasons for taking this course. Please respond to at least one of your classmates' introductions, as this is our opportunity to get to know one another as we begin this course."*

As with all activities in a course, students can be encouraged to participate by giving them a 1 or 2 point grade for posting and/or responding to a minimum number of other students' posts. It is important that the instructor participates in and leads these activities to show the students their importance. To follow this up, faculty can also provide an ungraded student lounge forum, where students can conduct off-topic discussions, and build community.

Biography assignments are another, more private, way to get to know the students, and faculty should provide welcoming comments when returning each of their submissions. A general welcome message can also help the students connect with you as the instructor, and should be considered a minimum way to establish social presence. A welcome message could be a quick five-minute video or audio message introducing yourself and the content of your course, as well as your expectations of the student. These can be accomplished by using a webcam, microphone, and free video editing tool such as Windows Movie Maker or iMovie to make your video, or recording your voice and editing it with a free audio editor like Pinnacle. You can also use a Web conferencing or lecture capture system to record and present your short message.

Future Implications

Although given a DE context here, each of these activities would greatly benefit blended courses, as well. When some face-to-face sessions are reduced in lieu of moving more content online, faculty need to help students connect more richly in both environments. Students may think that the online environment is less relevant then in-class sessions, but the social engagement developed online can illustrate to them that the online component, or LMS, is a classroom, too. This can be especially helpful in increasing engagement in large enrollment courses. By adding components to your course such as welcome videos, biography assignments, Web conferencing opportunities, "Introduce Yourself" forums, and customizable profiles, you can assist students' development of social presence and engagement in your course. This is especially important, as research has been shown that students' perceptions of social presence in online courses are a predictor of their perceived learning and satisfaction with the course (Richardson & Swan, 2003).

References

Richardson, J., & Swan, K. (2003). Examining social presence in online courses in relation to students' perceived learning and satisfaction. *JALN, 7*(1), 79.

BUILDING A SENSE OF COMMUNITY IN AN ONLINE ENVIRONMENT: STUDENT AUTOBIOGRAPHICAL VIDEOS

MICHELLE GACIO HARROLLE
NORTH CAROLINA STATE UNIVERSITY

Keywords: distance education, building communities, student video presentations

Framework

More universities have turned to alternate educational delivery systems such as distance education (DE) and online courses. However, as the learning environment is at a distance, many students have expressed isolation and a sense of not belonging to a community. This sense of community is an important component of successful online learning. In order to increase interaction among students and build a sense of belongingness for students in my DE courses, I assign DE students short and easy autobiographical video presentations using PowerPoint.

Making it Work

Students create autobiographical presentations using PowerPoint slides with photos and text boxes. They may use voice over or may add music to the background by inserting the audio or video files from the insert tab in PowerPoint. The videos are limited to 1–1:30 minute presentations. However, some students have asked for more time. Typically, I deal with time extensions on a case-by-case basis and will allow up to 2:30 minute videos.

In PowerPoint 2010, it is simple for students to save their presentations in a video format (Windows Media Video; .wmv); however in older versions of PowerPoint students should save the files as a PowerPoint Slide Show (.ppsx).

As part of the assignment, students post their videos (or PowerPoint Slide Show) to the online course discussion board, so the entire class (e.g., 30 graduate students) has access to the students' autobiographies. The videos could also be used for larger DE classes. Small discussion forum groups of 10–15 students could be used to increase students' interaction and engagement for larger courses.

Future Implications

To help build a sense of community and sense of caring during the live online synchronous course meetings held once a week, I quiz students on other students' video information at the beginning of each class. Within my lecture slides on Elluminate (online virtual classroom provided through our university's information technology office for faculty use), I will post a few facts about a student with accompanying photos, based on their videos/presentations, and will provide multiple choice answers from names of students in the class. Then, I informally poll the students to help them to get to know each other. Typically, this portion of the synchronous course meeting requires approximately 20 minutes of instructor's preparation time and 5–8 minutes of online classroom time each week.

These student videos have helped to create a sense of community among our DE cohort of students, as evident in the positive feedback from our students and our low attrition rate.

· · · · · · · · · · · ·   · · · · · · · · · · · ·

This sense of community is an important component
of successful online learning.

Online art galleries and clinical stories

Linda Felver
Oregon Health & Science University

Keywords: online learning tools; student engagement; deep learning

Framework

In my clinical pharmacology course, I use technology to promote student engagement and deep learning with online art galleries and clinical stories that support our classroom sessions. Each course topic we discuss has its own art gallery and clinical story section available online at the beginning of the term. Students use these for study and also have the opportunity to make two submissions of their own for extra credit points.

> I encourage students to draw pictures to help them learn side effects and how best to teach patients about the various classes of drugs.

Clinical stories are short, true scenarios with names and identifying details removed to preserve confidentiality. Submissions must include at least two "Questions for Thought" to help other students reflect on the clinical pharmacology of the situation during individual or group study. Writing these thought questions impels the student who submits the story to integrate and reflect on knowledge relevant to the clinical situation.

Art galleries consist of items created by students: photographs, cartoons, drawings, audio clips of original songs, animations, and other media. Each is accompanied by Questions for Thought. In class, I encourage students to draw pictures to help them learn side effects and how best to teach patients about the various classes of drugs. Knowing that they can receive extra credit for their drawings of Penny Cillin and her cousins encourages students to manipulate the ideas in their minds to express them in a visual way. This process provides a much deeper level of learning than rote memorization of lists.

Making it Work

These online learning tools are appropriate for both small and large classes. I use them with my classroom course for nursing students, but they can be adapted for courses in any discipline, especially where the desired outcome is application of knowledge or bridging the gap between facts, ideas, and real life.

I use the learning management system (LMS) provided by the university, to which all students already have access from their own and campus-based computers. Thus, no additional costs are involved in this use of technology. Because I mount the art galleries and clinical stories in HTML files, it was easy to move them when the university changed from a proprietary LMS to Sakai, an open source software LMS and collaboration environment created by a community of educators.

Since I already had an online site to support my classroom course, it was not difficult to implement this use of technology to enhance learning. Having an art gallery and clinical stories for each course topic required creation of 10 or more art galleries and an equivalent number of clinical story repositories. I created an art gallery template and one for clinical stories, to streamline the initial creation process. After creating separate files from the template and populating each with a few submissions of my own, I linked each one to its topic page online in a consistent location so that students would know where to find them. This process took a couple of weeks in small time segments sandwiched between my other responsibilities. In the art galleries, I provide alt text for all graphics, to allow access for visually impaired people who use screen readers, and transcripts for audio and video, to provide access for people with hearing difficulties.

Now that these electronic files are created, I can add new material to the growing collection each term so that students benefit from previous submissions. Students themselves generate the new material through their submissions for extra credit. In this beginning course, I do not have students post in a blog or wiki, to avoid confusing other students when there are pharmacology errors. I post only those submissions that are error-free. My screening process is synonymous with grading the extra credit, using the criteria I have posted online for students to see. In a more advanced course, I would have students post them directly for all to see.

Future Implications

In anonymous course evaluations, many students report that they found the art galleries and clinical stories very useful for learning. The Questions for Thought that students generate demonstrate their understanding of course material. Some students discuss their submissions briefly with me, showing depth of learning that surpasses course requirements. The outcome I see is epitomized by a student who emailed me that she began her clinical story submission to gain extra credit points. However, by the time she completed it, she realized that she had learned more deeply about three classes of drugs we had studied in class and had integrated her knowledge at a clinically applicable level. She was thrilled at her ability to retain and apply this material later. This example of deep learning rather than surface learning (Mentkowski & Associates, 2000) is why I keep using technology in this way.

Future Directions: The templates I designed work well on computer screens with any web browser but are not optimal for the tiny screens on smart phones and other mobile devices. At present, I am working with our Academic Technology department to design a new art gallery interface optimized for handheld devices. Based on the usefulness of online art galleries and clinical stories in engaging students and deepening their learning, I plan to make them available via this new mobile technology as well.

References

Mentkowski, M., & Associates. (2000). *Learning that lasts: Integrating learning, development, and performance in college and beyond*. San Francisco: Jossey-Bass.

Sakai Project, http://sakaiproject.org

She realized that she had learned more deeply about three classes of drugs we had studied in class and had integrated her knowledge at a clinically applicable level.

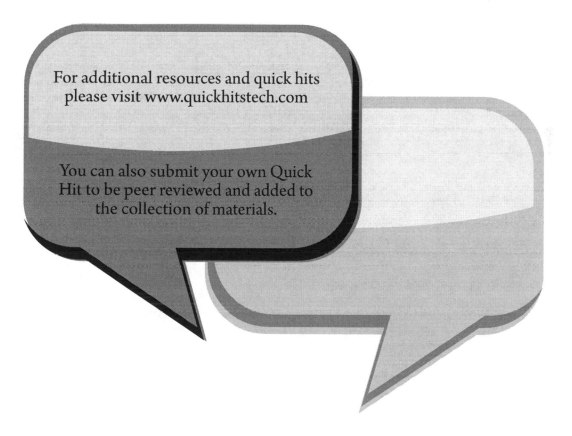

For additional resources and quick hits please visit www.quickhitstech.com

You can also submit your own Quick Hit to be peer reviewed and added to the collection of materials.

PROVIDING ACCESS

PROVIDING A SHORTER PATH USING DISTANCE EDUCATION TO ENHANCE ACCESS

JOAN ESTERLINE LAFUZE
INDIANA UNIVERSITY EAST

It was the first day of a two semester class in anatomy and physiology. We had finished the tour around the room, with a quick introduction and description of personal goals. During the break, several students stopped with questions or comments, but one woman waited patiently until all others had left the room and then said, "I just wanted you to know that I am eligible for student services, but I don't want to be treated any differently from the others. The only reason that I am telling you is because if I work hard enough I can make a C in this class. I just don't want you to think that my C is not because I am not trying."

Upon reflection, I decided to develop "voiceover" PowerPoint slides as a way of meeting the needs of not only this student, but also other students who may have difficulty learning the material at the quick pace set in my classes. To create a "voiceover" PowerPoint slide, I simply recorded myself as a I explained complicated concepts on each of my PowerPoint slides and briefly discussed how we would use the material covered in the PowerPoint slides in class to develop a deeper understanding of the material. After I distributed my "voiceover" PowerPoint slides to the class, this student stopped again during break. "Oh, thank you. It is exactly how I learn. I hear your voice, see the picture or words and have time to write it on paper."

In the same way that putting reading glasses on a student who is visually impaired can help them to see clearly, using the newer technologies may provide an opportunity for students to learn in meaningful ways. Over the almost two decades that I have used "distance education" technologies to "close the distance" between the classroom and the student learner, I have marveled over the power that technology may sometimes provide in opening doors that would be closed and locked to students who only now have access to the college education of their dreams. I have had a number of students move during the semester from traditional classrooms to online sections of courses that I teach in order to make it possible to follow deployed spouses or partners; to take care of children, spouses, partners or parents who are critically ill; or to take advantage of job or career opportunities that require relocation or shift change considerations.

Of course, my personal account overlaps greatly with the experiences of others. In this chapter, you will find Quick Hits from faculty who use technology to assist students in finding pathways to achieve their educational goals. As a whole, these submissions reflect several of the potential advantages of distance education as outlined in Steenhausen's (2010) executive summary of "The Master Plan at 50: Using Distance Education to Increase College Access and Efficiency." Specifically, the submissions in this chapter:

- Make undergraduate and graduate coursework more accessible to students who otherwise might not be able to enroll due to restrictive personal or professional obligations.
- Provide opportunities for students attending one campus to find and get credit for courses at other campuses (thereby potentially speeding their graduation).

- Allow campuses to increase instruction and enrollment without a commensurate need for additional physical infrastructure (such as classrooms and parking structures).
- Make possible statewide collaborations, including "virtual" academic departments that are taught by faculty from more than one campus.

Many of our students are restricted in completing course work in a traditional classroom setting by both personal and professional obligations. In the submission by Beth Goering (Indiana University Purdue University Indianapolis), a way of helping students 'internationalize' their education is described – without the students going abroad. Similarly, Laura Guertin (Penn State Brandywine) describes utilizing existing gigapixel panoramas for virtual fieldtrips in her courses.

In their submission, Grace Pinhal-Enfield, David DeFouw, and Nagaswami Vasan (New Jersey Medical School) describe the use of virtual microscopy in teaching histology. With virtual microscopy, "rather than being limited to a set of glass slide boxes created by one institution, our students have access to a broad repertoire of virtual slide images in an optimized, faculty-selected virtual slide box. Furthermore, in contrast to variable box-to-box slide quality seen with glass slide boxes, virtual slide boxes are uniform and all students have access to the same virtual images."

Additional advantages are illustrated in the Doppelgänger Professor, submitted by Elizabeth Jones (Notre Dame University of Maryland). In this Quick Hit, technology allows for a "blended learning solution in which core content was delivered online and a single faculty member met students at each location on a rotating schedule. By combining the efficiency of asynchronous online presentation with lively, on-site interaction, students received first-rate instruction and graduated on time; and the college provided affordable, high-quality services to a widely separated population using just one instructor."

References:

Steenhausen, P. (2010). *The master plan at 50: Using distance education to increase college access and efficiency.* Retrieved on July 14, 2011: http://www.lao.ca.gov/reports/2010/edu/distance_ed/distance_ed_102510.aspx

TO PODCAST OR NOT TO PODCAST

MARK URTEL AND EUGENIA FERNANDEZ
INDIANA UNIVERSITY PURDUE UNIVERSITY INDIANAPOLIS

Keywords: student perceptions of podcasts, podcasting best practices, academic broadcasts

Framework

Technology is being used extensively in higher education classrooms across the globe. Podcasting is one of these technologies. With the proliferation of iTunes, mobile devices, and free, (relatively) easy podcast-creating software, academic podcasting is exploding. If you are reading this, you may be wondering if you should join in. To help with your decision, we offer some simple guidelines on creating podcasts, some evidence on student usage of podcasts, and a little bit of reassurance.

What is podcasting?

Podcasting is a method of distributing audio or audio/video files via the Internet for playback on mobile devices and personal computers at the listener's convenience. Podcasts are almost always saved in MP3 format so they can be played on most any computer or mobile device. True podcasting combines the audio files with a subscription service (similar to that in iTunes) so that new podcasts are pushed to the subscriber. However, this is not necessary as users can elect to download podcast at will.

What technology is currently available for creating podcasts? Take advantage of the technology or teaching support center at your institution to learn about the most current hardware and software used to make an academic podcast. The learning curve in creating, editing, and posting academic podcasts has been greatly compressed over the last few years. Literally, a single podcast can be created, edited, and posted in less than two hours.

Making it Work

Guidelines on creating and using podcasts

Learn from others. Make yourself available to the emerging scholarship on academic podcasting. Learn from faculty whom have investigated this technology so that it positively contributes to your own teaching practices and is not just the "latest and newest shiny thing" in higher education with limited value.

Keep the end user in mind. Understand the student perspective so that you create a podcast that will be listened to and used within the framework of the course. While contemporary students are tech-savvy, remember that just because students use a technology in their social time and space does not mean they will use it in their academic time and space.

Don't make your podcasts re-runs. Avoid using podcasting only to "lecture capture"; evidence suggests that simply recording a scripted lecture and posting it as an academic podcast will lead to failure. Make academic podcasts that are fresh and alternative perspectives to course material. Or use a podcast to introduce a topic and guide student learning about it. The novelty tends to hook students and amplify their understanding.

Vary the perspective. Commit to creating podcasts that enhance and supplement course materials, e.g., interviewing national experts, textbook authors, and local and regional experts on timely topics or poignant elements of assigned reading that can amplify student understanding. In fact, these types of interviews can be viewed like a guest speaker in perpetuity. Interviewing an industry expert is invaluable as a tool; a brief yet particular interview can help clarify or expand on an element of the reading in a way that students can connect with outside of the class.

Use a podcast to introduce a topic and guide student learning

Don't think you will defeat students' social habits. Certainly create and post academic podcasts so students can download them using multiple mediums and technologies, but understand students view academic podcasts as just that … academic assignments. Research tells us students will probably listen to them at home or in the library on a desktop or laptop … not in transport on a personal listening device. And this behavior is both a compliment and a good thing as it shows students are viewing the podcasts as an academic pursuit and not a social activity. In addition, while they may not take advantage of the mobile possibilities of podcasts, they do appreciate the flexibility podcasts provide for any-time learning.

Brevity is best. Limit podcasts to 5–15 minutes, 30 minutes maximum, if you must. Remember that you are dealing with students who are used to listening to a 3–5 minute song. A podcast longer than 15 minutes can lead to a mental drift when listening. Of course, the length of the podcast is related to its purpose. For academic podcasts, focus at most on one or two themes or lecture highlights. Create a podcast that addresses a few discrete elements. Emulate the philosophy of the PechaKucha movement, which limits PowerPoint presentations to 20 slides at 20 seconds each. "It's a format that makes presentations concise, and keeps things moving at a rapid pace." (www.pechaKucha.org).

Value the podcast. Hold students accountable for the podcast by making the content evident on a course assessment. Whether you choose a weekly quiz or brief synopsis paper, you are making it clear to the students that you value the podcast content; as a result, students will value the podcast.

More is not better. Avoid feeling compelled to create an academic podcast for each class session or even each week, which could easily lead to this technology becoming overbearing and monotonous. Conversely, creating a single academic podcast for the entire semester may not indicate significance and students may simply not invest the time and energy to listen to that single podcast.

Future Implications

Student view of podcasts
Okay, you've spent time creating numerous, novel, innovative, and brief podcasts to enhance your course materials. How will the students respond to and use them? Research evidence suggests the following.

- When asked, students are positive about the idea of podcasts, but not all listen to them (listening rates vary between 40%–75%). In general, upperclassmen are more likely to listen to podcasts than underclassmen, and graduate students more than upperclassmen. Somewhat surprising, students with a lot of experience in downloading recreational content and those with little / no experiences with downloading recreational content have displayed similar academic podcast listening rates.
- Fortunately, students who do listen to course broadcasts say they help their understanding of course concepts and enhance their learning. This is especially true when it is clear the academic podcast has value in regard to course assessments (quiz, test, paper, etc.).
- Students view academic podcasts as separate from entertainment-related ones, and generally do not make use of syndication feeds for automatic delivery of academic podcasts but download them manually. More importantly, students will likely listen to the podcast on a desktop or laptop at home or on-campus. Additionally,

it is unlikely students will listen to the podcast on a mobile learning device while in-transport.
- Many non-native English speaking students find podcasts useful so that they can review in-class material that might be difficult to understand upon first hearing the material. So if you teach courses where English is a new language for the enrolled students, it is helpful if the podcast has elements that coincide with lecture notes or slides; again so they can listen to a podcast multiple times to help overcome comprehension difficulties related to language abilities. This can also help them prepare for course assessments.

But what about attendance?
Be assured, most students who listen to podcasts still attend class. Evidence shows that the use of podcasting has little or no impact on class attendance. Think of academic podcasts as a supplement to class, and not as a replacement for classroom instruction.

References

Audacity: free, open source software for recording and editing sounds. http://audacity.sourceforge.net/

Briggs, L.L. (2008). *Podcasting and education.* Retrieved from Campus Technology website July, 18, 2011: http://campustechnology.com/articles/57399/

Campbell, G. (2005). There's something in the air: Podcasting in education. *EDUCAUSE Review, 40*(6), 32-47. Retrieved July 18, 2011: http://connect.educause.edu/Library/ EDUCAUSE+Review/TheresSomethingintheAirPo/40587

How to podcast. Retrieved from Podcasting Tools website July 18, 2011: http://www.podcasting-tools.com/how-to-podcast.htm

Malan, D.J. (2007). Podcasting computer science E-1. *Proceedings of SIGCSE'07*, March 7–10, Covington, Kentucky.

What is Podcasting? Retrieved from Podcasting News website July 18, 2011: http://www.podcastingnews.com/articles/What_is_Podcasting.html

University Information Technology Services. (2011, March 21). *Where can I learn more about podcasting at IU?* Knowledge Base article retrieved July 19, 2011: http://kb.iu.edu/data/auwt.html

Urtel, M.G. (2010). *Academic podcasts: Student perspectives. Academic Exchange Quarterly, 14*(4), 117-122.

Think of academic podcasts as a supplement to class,
and not as a replacement for classroom instruction.

SOME ASSEMBLY REQUIRED: TEACHING ONLINE WITH GOOD INSTRUCTIONS

DUSTIN L. SHELL AND BRIAN A. WARNER
UNIVERSITY OF CINCINNATI

Keywords: instructions, scaffolding, interactive media, manual, online, hybrid

Framework

For many people, assembling Swedish furniture runs the gamut of emotion: The joy of success to the agony of defeat. If you haven't had this 'pleasure', consider the last time you felt incompetent using an instruction manual to assemble a new product. What caused this? Was it either too complex or too simplistic? I think we can agree that most of us are capable of assembling a product with the right instructions (and the right size allen wrench). More often than not, however, the process of deciphering the steps, processes, and meanings of those deceivingly confusing little pamphlets leads to high levels of frustration and despair. This example parallels the design of effective instruction through technology. Whether you're teaching a fully online or hybrid course, be it large or small, clearly articulating the organization and application of your content is essential to making it accessible in a meaningful way. The best way to approach effective design strategies is two fold: Keep instructions simple, then augment them with interactive media.

Figure 2.1. Satirical Ikea illustration.

Ikea is known for only using images with no text to demonstrate product assembly. This illustrates how unclear instructions may cause confusion. Image courtesy of Justin Spencer.

Making it Work

First, it is easy to get lost in course design, so keep it simple to start with; I recommend using your learning management system (Blackboard, Moodle, etc.) to structure your content. It's free and you probably already know how to use it. Start by writing an introduction to each new content module to bring context and relevance to the material. Never post an article, reading, or video without an explanation of how it fits into the bigger picture. Remember the Swedish furniture; even the brightest individuals will struggle putting the pieces together if they lack meaningful and easy to follow instructions. In terms of time commitment, expect to spend an extra hour preparing each new module depending on its complexity and length. Each time you teach a course, you will likely find new improvements to make on the instructions to help students 'assemble' your material in meaningful way.

clearly articulating the organization and application of your content is essential to making it accessible in a meaningful way.

• • • • • • • • • • • •

As eLearning development tools continue to evolve, facilitating online learning through good instructions will become even more important. For the first time, faculty will be asked to provide interactive learning opportunities that are contextual instead of linear. This brings me to my second step, pairing multimedia with your instructions.

I've found that pairing video and audio instructions with written ones reduces student questions and improves satisfaction. For example, Adobe Acrobat Professional is available at a low cost and can make a standard syllabus more interactive with comments, highlights, and audio feedback where students can hear you explain each assignment. Free applications and online services, such as Jing.com, allow you to capture your computer screen with audio recordings; essentially creating video "How-To's" of your course material. Showing your students what they need to do, while explaining key concepts is a powerful learning tool.

The end result is a guided learning module that walks learners through experiences while providing knowledge checks and supplemental learning. Our ability to use technology to facilitate learning experiences will be critical in the years to come. Good luck writing your instruction manuals!

THE OPEN SOURCE PHYSICS PROJECT ON ComPADRE

WOLFGANG CHRISTIAN AND MARIO BELLONI
DAVIDSON COLLEGE

Keywords: physics, astronomy, simulations, digital library, open source

Framework

The Open Source Physics (OSP, 2011) Project is a collection of online simulations and resources located on the ComPADRE National Science Digital Library (NSDL). The OSP Project seeks to reform undergraduate education by providing simulations and curriculum resources that engage teachers and students in physics, astronomy, computation, and computer modeling. The site is based on the integration of the ComPADRE NSDL with (1) a large collection of Java simulations for physics and astronomy teaching, (2) the Easy Java Simulations (EJS) modeling and authoring tool (Christian & Esquembre, 2007; Easy Java Simulations, 2011), and (3) the OSP code library and computational physics textbook (Gould, Tobochnik, & Christian, 2006).

Computers and computer-based instruction pervade our educational institutions, and much of experimental and theoretical science cannot be done without the aid of computers. Despite advances in teaching and research, computational instruction remains absent from many physics programs. Students are bombarded with simulated reality by instructors, textbook publishers, and Hollywood directors, but few students are prepared to critically assess these simulations and even fewer are asked to create their own computational models. A physics student might never critically evaluate a simulation's output or study a computational algorithm because it is not required for admission to undergraduate or graduate school and does not appear on the Scholastic Aptitude Test or the Graduate Record Examination.

Making it Work

The OSP project seeks to address this failure by providing resources to teach fundamental skills that every student should learn and use (Karplus, 1977; Hestenes, 1987). The computer models on the OSP site:

- Help students to visualize abstract concepts: The most obvious benefit of simulations is that they help students to visualize situations. In traditional instruction, students learn physics concepts via static pictures and construct incomplete or incorrect mental models that hamper their progress toward deeper understanding of physical concepts (Mayer & Moreno, 2002; Beichner, 1997).
- Are interactive and require student interaction: When solving physics problems, students often determine the appropriate equation without relying on

physics concepts (Maloney, 1994). In well-designed simulations, physical quantities (such as position or velocity) are not given, they must be determined. By determining relevant information early in the problem-solving process, students must understand the conceptual underpinnings of the problem (Christian & Belloni, 2003).

- Are more like real-world problems: Solving simulation-based problems and real-world problems require students to distinguish between relevant and irrelevant information (Ronen & Eliahu, 2000). Simulations, just as laboratories, can also reinforce uncertainty in measurement and thus uncertainty in results. Simulations, therefore, can bridge the gap between theory and the real world (Zacharia & Anderson, 2003).
- Use multiple representations to depict information (Van Heuvelen & Zou, 2001): The idea that students learn best when they see the same ideas presented in different ways is not new. Simulations can depict motion, but they can also simultaneously depict the information in a different way via graphs and tables that change with time and can also provide the opportunity to investigate numerous alternate scenarios (Rieber, Tzeng, & Tribble, 2004).
- Can improve assessment of student understanding: Simulation-based resources can provide a superior assessment vehicle compared to traditional paper-based questions (Dancy & Beichner, 2005). Dancy compared student responses to traditional exercises with responses to nearly identical simulation-based exercises and found that the simulation-based exercises were more valid for determining whether students understood a given concept.

Simulations can depict motion, but they can also simultaneously depict the information in a different way

• • • • • • • • • •

This interplay of computation, theory, and experiment can lead to new insight and understanding that cannot be achieved with only one approach, and, in many cases, computation is the primary or sole means to solve new and interesting problems in physics and the other sciences.

Figure 2.2. The Roller Coaster item and its subdocuments.

There are currently over 400 items in the OSP Collection and many of these entries have multiple support documents. For example, the "Roller Coaster" item shown in Figure 2.2. and easily found by searching the collection for "energy conservation" has multiple subdocuments including three ready-to-run Java simulations for college-level and high school physics, a middle/high school lesson plan and student worksheet, an applet page, and the source code. Users need only click on a link to download these documents to their desktop.

Future Implications

As with all simulations created with EJS, users can examine, modify, and recompile the model for redistribution. The item is therefore useful to teachers who need simulations for their teaching, to teachers wanting to modify existing simulations, and to computational physics teachers who wish to study the underlying algorithms.

Despite its current focus on upper-level physics, the OSP Collection fall 2010 usage statistics show an average of 35,000 page views, 9,000 visitors, and 7,000 downloads per month, and between 2009 and 2010 (ComPADRE Webmetrics, 2010), the usage of the OSP Collection has grown twenty percent. ComPADRE also supports personal resource collections, personal profiles, discussions, group Web pages, and an integrated wiki.

ComPADRE's use of standardized education and library metadata broadens the potential avenues for dissemination of OSP content. The ComPADRE resource metadata is available in IEEE Learning Object Metadata (LOM), standard Dublin Core, and NSDL Dublin Core formats. The collection metadata can be harvested by partners through the Open Archives Initiative OAI-PMH protocol and is being used to provide federated searching with a number of other projects including the NSDL, MERLOT, and the SAO/NASA Astrophysical Data System (http://adswww.harvard.edu).

References

Beichner, R. (1997). The impact of video motion analysis on kinematics graph interpretation skills, *Am. J. Phys., 64* (10), 1272–1277. doi:10.1119/1.18390

Christian, W., & Belloni, M. (2003). *Physlet® physics: Interactive illustrations, explorations, and problems for introductory physics*, Prentice Hall's Series in Educational Innovation. Upper Saddle River, New Jersey: Prentice Hall.

Christian, W., & Esquembre, F. (2007). Modeling physics with Easy Java Simulations, *The Physics Teacher*, 45 (10), 475-480. doi:10.1119/1.2798358.

ComPADRE Webmetrics (2010). ComPADRE Webmetrics provided by Google Analytics and ComPADRE Server logs, August 2010.

Dancy, M.H., & Beichner, R. (2005). Impact of animation on assessment of conceptual understanding in physics, *Phys. Rev. ST Phys. Educ. Res. 2*, 010104. doi:10.1103/PhysRevSTPER.2.010104

Easy Java Simulations (2011). Retrieved February 16, 2011 from the Easy Java Simulations Web page: http://www.um.es/fem/EjsWiki.

Gould, H., Tobochnik, J., & Christian, W. (2006). *An Introduction to Computer Simulation Methods*, Boston, MA: Addison Wesley.

Hestenes, D. (1987). Toward a modeling theory of physics instruction, *Am. J. Phys. 55* (5), 440-454. doi: 10.1119/1.15129

Karplus, R. (1977). Science teaching and the development of reasoning, *Journal of Research in Science Teaching*, 14, 169–175. doi:10.1002/tea.3660140212

Maloney, D.P. (1994). Research on problem solving: Physics, in Gabel, D. (Ed) *Handbook of Research on Science Teaching and Learning*, New York: MacMillan.

Mayer, R. E., & Moreno, R. (2002). Animation as an aid to multimedia learning, *Educational Psychology Review*, 14(1), 87-99.

OSP. (2011). Retrieved February 11, 2011 from the Open Source Physics Collection on ComPADRE: http://www.compadre.org/OSP/.

Rieber, L.P., Tzeng, S., & Tribble, K. (2004), Discovery learning, representation, and explanation within a computer-based simulation: finding the right mix, *Learning and Instruction*, 14, 307-323. doi:10.1016/j.learninstruc.2004.06.008

Van Heuvelen, A., & Zou, X. (2001). Multiple representations of work-energy processes, *Am. J. Phys. 69* (2), 184-194. doi: 10.1119/1.1286662

Zacharia, Z., & Anderson, R.O. (2003). The effects of an interactive computer-based simulation prior to performing a laboratory inquiry-based experiment on students' conceptual understanding of physics, *Am. J. Phys. 71* (6), 618-629. doi: 10.1119/1.1566427

Acknowledgements

Partial funding for OSP was obtained through NSF grants DUE-0442581 and DUE-0937836. Opinions expressed here are not those of the NSF.

USE OF TEAM VIEWER SOFTWARE TO ASSIST STUDENTS

KAREN BANKS
INDIANA UNIVERSITY BLOOMINGTON

Keywords: online, free, office hours, maximize learning

Framework

It is not always possible for students to come to your office for help. If you have a student who is confined to their room due to an illness, but is well enough to work on an assignment you can help them with the Team Viewer software. If a student is having problems using software or correcting an assignment, you can try to explain the solution in a long e-mail or you can show them using the Team Viewer software. If your students tend to work on their assignments in the evening, but you do not want to be in your office during those hours, you can create a virtual office with the use of the Team Viewer software. Team Viewer is a free customer support software, which allows an instructor to take over a student's computer to assist with schoolwork.

Making it Work

For Faculty
1. Go to http://www.teamviewer.com/download/index.aspx
2. Under "All-In-One: TeamViewer full version", click the Download button.
3. Click Run, and then Run again.
4. TeamViewer will ask if you wish to install the software or just run it on your computer. This is a very useful option because you can run this software in a Student Technology Computer (STC) lab, you do not have to install the software.
5. After you have accepted the terms of agreement, TeamViewer will ask for the password and ID of the other computer.

For Students
1. Go to http://www.teamviewer.com/download/index. aspx
2. Under "For the instant customer: TeamViewer Quick-Support", click the Download button.
3. Click Run, and then Run again. This is a very useful option because you can run this software in a Student Technology Computer (STC) lab, you do not have to install the software.
4. TeamViewer will provide an ID and password. This ID and password changes for each session.
5. The student e-mails or phones the instructor the ID and password.

Once the ID and password have been entered, the instructor will have control of the student's computer and can assist the student with the problem. The student also has control of their own computer so the instructor can ask the student demonstrate the problem. The student cannot see the instructor's computer.

To help students feel comfortable with the software, ask students to visit a lab in pairs to practice using the software. One student should play the role of the instructor and the other should play the role of the student. Then they should switch roles. Students will be more likely to use the software once they see that they have to give the instructor a new password each time they request help and they understand what the instructor can see. This role playing exercise will take between 10 minutes to 30 minutes.

Future Implications

Outcomes/Assessment
I have been able to help some very panic students who have run into technology trouble through no fault of their own. Often a student is clicking in the wrong place, on the wrong hyperlink, or is making a small conceptual error that a five minute session in Team Viewer will resolve. This quick problem resolution is greatly appreciated by stressed-out students and makes for a better learning environment. If a student is unable to attend class due to a medical reason, but is able to work on the course content, I can help that student to keep up with the work. Students are very grateful for the help and find the software very easy to use. Some students go on to use the application to solve technology problems for their parents.

Future Directions/ Modifications/ Hybrid context
The success of online classes has shown us that we don't have to be face to face for all successful interactions with students. The use of typical online class technology for regular classes needs to be considered especially with classroom space at a premium.

UTILIZING EXISTING GIGAPIXEL PANORAMAS FOR VIRTUAL FIELDTRIPS

LAURA GUERTIN
PENN STATE BRANDYWINE

Keywords: virtual fieldtrip, panorama, technology

Framework

Since 2004, gigapixel panoramas have been constructed from locations across the planet to outer space. Originally designed by NASA for rovers to photodocument the Martian surface, the hardware and resulting imagery is now accessible to anyone. The free, online database of images known as "gigapans" (http://gigapan.org) democratizes information and makes panoramas accessible to anyone with a computer and access to the internet. Viewers of the online gigapans can navigate across an image and zoom in to see details on everything from rock art and cave art, to landscapes in National Parks to the South Pole.

Making it Work

As is it not always possible for an instructor to take a class on a fieldtrip, especially to distant locations, a gigapixel panorama provides visual access to sites that can enhance course content. An instructor may lead a "show and tell" fieldtrip while showcasing gigapans in the classroom and calling attention to image details. In addition, students may explore the images outside of the classroom; this allows students to control what they zoom in to on the image and control the amount of time spent viewing different parts of the image. Students may be required to complete a log book and/or answer a set of guided questions based on what they see in the image, just as an instructor would require on an actual fieldtrip.

Future Implications

Gigapixel panoramas have been taken across the globe in a variety of indoor and outdoor settings. The online gigapan collection can be utilized by any instructor in any discipline to encourage students to engage in material recorded as a snapshot in time. For example, an art instructor may want students to explore the textures of oil on linen paintings at the Hawaii State Art Museum. Business instructors may virtually take students to a trading floor in Chicago. Biology instructors may have students explore an insect collection, and anthropology instructors may have students explore the largest open-air market in Central America. For astronomy instructors, NASA Ames stitched together panoramas from the Apollo 16 and 17 missions for panoramas of the Moon, and there exist gigapans of the Martian landscape. Certainly, sitting in front of a computer will never substitute for visiting and experiencing these actual locations. The sounds and smells cannot be recorded in an image. But when it is not possible to bring students to places and environments across the globe, a gigapixel panorama can engage students in exploring these distant locations by providing students the power to explore across the panorama.

Suggested gigapixel panoramas appropriate for a virtual fieldtrip in various disciplines can be found at: http://tinyurl.com/quickhitsgigapan

---

SERVICE-LEARNING AT THE SEAL INDIANA MOBILE PROGRAM

ARMANDO E SOTO-ROJAS
INDIANA UNIVERSITY SCHOOL OF DENTISTRY

Keywords: service-learning, course management system

Framework

The Seal Indiana (SI) Program is a statewide mobile dental program that provides preventive oral health services for children who do not have adequate access to dental care. The Indiana State Department of Health (ISDH) and Indiana University Purdue University Indianapolis (IUPUI) provided start-up funding for the program, which began in March 2003. Services provided by SI include dental sealants, examinations, x-rays and fluoride varnish. The educational goals are to provide service-learning experiences for dental students, foster greater understanding of issues related to community oral health, and greater access to dental care. Since the inception of the program, approximately 700 4th year dental students have worked providing preventive dental services including dental sealants in the state of Indiana. I have participated in the program since 2004 and since 2006 I have been involved in the assessment of students' evaluations using Oncourse. In 2007, I became the SI Associate Director and am now the Director; I teach dental students and provide services 2 days a week.

The program uses portable dental units and equipment. The SI team serves an average of 20–25 children who are the least likely to receive care. Before and after their rotation, the students complete Oncourse assignments, surveys and write reflective essays.

Oncourse provides IU students, faculty, and staff with a powerful environment in which to collaborate and learn. IU developed Oncourse to allow for innovative ways of accessing and sharing materials and information. Oncourse offered Seal Indiana a straightforward way to create a web site through which students and faculty can access course syllabi, online quizzes, and surveys. Dental educators have recommended utilization of computer-based and web-based information technology to enrich student learning. Eighty-six percent of dental schools have expanded use of already implemented learning instructional technology and most (82%), if not virtually all, dental schools have additional plans for further informatics and technology expansion (Kassebaum, 2004).

Making it Work

Before each SI rotation by fourth year dental students, they receive an email from me providing instructions about their required rotation and Oncourse assignments and surveys. Once students log into Oncourse they are required to view an orientation video. After reading the syllabi students complete the pre-rotation Oncourse survey and assignment. No grade is assigned for written reflections.

Using a course management system like Oncourse has enhanced the service-learning experience of dental students; it allows the students to reflect on their experiences and think about this as a different part of their work that is not only to provide the services but also to assess firsthand cultural and socioeconomic differences in the population they are servicing. By completing this course students have a better understanding of their role in society and are able to connect their experience with other aspects of learning their profession. This is difficult to achieve in a traditional setting using a lecture format.

In the Pre-Rotation Assignment students are required to use web based resources and assess Indiana dentist and population statistics, such as: ratio of dentists to population by county, report percentages of individuals living below poverty level, racial distribution, information about Hoosier Healthwise and Head Start programs. They are required to read articles posted in the resources section and answer questions on sealants and service-learning. Pre and post-rotation surveys inquire about, age, gender, program, racial background, service-learning experience, community service and cultural differences.

The post-rotation assignment focuses on written service learning reflections: "what did you do", "so what" how does it connect with your learning and life goals, and "now what" (how could this impact beliefs, attitudes and actions). Students are encouraged to write a letter to legislators to support the program and to briefly describe a significant moment/event that was related to the rotation. Finally an evaluation of the program enquires about the strengths and weaknesses and the students rate the overall experience.

I review students' responses and reply to them sending an e-mail pointing important and interesting aspects about their service learning and dental this would otherwise not be possible in a lecture or on site. I highlight "most helpful" comments and bring these to the group reflection session that is held following students rotation. This learning mechanism creates an incentive to reflect, write and select useful reflective comments. Discussions lead to debate within the group.

Examples of Oncourse Responses

"… Seal Indiana rotation was an experience that strengthened my development in the dental field by interacting and treating children. It also helped me learn more about my personality and flexibility to interact with all patient populations." Clearly the student was able to recognize this by responding to this web course

"…this experience will influence my practice on communicating with kids. I was able to understand disparities in access to dental care. This was in large part due to the number of children who told me they had never seen a dentist. It was easy to see that the children did not come from a family with a lot of money either, which led me to believe was a part in the lack of access to dental care." Through the use of this technology students have the incentive to reflect, write and express goals and values in life.

Future Implications

The examples above demonstrate how this process facilitates the student's rotation with the SI program. The use of Oncourse enhances community participation and several forms of evaluation for their SI rotation including self-assessment. The groups are generally of 100 students and the rotation is on average 3 students a week throughout the year. Without the use of this technology it would be almost impossible to achieve what students and faculty accomplish through reflection using this web-based course. The students don't assess the web course but in general suggestions to reduce the size of this is commonly stated. Future plans include research to do content analysis and assess areas that enhance student participation and learning and eliminate questions that seem redundant.

1. The Oncourse student responses comments and suggestions provide differing views of education, dental education techniques, service-learning applications and concepts.

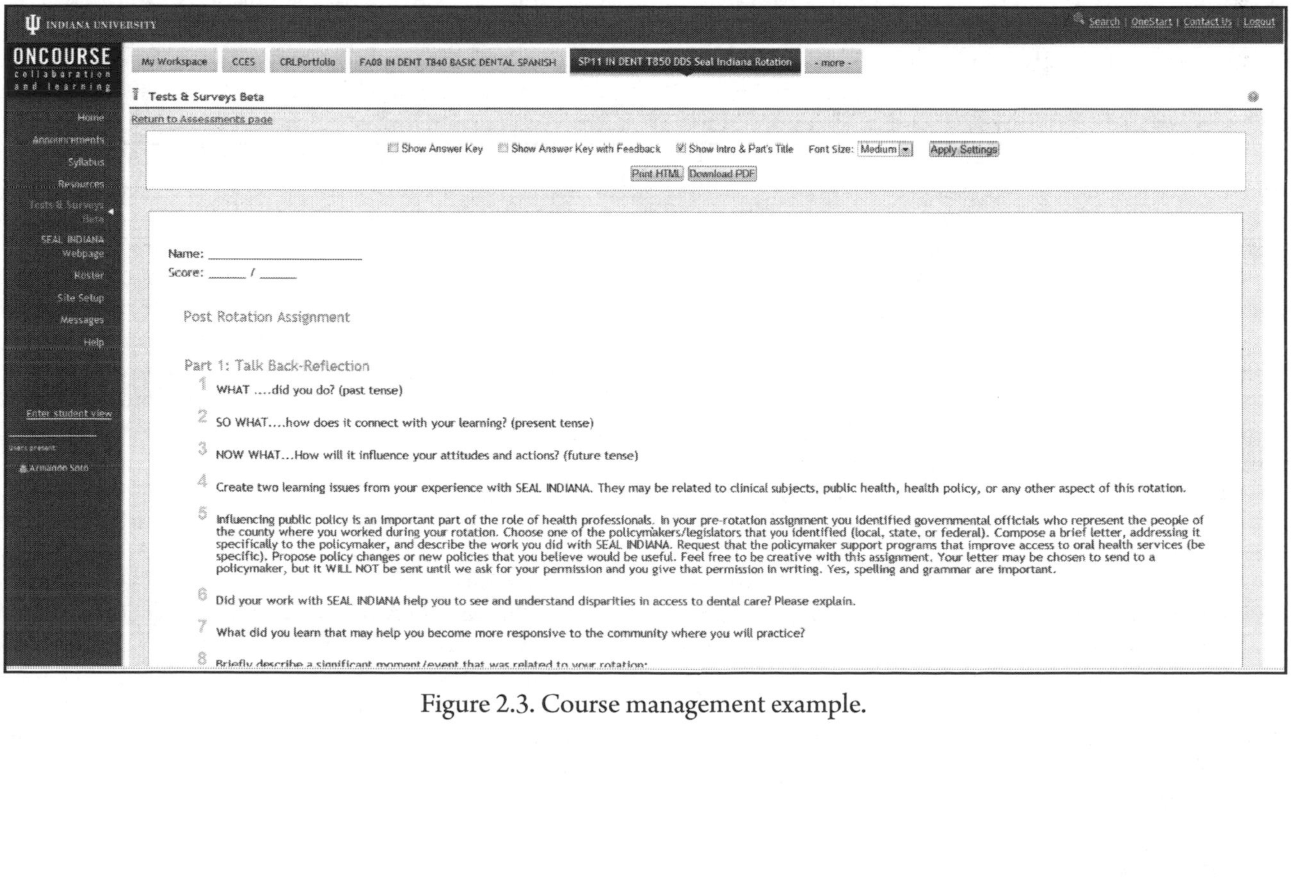

Figure 2.3. Course management example.

2. Students do not receive grades but a pass or failed. Responses to students include assessment of their concerns and suggestions to the program or the course.
3. During the reflection sessions the group discusses the individual comments, suggestions to the course and learning outcomes of their participation.

References

Kassebaum, D.K., Hendricson, W.D., Taft, T., & Haden, N.K. (2004) The dental curriculum at North American dental institutions in 2002-03: A survey of current structure, recent innovations, and planned changes. *Journal of Dental Education, 68*(9), 914-931.

Developing medical education teaching applications for mobile devices

Ralph A. Gillies
Georgia Health Sciences University

Keywords: medical education, mobile devices, clinical laboratory tests, internet, website

Framework

Medical learners are increasingly employing electronic learning content to increase their knowledge and understanding of medically related topics. As a result of the popularity of mobile devices (e.g., iPhone) that can host learning and clinical applications (iMedicalApps, 2010) and/or access to the Internet, these devices have become an excellent opportunity for educators to disseminate learning content. *MedLab Tutor* is an example of such a mobile device application; it was developed to assist medical learners in reading and interpreting common medical labs (e.g., CBC and CMP). The application provides learners with a resource that is accurate and presents content in a manner consistent with adult learning principles (i.e., relevant, interactive, information presented via multiple modes and with increasing complexity). The application has been published at Apple's iTunes App store and has been downloaded for free by thousands of users in dozens of countries. For more details, http://itunes.apple.com/us/app/medlab-tutor/id383650731?mt=8. An accompanying website with the same content is being developed for learners who do not have an iPhone device (see http://www.mcg.edu/mobile/medlab/index.html).

Making it Work

To ensure the content of this application was relevant and presented in a manner useful for learners, a series of focus groups were held during development of the application. First, a group of physician faculty suggested that the initial content should address the basic clinical labs and include case examples to illustrate their use. In two follow-up groups, medical students prompted the addition of increased details of lab components, the addition of learning exercises for application of concepts and review, and more streamlined flow of screens for technologically savvy users. The students' request for the application to assist in their diagnostic work-ups was not included given the application is not a clinical tool and such clinical reasoning is a more complex learning goal. Prior to publication, all clinical content was reviewed by a set of physicians to ensure clinical accuracy.

Future Implications

Medical educators can benefit from MedlLab Tutor and similar mobile device applications in two ways. First, educators can integrate this and similar teaching resources into their existing curriculum. Tools like *MedLab Tutor* can serve as a primer for discussing content or as a follow-up assignment to reinforce presented material. Second, educators can use *MedLab Tutor* as a template for developing similar applications on their own. With the assistance of technical support staff, the format of this application can readily be translated to address other medical education topics.

Given today's medical learners are already employing and creating these mobile and online learning tools, educators have an impetus to develop useful, accurate tools of this kind and influence how these tools are integrated into existing training. Finally, these mobile and online tools provide viable options for educators faced with increased numbers of learners, varied learning styles and experiences of learners, and decreased faculty and learner time for teaching and learning.

References

IMedicalApps (2010). Mobile Medical App Reviews & Commentary: Top 20 Free iPhone Medical Apps For Health Care Professionals. Retrieved February 1, 2011, from http://www.imedicalapps.com/2010/12/bes-free-iphone-medical-apps-doctors-health-care-professionals/

MAKING TECHNOLOGY-ENHANCED CLASSROOM PRESENTATIONS ACCESSIBLE TO STUDENTS WITH SENSORY IMPAIRMENTS

SHERYL BURGSTAHLER
UNIVERSITY OF WASHINGTON

Key words: sensory impairments, accessibility

Framework

What might be your first response when a student who is blind enrolls in your course? Would you be able to look forward to the unique perspective this student brings to the class or would your thoughts be dominated by concern regarding accommodations that this student might require? An important first step to creating a welcoming and inclusive classroom environment for students with disabilities is to truly value diversity in all of its many forms—to see, in this case, differences in visual abilities as simply a normal part of the human experience.

As growing numbers of individuals with disabilities are attending college, the importance of delivering content that is accessible to students with a wide variety of characteristics is hard to overstate. By developing my presentations using principles of "universal design" I avoid erecting potential barriers to students with sensory impairments in technology-enhanced on-site instruction.

Being proactive in addressing potential access barriers to technology-rich presentations can reduce the need for accommodations by specific students.

• • • • • • • • • •

"Universal design" (UD) is defined as "the design of products and environments to be usable by all people, to the greatest extent possible, without the need for adaptation or specialized design" (Center for Universal Design, 2008, p. 1). The UD approach recognizes that individuals within a group, such as an academic course, may have diverse cultural and language backgrounds; interests; and abilities and disabilities associated with learning, attention, mobility, sensory perceptions, spelling, and reading. UD specifically benefits both disabled and nondisabled students. For example, the UD feature of captions on videos benefits students who are deaf but is also useful to students for whom English is not their first language and those whose learning preference is written rather than spoken language. Being proactive in addressing potential access barriers to technology-rich presentations can reduce the need for accommodations by specific students.

Making it Work

The Center for Applied Special Technology (CAST, n.d.) has for many years promoted the use of educational technology that is accessible to and usable by all students. CAST's three universal design for learning (UDL) principles "form a practical framework for using technology to maximize learning opportunities for every student" (Rose & Meyer, 2002, p. 5):

Multiple means of representation, to give learners various ways of acquiring information and knowledge;

Multiple means of action and expression, to provide learners alternatives for demonstrating what they know;

Multiple means of engagement, to tap into learners' interests, offer appropriate challenges, and increase motivation. (CAST, n.d., p. 1)

At The Center for Universal Design in Education (CUDE), hosted by the DO-IT Center that I direct at the University of Washington in Seattle (Disabilities, Opportunities, Internetworking, and Technology [DO-IT], n.d.), staff and collaborators in multiple projects (DO-IT, 2007) operationalized the principles of UD and UDL. Motivated to a great degree by requests of postsecondary faculty for practical strategies for applying UD to specific instructional products (e.g., websites) and environments (e.g., classroom presentations), we created and validated a checklist of universal design of instruction (UDI) practices (Burgstahler, 2011). The UDI checklist reveals how UD can be applied to the class climate, physical environments/products, delivery methods, information resources/technology, interaction, feedback, and assessment. For each practice on the checklist, references are made to UD principles and UDL guidelines for which the example is most relevant.

The first step is simply to consider the diverse characteristics your students might have with respect to sensory and physical abilities, learning styles and challenges, gender, race/

ethnicity and social-economic status. Then, I suggest that you review the examples in CUDE's UDI checklist (Burgs-tahler, 2011) and assess

- which strategies you already employ,
- those that you employ to some degree, and
- practices that you would like to adopt in the future (and record a targeted date for implementation).

The result will be a step-by-step UDI implementation plan designed for you. As far as making a technology-enabled on-site presentation accessible to those with sensory impairments, a good exercise is to imagine you have both a blind student and a deaf student (with a sign language interpreter) in your audience. How could you ensure that these two students have access to the content you present?

Listed below are some relevant practices gleaned from the UDI checklist.

- As you prepare your images that will be projected on a screen, select large, bold, simple fonts and high contract, uncluttered backgrounds. Avoid crowding too much content on a single image.
- When you deliver your presentation, describe orally all text and other relevant content projected on a screen.
- Use captioned videos and provide transcriptions for audio presentations.
- Provide the syllabus and other printed materials in an electronic format on a website; make sure that they are available in a text-based format so that blind students using screen reader technology can access the content.
- Supplement in-person contact with online communication.

Many UDI practices benefit students who do not have disabilities. For example, I have found that speaking the content of my overhead visuals not only makes my content more accessible to students who are blind, but also to those who are sitting in the back of the room, who learn better when content is both seen and spoken, or for whom English is their second language.

Future Implications

Access issues will likely arise for students with sensory impairments when instructors use digital media in the classroom after considering only a narrow range of characteristics of potential students. The application of UD to instruction holds promise as faculty try to effectively teach a student body that is increasingly diverse. Consistent with other applications of UD, courses that employ UDI are welcoming, accessible, and inclusive for all students, without giving unfair advantage to anyone.

Resources

Good places to start in learning more about how the UD approach can be applied in your class include:

- The Center for Universal Design http://www.ncsu.edu/www/ncsu/design/sod5/cud/
- The Center for Universal Design in Education http://www.uw.edu/doit/CUDE/
- National Center on Universal Design for Learning http://www.udlcenter.org/

Acknowledgements

This chapter is based on work supported by the National Science Foundation under grant #HRD-0833504 in Research in Disabilities Education (RDE) and #CNS-0837508 in Computer and Information Science and Engineering (CISE). Any opinions, findings, and conclusions or recommendations expressed in this material are those of the authors and do not necessarily reflect the views of the National Science Foundation.

References

Burgstahler, S. (2011). *Equal Access: Universal Design of Instruction*. Seattle: University of Washington. Retrieved July 1, 2011: http://www.washington.edu/doit/Brochures/Academics/equal_access_udci.html

Burgstahler, S. E. (2008). Universal design of instruction: From principles to practice. In S. E. Burgstahler & R. C. Cory (Eds.), *Universal Design in Higher Education: From Principles to Practice* (pp. 3-20). Boston: Harvard Education Press.

Center for Applied Special Technology [CAST]. (n.d.). *What is universal design for learning?* Retrieved July 1, 2011: http://www.cast.org/research/udl/

DO-IT (Disabilities, Opportunities, Internetworking, and Technology). (n.d.). Seattle: University of Washington. Retrieved July 1, 2011: http://www.washington.edu/doit/CUDE/

DO-IT. (2007). *AccessCollege: Systemic Change for Postsecondary Institutions*. Seattle: University of Washington. Retrieved July 1, 2011: http://www.washington.edu/doit/Brochures/Academics/access_college.html

The Center for Universal Design [CUD]. (2008). Raleigh: CUD. Retrieved July 1, 2011: http://www.design.ncsu.edu/cud/about_ud/about_ud.htm

The Center for Universal Design in Education [CUDE]. (n.d.) Retrieved July 1, 2011: http://www.washington.edu/doit/CUDE

||||||||||||||||||||||||||||||||||||||||||||||||||||||||||||||||||||||||||||||||||||||||||||||||||||||||||||||||||

BLOGGING IN THE CLASSROOM

PATRICK FENG
UNIVERSITY OF CALGARY

Keywords: blogging, self-reflection, new media, community

Framework

One of the things I have students in my new media class do is contribute to a class blog. I have found this to be a useful activity for three reasons. First, blogging is a way for students to reflect on ideas discussed in class. Second, blogging allows students to interact with one another outside of class. Third, for a course on new media, it makes sense that students use new media tools as part of their learning experience. The end result is students who are more reflective and interactive, both in and out of the classroom.

Making it Work

The assignment works as follows. Students are asked to post one entry per week to the class blogging site; posts may be on any topic as long as it relates to the course in some way. Students are also required to comment on at least two of their classmates' posts each week. Over the next eight weeks, these posts and comments develop into a compilation of the class' thoughts and opinions. Afterwards, students write a short reflection paper where they discuss their blogging experiences; they then submit a portfolio consisting of their best posts and comments plus their reflection paper. Portfolios are graded based on originality, thoughtfulness, and quality of writing. I find the assignment works best for smaller classes.

Setting up a class blog is straightforward. I worked with a programmer from our university's Teaching and Learning Centre to set up a site specific to my needs, but this isn't essential. Many blogging platforms are available online that are free and easy-to-use; signing up for an account takes just a few minutes, after which you can create and customize your site. Blogging requires no particular computer skills beyond those students use every day. In addition, there is no cost to students or the university. One concern students might have involves posting thoughts online, where they might be read by anyone; if this is an issue, set the privacy settings on your class blog so that it is private and/or blocked from search engines.

Future Implications

The response from students has been very positive. Students appreciate the open-ended and informal format of blogs, which seems well-suited for critical thinking and self-reflection. Having students blog on a regular basis encourages a level of reflection that is difficult to achieve through lectures alone. As I explain to students, the goal is not to arrive at "the right answer"—as there will always be multiple ways of looking at an issue—but rather to come to well-reasoned positions and to thoughtfully consider the positions of others. While some are hesitant at first, by the end of the course students report having a better appreciation for this medium and a few even decide to continue blogging. More importantly, students report feeling more connected to their classmates—even those they did not interact with—because they got to read their classmates' posts and comments. In this way, blogging in the classroom contributes to a sense of community among students.

||||||||||||||||||||||||||||||||||||||||||||||||||||||||||||||||||||||||||||||||||||||||||||||||||||||||||||||||||

VIRTUAL MICROSCOPY AS A REAL AND EFFECTIVE TOOL FOR TEACHING HISTOLOGY

GRACE PINHAL-ENFIELD, DAVID O. DEFOUW, AND NAGASWAMI S. VASAN
NEW JERSEY MEDICAL SCHOOL

Keywords: virtual microscopy, teaching histology

Framework

There has been an exciting and expanding movement involving the use of virtual imaging in many areas of education. Virtual imaging has become an effective and readily adaptable learning medium in many fields such as music (e.g., virtual piano), sports (e.g., virtual golf), and medical sciences (e.g., virtual colonoscopy and virtual microscopy).

Virtual microscopy (VM) has become a useful tool for teaching undergraduate, graduate, and medical histology. In VM, computers are used to visualize images of histological slides rather than viewing glass slides with light microscopes. While employing many traits and functions of traditional microscopy, VM is an extraordinary instrument for exploration of histology beyond the confines of microscopy. Advantages of VM in teaching histology include access to an extensive repertoire of specimens; selection of optimal specimens by histology faculty; uniformity of slides among students; convenience due to internet accessibility; multiple viewer format for efficient and effective teaching, learning, and assessment; and overwhelmingly favorable responses from the current technologically-savvy generation of students.

There are many similarities between VM and traditional microscopy. Because virtual slides are acquired from actual histological glass slide specimens, virtual slides exhibit the same properties as glass slides, such as artifacts and real staining (no pseudocoloring). Virtual slides also allow for navigation and observation at different magnifications. Some virtual slides may even feature the ability to focus through different planes of the tissue. Thus, the use of computers and internet servers in VM provide many advantages.

Making it Work

VM provides access to thousands of digitized histological virtual slide images, obtained from high-resolution scanning (by specialized scanners such as Hamamatsu's Nano-Zoomer or Olympus's VS110) of real histological glass slide specimens contributed by multiple institutions. For example, Olympus exhibits thousands of digitized virtual slides in their WebSlide database and faculty members at our institution have selected approximately 200 virtual slides for our

school's virtual slide box. Therefore, rather than being limited to a set of glass slide boxes created by one institution, our students have access to a broad repertoire of virtual slide images in an optimized, faculty-selected virtual slide box. Furthermore, in contrast to variable box-to-box slide quality seen with glass slide boxes, virtual slide boxes are uniform and all students have access to the same virtual images. Thus, consistency is achieved among all students. Because there are no slide box differences between students, faculty can comfortably test student knowledge on all structures of interest that are known to be present in the faculty-selected, optimized virtual slide boxes. Lastly, VM is cost effective with a one-time license fee and minimal maintenance compared to purchase and repair costs required for glass slides and microscopes. Further, the virtual slide box can be simultaneously accessed by multiple users within different courses.

VM is relatively easy to use and can be quickly learned by most inexperienced users.

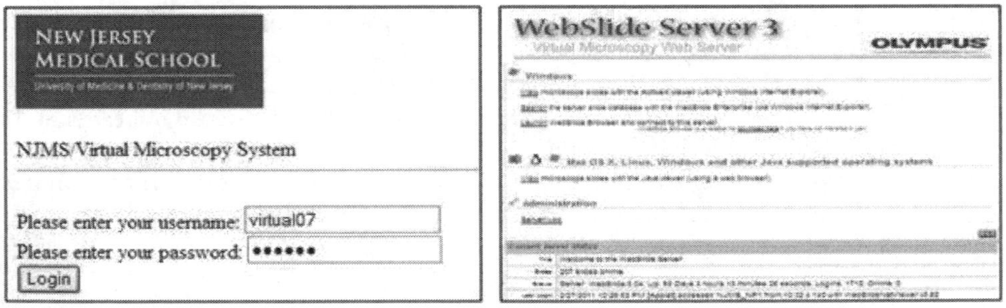

> Rather than being limited to a set of glass slide boxes created by one institution, our students have access to a broad repertoire of virtual slide images in an optimized, faculty-selected virtual slide box

Figure 2.4. VM allows for internet access to slides on a server.

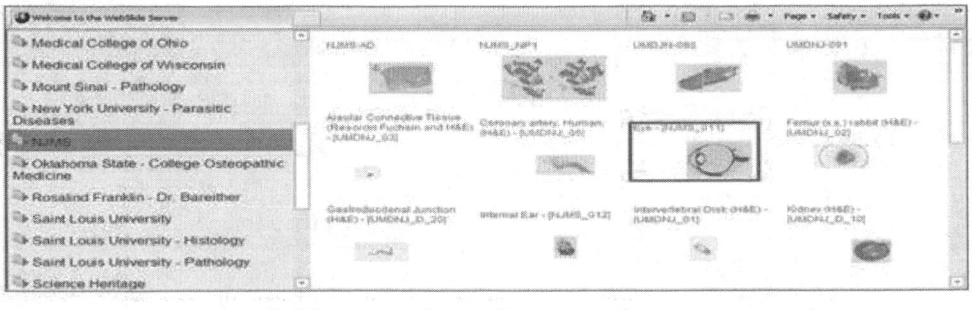

Figure 2.5. Virtual slides can be located by a specific accession number.

1. Once a school establishes a contract with a provider (e.g, Olympus) and faculty have selected virtual slides for an institution-specific virtual slide box, multiple registered computers can log onto an internet server for access to the virtual slides. Users can access virtual slides using any common Web browser such as Internet Explorer, Netscape, Mozilla, or Safari, and there are viewers available for any computer platform such as Mac, Linux, or PC. Use of the virtual software (e.g., WebSlide Enterprise from Olympus) allows for convenient search and view of virtual slides located on a server (Figure 2.4).

2. Virtual slides can be found by entering a search term (e.g., "eye") or by locating a specific, predetermined webslide accession number (e.g., NJMS_011, as shown in Figure 2.5).

3. Once a virtual slide image is opened, there are many ways to view the specimen. Examples of VM features include use of drop-down menus and a mouse (by clicking or scrolling) or keyboard to navigate through the virtual slide box database; navigation through a virtual slide and/or an interactive thumbnail (in which you can view and change your location on the larger virtual slide image); changing magnifications (and focus on some specimens) (Figure 2.6); viewing multiple images simultaneously for compare-contrast strategies (Figure 2.7); measuring area and length; indicate area of interest with a pointer; and viewing annotations on virtual slides. An especially valuable and highly used feature is the ability to copy images onto a clipboard for labeling by using the CNTRL+C function, as performed to create the figures in this article.

4. We have provided our students with a detailed lab guide that describes and directs them to find morphologic features that can be identified on a specific virtual slide image. Students are expected to work together to compare/contrast the virtual slide image with atlas and textbook descriptions. In addition to providing focus and direction through a lab guide, we have also presented labeled images to allow the students to confirm their own findings.

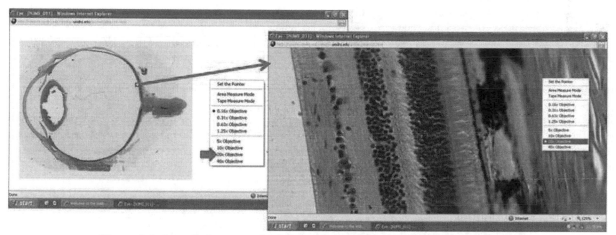

Figure 2.6. Specified region of a slide can be viewed at higher magnifications.

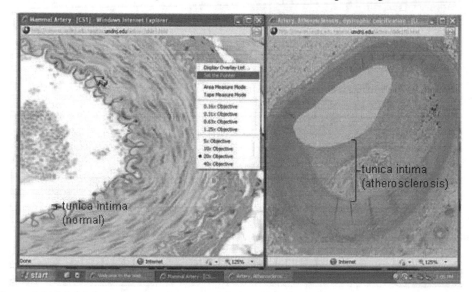

Figure 2.7. Multiple images can be accessed simultaneously for compare-contrast studies.

Future Implications

Impacts of VM feature interactive, student-directed learning with the ability to study virtual slides and reinforce knowledge through labeling at student convenience. VM is an invaluable tool because it allows accessibility online from a server by any registered computer for self-spaced, distance learning at any time. Thus, study of histology slides is not limited to labs with microscopes during specified hours of operation, but is available at anytime and from anyplace due to the convenience of using a computer and the internet. At our school, VM has enabled the integration of histology into our gross anatomy curriculum as students study virtual slides from the comfort of their laptop to reinforce studying gross anatomy material. VM allows students to study (and faculty to teach) in an open group format with exchange of ideas for more effective and collaborative learning (compared to limitations posed by a one-viewer light microscope). Furthermore, the reality and trend of reduced instructor-student contact hours and associated need for more efficient and effective self-learning by students, can evolve into a positive outcome by adopting VM. In addition, because VM is computer-based, images can be captured, labeled, and saved for future reference. This allows for interpretation, review, and clarification/feedback from fellow classmates and instructors. Thus, use of VM can result in increased study time, deeper understanding, improved knowledge retention, improved academic performance, higher student satisfaction, and effective team learning. As a result of the benefits of VM, such as uniform slide boxes among students and projection of virtual images onto a large screen for simultaneous testing, our school has been able to improve our histology practical examinations. Despite an increased level of difficulty of our histology practical questions, we have seen greatly improved academic performance.

In summary, students and instructors at many institutions have adapted well and flourished with the use of VM. This is particularly noteworthy as schools attempt to redesign the curriculum with the current needs and learning styles of a technology-driven generation of students, who are faced with decreasing instructor-driven modalities.

Author note

This work was supported by the Department of Cell Biology and Molecular Medicine at the New Jersey Medical School, University of Medicine and Dentistry of New Jersey.

References

Johnson, C., & Ahlouist, D. (1999). Computed tomography colonography (virtual colonoscopy): A new method for colorectal screening. *Gut, 44*(3), 301-305.

Goldberg, H.R., & Dintzis, R. (2007). The positive impact of team-based virtual microscopy on student learning in physiology and histology. *Advances in Physiology Education, 31,* 261-265.

Harris, T., Leaven, T., Heidger, P., Kreiter, C., Duncan, J., & Dick, F. (2001). Comparison of a virtual microscope laboratory to a regular microscope laboratory for teaching histology. *The Anatomical Record, 265,* 10–14.

"IT'S A SMALL WORLD AFTER ALL:" USING TECHNOLOGY TO INTERNATIONALIZE CURRICULUM

BETH GOERING
INDIANA UNIVERSITY PURDUE UNIVERSITY INDIANAPOLIS

Keywords: internationalizing curriculum, readily available technologies

Framework

Internationalizing curriculum, or the "process of integrating an international, intercultural, or global dimension into the purpose, functions, or delivery of post secondary education," (Knight, 2003) has become a priority in higher education. The emphasis placed on internationalizing the curriculum is well-founded because research shows that integrating intercultural/international encounters into the college curriculum is linked with a variety of positive academic, economic, and social outcomes (Green & Olson, 2008). Traditionally, efforts to provide students with international experiences have consisted of student exchange or study abroad programs. While these programs have demonstrated value, only about 50% of college students report that they plan to participate in a study abroad program (American Council on Education, 2008). The other half, for a variety of reasons including concerns about costs, career or family obligations, or anxiety about safety, "do not want to or are unsure about" study abroad (American Council on Education, 2008).

Making it Work

I have found that technology is a useful tool for internationalizing the learning experience of students who cannot (or choose not to) leave the country. I have experimented with a variety of technological tools in my efforts to internationalize my students' college experience, and I would like to share three particularly successful "experiments" with you. Using technology to build bridges across cultural divides within the academy is nothing new. Universities have utilized elaborate video conferencing technology and global seminar rooms to enable students from multiple cultures to learn together. These "high-tech" approaches to internationalizing curriculum are great, but they require technology that many schools do not have, and using them is often restricted by differences in time zones (i.e., a reasonable time to meet in Indianapolis is the middle of the night in Russia). Consequently, I have, instead, chosen to focus on ways to use generally available technologies to internationalize the educational experience of students. Most students have access to the internet, so even in a world with a widening technology gap, it is relatively easy to implement the tips presented below. Furthermore, these experiences could be easily modified and adapted to a wide variety of academic fields.

E-mail Partners (Implemented in an undergraduate Organizational Communication course):   Students from IUPUI were paired as e-mail partners with students in a comparable class at a university in Russia. Before the class began, the professors, who had met at an international conference, agreed upon case studies that would be assigned in both classes. Throughout the semester, the U.S.-Russian student pairs used e-mail to discuss and analyze the case studies. The specific tasks given the pairs changed throughout the semester. Initially, each student was asked to write an individual paper summarizing the perspective of his/her partner and highlighting key differences. Later in the semester, students were asked to hypothesize possible culturally-grounded explanations for the differences they observed in how the cases were being perceived. By the end of the semester, the partners were asked to collaboratively write an analysis, with recommendations for improving communication in the organization depicted in the case. In this case, student learning was assessed through the written work they submitted for evaluation. By examining the cases through their own and another's cultural lenses, students on both sides of the Atlantic learned a great deal about the subject matter as well as about cultural differences in communication within organizations.

Forum Interviews with Practitioners (Implemented in an undergraduate Intercultural Communication class): This strategy utilized the "Forum Discussion" tool in our university's online-learning environment. Throughout the semester, I used my personal and professional networks to arrange for "international guests" to participate in week-long forum discussions with students enrolled in the class. The invited guests varied, depending on the course content. One week, it was a professor from Russia who talked with students about communication within the Russian educational system. The next week, a German businessman answered students' questions about how communication in business

contexts varies across cultures. Finally, a doctor with considerable experience working with culturally diverse patients was available to talk with students. In this case, student learning was assessed through their participation in the online forum discussions. Students responded very favorably to this use of technology, and the international guests also reported enjoying the opportunity to interact with American college students.

Multimedia Project Presentations: This strategy actually evolved as a solution to a particular problem that arose in a graduate-level Advanced Intercultural Communication class. Half the class consisted of exchange students visiting our campus for the semester. Because of different academic calendars in their home universities, several of the visiting students needed to leave before our semester was over. Technology to the rescue! Students had completed applied projects, and I replaced the in-class oral presentations that were originally scheduled for the last few weeks of the semester with multimedia presentations posted by the students on our online teaching site. Students were given the freedom to present their work in any format they chose. To ensure that students would have the skills to complete the assignment, they were all introduced by the professor to wikispaces. Wikispaces (http://www.wikispaces.com) is a website that supports collaborative work, and its basic service is free. The site offers tutorials that introduce users to the various wiki functions. Several of the students did, indeed, create wikis describing their projects. Others selected other ways of presenting their research. One student created an interactive pdf file, and another posted a series of PowerPoint presentations. Through the use of technology, the challenges of meshing international academic calendars in real space and time were mediated to the benefit of all.

Future Implications

Technology has the potential to enhance pedagogy in so many ways. This volume of Quick Hits is filled with many impressive and creative ways in which technology, with all its bells and whistles, can engage students and facilitate learning. But, what I like about the three strategies I have shared with you here is that they produce positive results with relatively simple technologies. They utilize technologies that are generally available, so special arrangements usually do not need to be made to implement the strategies. Because they rely on asynchronous means of communication, negotiating different time zones is no problem. Most important, though, is that they have the potential to bring the world to the students, providing students who may not be able to take advantage of study abroad programs with valuable exposure to international perspectives.

References

American Council on Education, Art & Science Group LLC, and the College Board (2008). *College-bound students' interests and other international learning activities: A special edition of student poll*. Baltimore, MD: Art & Science Group.

Green, M. F., & Olson, C. (2008). *Internationalizing the campus: A user's guide*. Washington, D.C.: American Council on Education Center for Institutional and International Initiatives.

Knight, J. (2003). Updated internationalization definition, *International Higher Education*, 33, 2-3.

The inverted hybrid science classroom

Janet E. Hurn
Miami University, Middletown

Keywords: hybrid, science, physics, student response system, collaborative, engagement

Framework

Students in my introductory physics classes were often showing up ill prepared for class or not at all. In addition, their problem solving skills were not improving over the course of the semester. Changes were made to this small (<20) lecture based introductory physics classroom over a three year period. Lecture material was moved online via Articulate Presenter. This software allows for flash delivery of visuals and audio as well as allowing for student interaction with the material. With this additional outside work, class time was reduced 50 minutes per week. After watching this material, students are expected to arrive at class (50–75 minutes) prepared for a short quiz taken via TurningPoint clickers that they had purchased ($30–50). The clickers allow for immediate results that inform a short concept review that follows. The rest of class time is spent in a variety of ways. For example, one activity is for the students to complete "homework" problems in groups and respond via the clickers. The Eno Interactive white board is used to present the problems and outline a solution. These boards are saved and uploaded to the learning management system for students to review later. Any type of electronic white board or document camera would be suitable ($500–$3000). Groups also work to solve problems presented in class demonstrations. Students must then submit homework problems via WebAssign ($60–$90). This encourages each student to participate during group work. The cost of WebAssign includes their E-textbook. The total cost to the student is $90–$140 as opposed to the $200 tag on the paper book alone.

Making it Work

These changes were implemented in stages. It took almost two years to create the online lectures. Clickers were added next but the brand changed from Einstruction to TurninPoint (to align with the university's standard clickers), which has added some additional work. Students can now use them throughout their college careers at Miami in other classes. The WebAssign implementation was the missing piece to holding students accountable for their work in class.

Future Implications

These observations are anecdotal for the most part. Student attendance has improved. Students value the work we now do in class rather than me just talking "at" them. Students are more engaged, and they communicate with me and each other considerably more. Student problem solving has improved immensely as seen on test scores. Scores on conceptual questions have decreased slightly however. Students state that they enjoy the inverted format and enjoy coming to class. (Based on SGID responses and student personal reflection blogs.)

I would like to add more demonstrations for discussion and problem solving. These require more inquiry and critical thinking by the students to determine what information is needed to answer a question. I also want to add some student project elements which move the onus of responsibility for learning to the student — i.e. Google Science Fair type project, and water rocket building. I will never go back to a traditional lecture classroom model.

Students are more engaged, and they communicate with me and each other considerably more.

• • • • • • • • • • • •

THE PHYSLET PROJECT

MARIO BELLONI AND WOLFGANG CHRISTIAN
DAVIDSON COLLEGE

Keywords: physics, Physlets, simulations, digital library

Framework

A decade ago, my collaborators and I began a multi-university effort to create Web-based pedagogy and technology which resulted in the development of the Just-in-Time Teaching (JiTT) method (Novak et al., 1999) and the creation of the Java applets known as Physlets. The Physlet Project (2007) has resulted in over 1,500 curricular items (Physlet Resources, 2008) and three books with translations into four languages (Christian & Belloni, 2003; Esquembre, Martin, Christian, & Belloni, 2004) and are one of the most well known and most widely used innovations for college and university instruction in the U. S. (Henderson & Dancy, 2009). *Physlet Quantum Physics* (Belloni, Christian, & Cox, 2005) extended Physlet teaching innovations to upper-level physics, but is also appropriate for the teaching of quantum chemistry.

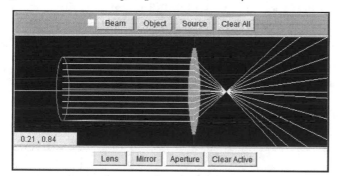

Figure 2.8. The Optics bench Physlet showing a beam of parallel light rays incident on a lens.

We created this Physlet to demonstrate the optical properties of ideal lenses and mirrors. Students can add/remove optical elements to simulate a wide range of optical experiments and devices.

Making it Work

The suite of 40 applets we created at Davidson College is known as Physlets (Physics applets). They are small, flexible Java applets that can be used in a wide variety of applications (see Figures 2.8-2.10) and run on any platform with almost any Web browser. Many other Physics-related Java applets are being produced around the world, however the applets we call Physlets have attributes that make them especially valuable for education:

- Physlets are simple. The graphics are simple; each Physlet is designed to deal with one facet of a phenomenon,

such as the Optics bench shown in Figure 2.8. This keeps Physlets relatively small (the Optics bench Physlet is only 46.2kb) and removes details that could be more distracting than helpful to students. Students can also take simple measurements as shown with the yellow box in Figure 1 which indicates the position of the cursor.

- Physlets are flexible. All Physlets can be changed and controlled with JavaScript as shown in Figures 2.9 and 2.10. The Optics bench can be used for almost any problem involving ideal lenses or mirrors (magnifying glasses, telescopes, microscopes, cameras, eyes, eye glasses, etc.) and in any discipline where optics is important (astronomy, biology, engineering, etc.).
- Physlets pedagogy is agnostic. Physlets can be used as an element of almost any curriculum with almost any teaching style (Titus, 1998; Dancy & Beichner, 2005). While Physlets work well with interactive engagement methods such as JiTT, they can be also used as lecture demonstrations and homework (see Figure 2.10). For example, the Optics bench in Figure 1 has been used as an in-class demonstration and as part of an introductory optics laboratory, while the telescope simulation in Figure 2 has been used as a demonstration in an astronomy class.
- Physlets are freely distributable for noncommercial use. The Physlet archives which contain the compiled Java programs can be freely downloaded from the Davidson WebPhysics server (Physlets, 2007). These files can also be mirrored on a local hard drive or on a noncommercial site in order to provide students easy access to Physlet-based materials.

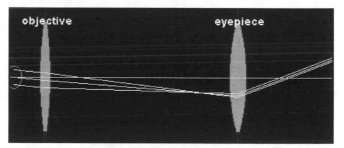

Figure 2.9. Using the same Physlet shown in Figure 2.8, we can create a virtual telescope by using JavaScript. The green circle represents a distant object whose parallel light rays pass through the telescope (the objective and the eyepiece). While the light rays from the source remain parallel, the angle from the optical axis is increased which magnifies the object without distorting it.

An example of a Physlet-based problem is shown in Figure 2.10. Students access the Physlet and are told, "A point source is located to the left of an ideal mirror. You can drag this point source to any position (which is given in centimeters). Find the focal length of the mirror." Students are not given any other information; they must interact with the Physlet to determine a strategy to answer the question. The standard novice problem-solving approach of "plug-n-chug" will simply not be effective. Successful students conceptualize the problem first (What does a focal length mean?) and find that there are at least 4 unique ways to successfully answer this question.

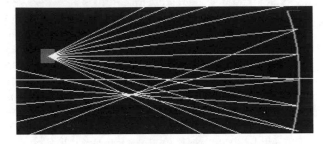

Figure 2.10. The Optics bench Physlet written as a homework problem.

Future Implications

We have recently recompiled and packaged Physlets (the applets themselves) in a single Java archive (or jar) file (Physlet Jar, 2011) which is being distributed from the ComPADRE digital library (OSP ComPADRE, 2011). In addition, Pearson Education, the English language publisher of Physlet-based curricular material, has agreed to allow teachers to post Physlet-based exercises from our books on personal and non-commercial education websites without seeking additional permission provided that the original copyright notice remains in place. This agreement will allow us to more easily distribute Physlet-based materials through ComPADRE.

References

Belloni, M., Christian, W., & Cox, A. J. (2005). Physlet® quantum physics: An interactive introduction. Upper Saddle River, NJ: Prentice Hall's Series in Educational Innovation.

Christian, W., & Belloni, M. (2003). Physlet® physics: Interactive illustrations, explorations, and problems for introductory physics. Upper Saddle River, NJ: Prentice Hall's Series in Educational Innovation.

Dancy, M.H., & Beichner, R. (2005). Impact of animation on assessment of conceptual understanding in physics, Physical Review Special Topics - Physical Education Research, 2(1), 010104-1 – 010104-7.

Esquembre, F., Martin, E., Christian, W., & Belloni, M. (2004). Fislets: Enseñanza de la física con material interactive. Upper Saddle River, NJ: Prentice-Hall, España,

Henderson, C., & Dancy, M. (2009). The impact of physics education research on the teaching of introductory quantitative physics in the United States, Physical Review Special Topics - Physical Education Research, 5(2), 020107-1 – 020107-9.

Novak, G., Patterson, E., Gavrin, A., & Christian, W. (1999). Just-in-Time Teaching: Bending active learning with web technology. Upper Saddle River, NJ: Prentice Hall.

OSP ComPADRE. (2011). Retrieved February 23, 2011 from the ComPADRE OSP Web site: http://www.compadre.org/OSP/.

Physlets. (2007). Retrieved February 23, 2011 from the Physlet Project Web site: http://webphysics.davidson.edu/Applets/Applets.html.

Physlet Jar. (2011). Retrieved February 23, 2011 from the ComPADRE OSP Web site: http://www.compadre.org/OSP/items/detail.cfm?ID=10710.

Physlet Resources. (2007). Retrieved February 23, 2011 from the Physlet Project Resources Web site: http://webphysics.davidson.edu/physlet_resources.

Titus, A. (1998). Integrating video and animation with physics problem solving exercises on the world wide web, Doctoral Dissertation, North Carolina State University.

PODCAST TECHNOLOGY SELF-DIRECTED LECTURING FOR FLUORIDE TOXICITY

ARMANDO E SOTO-ROJAS AND E. ANGELES MARTINEZ-MIER
INDIANA UNIVERSITY SCHOOL OF DENTISTRY

Keywords: podcasts, Adobe Presenter, PowerPoint

Framework

I am the module director of the T562 OBF II, Caries Etiology Diagnosis and Management. The goal of the course is to establish knowledge necessary for attaining competencies related to the management of oral diseases of microbial etiology, particularly dental caries and periodontal disease.

Successful students are expected to become competent in the use, advantages, disadvantages, indications, and contraindications of the different strategies to prevent dental caries. One of those strategies is the use of fluoride and this paper focuses on the use of technology to understand fluoride's toxicity and reinforce understanding of the mechanism of action, kinetics, and metabolism of fluoride.

A podcast for a self-directed lecture on fluoride toxicity was created to meet these objectives. The term podcast was first used in 2004 and is a combination of iPod and broadcast (Rainsbury, 2006). Podcasts are media files that are distributed via the internet, through course management systems, and played on computers and handheld devices. Students can listen to, study, and watch podcasts on their computer or download to a portable device such as a droid or an iPhone. Dental students are now more mobile and versatile than ever. They often find themselves multitasking, working in various lectures and projects, or sometimes located at some distance from the school. Therefore, the idea of being able to study and learn without being linked to a classroom or a tight schedule is very attractive to dental students (Jahm, 2008). On the other hand, in a pedagogical context, a disadvantage is that a podcast is essentially a passive learning experience focused on an audio or audio/video facility alone (Johnson, 2006; Palmer, 2007).

Making it Work

The specific objectives of this podcast are to describe the effects of acute fluoride toxicity on the various organ systems, describe clinical signs and symptoms of fluoride toxicity and first aid, discuss the implications of the use of fluoride supplements and infant formulas, describe likely sources that may result in acute fluoride toxicity, and calculate lethal and probable toxic doses of fluoride.

This fluoride toxicity lecture was recorded by Dr. Martinez-Mier and was distributed over the internet as an audio podcast. The podcast was created utilizing Adobe Presenter plugin with PowerPoint using the lecture previously given by Dr. Martinez as a template along with images, examples, tests, and exercises. The understating of fluoride toxicity requires dental students to use complicated formulas and mathematical constants to calculate lethal toxic doses for simulated cases. Students would spend on average 30 minutes working on this podcast and it allowed the students the opportunity to review mathematical calculations at their own pace and to solve the practice cases as many times as they felt they needed.

The initiative to create this podcast was driven by students. The project involved collaboration among dental students, faculty, and staff from the Information Technology Department. In the past, our student evaluations of this lecture repeatedly demonstrated that some students required more time than allocated in the course for the topic of fluoride toxicity. As a result, we decided to implement this podcast technology in our course as a tool to enhance the learning experience and allow students to progress at their individual pace. Students can keep and review this lecture at any point in time and can use this as a reference source of information.

Future Implications

Dental students evaluated this new technology through course evaluations and the majority agreed that the "use of podcast within the course enhanced their learning" and that "the use of electronic resources enhanced my learning." However, some of the comments and suggestions made by students were: "The fluoride toxicity equations should have been explained more conceptually so that we could have understood what we were computing, rather than just memorizing equations," "a focus group and watch a few students work the problems after listening or working to the podcast might help improving the technology." Finally, a link to knowledge base articles will be added in the update of this podcast. All of the dental students that have used this podcast over 2 years have passed their fluoride toxicity exam and were knowledgeable in the area.

The podcast lecture was designed for the Oncourse course management system but could be used in any course requiring the use of technology regardless of the content being addressed. Developing course-specific podcasts requires time; the creation of this 1/2-hour lecture took several hours of faculty time.

References

Jham, B.C., Duraes, G.V., Strassler, H.E., & Sensi L.G. (2008). Question in cyberspace. Joining the podcast revolution. *Journal of Dental Education.* 72(3), 278-281.

Johnson L., & Grayden, S. (2006). Podcasts: An emerging form of digital publishing. *International Journal of Computerized Dentistry*, 9, 205–218.

Palmer, E.J., & Devitt, P.G. (2007). A method for creating interactive content for the iPod and its potential use as a learning tool: Technical advances. *BMC Medical Education*, 7, 32.

Rainsbury, J.W., & McDonnell, S.M. (2006). Podcasts: An educational revolution in the making? *Journal of the Royal Society of Medicine*, 99, 481–482.

We decided to implement this podcast technology in our course as a tool to enhance the learning experience and allow students to progress at their individual pace.

USING WEB-BASED VIDEOCONFERENCING TO EXTEND THE F2F EXPERIENCE TO DISTANCE LEARNERS

FRED T. HOFSTETTER
UNIVERSITY OF DELAWARE

Keywords: distance learning, distance education, eLearning, videoconferencing, Dimdim, Adobe Connect, chat, chatroom, screen sharing, best practice, guidelines, F2F, face to face

Framework

Delaware is a long and narrow state that creates logistical issues for downstate students to attend classes on the University of Delaware's main campus located in northern part of the state. To solve this problem, we are investigating the use of web-based videoconferencing to extend the face-to-face experience to distance learners. We began with a cloud-based collaboration service called Dimdim that provided real-time videoconferencing, chatroom, and screen sharing. When Salesforce.com acquired Dimdim in January 2011, we switched to Adobe Connect, which currently hosts the videoconferencing, chatroom, and screen sharing aspects of the project reported here.

Making it Work

To gauge the effectiveness of this project, students have been journaling in an online discussion forum about their experiences with Dimdim and Adobe Connect. We are conducting a thematic analysis of these journal entries, which are overwhelmingly positive.

In addition to the obvious advantages of saving gas and commuting time, web-based videoconferencing opens up a new channel of communication that adds an innovative layer of interaction to the course. Multiple students can ask questions at once, and students like how the chatroom queues their questions. As one student put it, "Since we can chat, Fred has answered every single one of my questions even though he's on campus and I'm at home in my study. Chatting also makes me feel like I've gotten to know some of my classmates, even though we're not physically interacting." Managing the chat enables the professor to decide when and how to work the student questions into the presentation, and the result is a classroom session that is more coherent and responsive to student needs. In the meantime, students can carry on side conversations. The students perceive this as forming subgroups. As one student said, "Having subgroups can ... differentiate learning ... because everyone is on a different part of the technology spectrum." As another student put it, "One added benefit is that, through chat, students can carry on side conversations without taking up class time."

An interesting multimedia question arose regarding campus use of videoconferencing, namely, what should be on camera? Many students maintain that it is the view of the instructor that makes them feel most present. Others like a camera placement that provides a view of the class including both the professor and the students. As one student said, "... that will really give remote users a feeling that they actually belong to the class." We discovered an interesting multimedia solution when I brought a handheld mirror to class and held it in front of the laptop's built-in camera, which normally shows a head-shot of the professor. When held up to the laptop's camera, the mirror makes the camera view the students attending class on campus. Of course, a more advanced solution would be to use an external, repositionable camera to capture the classroom participants. We got that working with a Creative USB Live Cam as well as a Canon ZR series camcorder with Firewire, but the mirror is more cost-effective.

Students like how Dimdim and Adobe Connect give the professor virtual microphones and a camera that can be assigned to different students during the class. The students used game-style headset mikes that enabled us to avoid the audio feedback than can otherwise occur if students use loudspeakers instead of headsets.

Students especially like how they can adjust the zoom to make the shared screen larger or smaller. As one student reported: "Just sat in on my first lecture from home. I could hear Dr. Hofstetter perfectly and it was also visually clear. If there was something I couldn't quite read in small print, I would simply adjust my zoom and then zoom back in if I wanted to write something on the chat wall."

Future Implications

Informed by this analysis, we are compiling best-practice guidelines for professors to use videoconferencing. Still to be determined is whether using Dimdim or Adobe Connect successfully requires that the instructor have the technological skills of this particular professor, who is an educational technologist. Our hope is that by identifying the specific skills instructors need, our best practice guidelines will enable most faculty to become facile with Web-based videoconferencing. So far, the guidelines recommend the following best practices:

- When sharing the instructor's desktop, keep the chatroom visible so the instructor can see the conversations happening in chat.

- If a wired Internet connection is available, turn off wireless to avoid connection issues that can occur if there is a weak wireless signal.
- Students who do not have a microphone can communicate just fine in the chatroom, and they can hear the instructor through their computer's speakers. If you are using a microphone, on the other hand, you must plug in a headphone, turn off your speakers, and listen through your headphone in order to avoid echo caused by audio feeding back through the speakers.
- Ask some of the students who are attending class locally to log on to the videoconference so they can alert the professor if any problems occur that the instructor is not aware of.

UNIVERSITY/SCHOOL PARTNERSHIP: USING TECHNOLOGY TO COLLABORATE WITH MIDDLE SCHOOL WRITERS AND CREATE MORE INFORMED TEACHERS OF WRITING

SUSAN R. RIDOUT, GARY PINKSTON, AND JANE RIEHL
INDIANA UNIVERSITY SOUTHEAST

DEBBIE SCHWEITZER
JEFFERSON COUNTY PUBLIC SCHOOLS, LOUISVILLE, KENTUCKY

Keywords: writing, collaboration, mentors

Framework

Indiana University Southeast students review middle school students' writing pieces during face-to-face conferences and online during "electronic conferences." Sixth and seventh grade language arts students are paired with pre-service Education students (mentors), but the project could easily be undertaken with English composition students serving as mentors. As an added bonus, in addition to seeing improvement in the writing abilities of the youngsters, we often see writing skills of the college mentors improve.

Making it Work

1. The middle school language arts teacher and the school technology coordinator travel to the University and conduct a presentation on portfolio pieces and the legal uses of student electronic communications. Mentors are assigned their students, and the mentors send an electronic "hand shake," sending their pictures and a few words of introduction.
2. Face-to-face conferences are held between mentors and their middle school students. Technology is utilized to add interest to the conferences as mentors use YouTube videos and self-developed PowerPoint presentations focused on specific writing elements.
3. Middle school students revise their writing pieces and use an electronic drop box to submit their work to their mentors. The mentors then electronically respond, offering additional comments, suggestions or encouraging words.

During this project, all of us — the classroom teacher, school technology coordinator, and university professors — monitor the activities to ensure that best practices for integrating technology and teaching writing are evident; we see mentors creatively use technology during the face-to-face conferences and also providing excellent face-to-face and electronic feedback.

Audience: Education Faculty and/or Writing Composition Faculty

Tools: The school's web-based communication system. (We use Jefferson County Public Schools' Angel Environment, much like OnCourse.) A protected environment is best, as we can monitor any exchanges between students and mentors.

Implementation Time: We were able to implement this using a one semester time frame. The first semester, we had two planning meetings and several electronic communications prior to the assignment of students. We now plan everything via e-mail. We meet one day for training the mentors and one day for face-to-face conferences. Electronic conferences between the middle school students and their mentors take place outside of class time.

Future Implications

The public school teachers have evidence from their evaluations of writing pieces (and from higher writing scores on portfolio pieces) that students' writing skills have improved. Wouldn't it be great if all young writers had this kind of support?

On post-project questionnaires, mentors also state their own abilities to write have improved. Mentors continue to amaze us with their highly creative and effective use of technology to support young writers. It truly is a win-win situation as relationships are built and skills are strengthened.

DOPPELGÄNGER PROFESSOR: HIGH-TOUCH DELIVERY TO LOW-DENSITY POPULATIONS

ELIZABETH H. JONES
NOTRE DAME OF MARYLAND UNIVERSITY

Keywords: hybrid delivery, blended learning, multiple campuses

Framework

The mission called for scheduling a required course at multiple, distant campuses, yet no single campus had enough students to warrant creating a section. Additionally, the students at this traditional, yet progressive, institution expected face-to-face interaction with their instructors. *Doppelgänger Professor* emerged as a blended learning solution in which core content was delivered online and a single faculty member met students at each location on a rotating schedule. By combining the efficiency of asynchronous online presentation with lively, on-site interaction, students received first-rate instruction and graduated on time; and the college provided affordable, high-quality services to a widely separated population using just one instructor.

Our small, liberal arts college has a growing population of adult undergraduate and graduate learners, but struggles to offer all required courses at all three of its campuses each term. The business department offers a master's degree in management at the main campus, and at satellite facilities 35 miles north and 115 miles south. While course content is equivalent at all three locations, the main and southern campuses offer 10-unit courses spread over a traditional semester; whereas the northern campus, in a recent innovation, provides cohort-based, compressed, 7-unit classes presented over seven consecutive weeks.

To meet several needs, the school has begun converting adult courses to hybrid delivery. This not only generates stronger learning outcomes than online or face-to-face alone (U.S. Department of Education, 2009) but also increases the scheduling flexibility prized by adult learners. Hybrid delivery alone, though, addresses only part of the problem.

Making it Work

I teach the master's capstone course, Leadership and Organizational Development, which is reading and writing intensive, requires inclusive programmatic assessments, and was previously offered only in a 10-unit format. Preliminary enrollments one term revealed another part of the problem: there were only four learners in the south, seven in the north, and seven on main campus. I was already committed to two other, fully enrolled, evening courses, but fortunately I had previously piloted a 10-unit, half-online/half-on-site blended version of the course at main campus with good results. The solution to our newest problem emerged after intense discussion: the school would provide 7-unit, compressed,

blended delivery with online content and two face-to-face sessions at each campus. Although students might reasonably expect a hybrid course, most would not expect timeline compression, and none would anticipate multi-campus personal presentations. To facilitate the process, I began intensive email communication with students six weeks prior to the course, notifying them of the format; providing a draft syllabus; and encouraging each to work directly with me. Additionally, the school provided full access to Blackboard online components (e.g., discussions, rubrics) two weeks before the start date.

Blended learning demands more of both students and faculty. Compressing the timeline while retaining all required elements also creates additional challenges. The integrated implementation process is deceptively simple: deploy content identified for mastery online, and then present enrichment and engagement materials on-site, linked to online elements so that all students have covered foundation materials before meeting face-to-face. Using a single timeline for online units while providing face-to-face instruction to students engaged in different portions of the course requires careful temporal decoupling of the on-site and online activities. This decoupling also allows learners to meet at any campus, enabling them to better resolve conflicts with work.

As with any such project, existing material must be re-purposed or a new course specifically created. Compression necessitated rewriting and re-sequencing of existing online lessons, deletion of lesser reading assignments, streamlining of a major case study, and elimination of a supporting case study. Decoupling proved more challenging, yet resulted in highly productive use of on-site time: I included only highly-focused, team-based activities such as values and personality assessment exercises. In the 10-unit hybrid version, online lessons, discussions, and activities had been assigned for weeks not having on-site sessions; however, in the 7-unit offering, all three were created for all units. This enabled the same syllabus to be followed regardless of when face-to-face sessions actually occurred.

In order to make learning rich but not overwhelming, I strategically staggered on-site meetings throughout the term, with online instruction provided between face-to-face sessions. I used online presentation of introductory and final instructional units, augmented by real-time chat, to ensure consistency and cohesion. Our face-to-face sessions met Monday, Friday, or the following Monday during units 2/3 and 5/6. In a traditional 15-week term, I would have met with three sections three times, possibly rotating sequentially on the same evening of on-site weeks.

A fully functional online learning management system is indispensable to blended learning, yet no highly sophisticated components are needed. Basic features such as online chat and a discussion board for graded activities proved sufficient to the task. My course encountered no online difficulty; however, I am fully conversant with Blackboard and experienced at delivering online curricula, and all of my students had at least modest technical savvy.

Future Implications

The course received positive feedback: students especially appreciated the flexibility, though most wished for more face-to-face time and several struggled with the intensity of the writing assignments. I gained satisfying insights from creatively meeting the challenge. An unanticipated benefit to the school also emerged: inclusion of learners from across the program provided benchmarks on cross-campus consistency of instruction and learning. Additionally, the compressed hybrid format facilitated identification and remediation of writing problems because I gave each learner weekly feedback.

Using Doppelgänger Professor — a single faculty member with multi-site blended learning — institutions can stay within budget, yet offer needed courses more frequently on satellite campuses. This mode seems most appropriate for upper-level courses serving adult and self-disciplined traditional students. The benefits to students and institutions are obvious, but the cost-benefit picture for faculty members is mixed. I found serving three campuses in a compressed term exhilarating, but starkly demanding. Many instructors would balk at this if not offered compensatory time or resources to offset its added burden. The institution should reimburse the faculty member for mileage, and consider remuneration for the extra work involved in converting the course and meeting with multiple sections, especially when significant travel is required several evenings in a single week. Even with the costs of added compensation, though, this approach generates dramatic net advantages for dispersed student bodies and creatively engaged institutions.

Reference

U.S. Department of Education. (2009). *Evaluation of evidence-based practices in online learning: A meta-analysis and review of online learning studies.* Washington, D.C.: Office of Planning, Evaluation, and Policy Development. Retrieved from www.ed.gov/about/offices/list/opepd/ppss/reports.html.

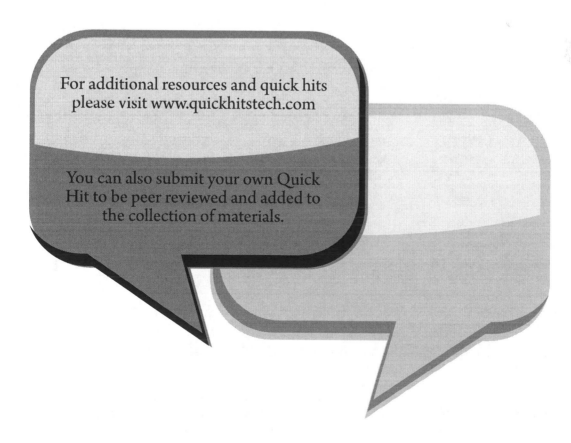

For additional resources and quick hits please visit www.quickhitstech.com

You can also submit your own Quick Hit to be peer reviewed and added to the collection of materials.

Enhancing Evaluation 3

Assessment: An opportunity to demonstrate excellence

Robin K. Morgan
Indiana University Southeast

Whatever else the Scholarship of Teaching and Learning (SoTL) may represent, the discipline clearly embraces an uncompromising ethic of quality control and accountability in the teaching-learning dynamic. Simply put, those who are passionate about being good teachers recognize the necessity of placing their teaching practices under the microscope, evaluating the results of such assessment, both good and bad, and reflecting on how to use such findings to improve teaching outcomes. This exercise in continuous assessment exemplifies, in many ways, the scientific attitudes of critical thinking and skepticism, and benefits a multitude of stakeholders, including the faculty themselves, their home institution, and, most notably, the students who stand to gain the most from this self-reflective endeavor.

The submissions in Chapter 3 converge on several dimensions of this assessment process. Evaluating teaching effectiveness requires that the spotlight fall on both principal players, teacher and student alike. Neither has escaped the scrutiny of the present authors. Proper assessment benefits both, and this is nowhere more apparent than in the decision to engage both formative and summative assessment in one's class. Formative assessment provides important early data for the instructor while simultaneously offering useful and timely feedback to the student, ideally reducing "surprises" on more summative measures. Several of the current submissions demonstrate methods of providing formative feedback. Three submissions, for example, outline various techniques of using personal responses systems, or clickers, in providing real time formative feedback. Similarly, Amy Zink, in her submission, describes how she uses Google Docs to gather feedback on what students know so that she can plan her lessons accordingly. She then describes how she uses the same data to evaluate the effectiveness of her teaching.

Although some form of course and instructor evaluation is in place in most colleges and universities, the data generated by such tools seldom engender confidence. Such instruments may offer valid information regarding student likes and dislikes, for both content and instructors, but may tell us precious little about what has and has not been mastered by the student as a result of their exposure to the course. Several of the present submissions address this issue. Michelle Gacio Harrolle, for example, describes her efforts to have students create a personal video demonstrating skills learned in class. Robin Lightner uses WebQuests specifically designed to meet the course's learning objectives. Both of these approaches provide much more detailed information about the quality of student learning than traditional course evaluations.

The authors of the current offerings remain of one voice in advocating for the ongoing assessment of teaching effectiveness. That this task can take many forms and provide an assortment of meaningful information is also apparent. For those of us who entered the academy roughly a generation ago, such developments are nothing short of remarkable. However, in spite of the varied and innovative ideas contained in these submissions, it is clear that, as a profession, we have a long way to go in 'closing the loop' on course evaluation. Technology holds promise as a quick and efficient method of collecting data about how well our teaching methods enhance student learning. The next step is to adjust our methods based on our collected data and then, once again, assess our effectiveness. Through reflecting on these efforts, it may be that changes that benefit student learning may occur beyond the classroom. That is, curricula or student advising changes may be necessitated to truly assist students in achieving their academic goals.

For additional resources and quick hits please visit www.quickhitstech.com

You can also submit your own Quick Hit to be peer reviewed and added to the collection of materials.

Google-Doc surveys for teaching Hispanic culture

Amy Zink
Indiana University Southeast

Keywords: Google, survey, culture, Spanish

Framework

My mother always said "Fall in love with a doc" and now I have. A Google-Doc.

One of the advantages of teaching Spanish is the opportunity to expose students to the values and practices of the Hispanic culture. Recognizing that behavior, including our own, has a cultural context helps students progress from an ethnocentric to an ethno-relative point of view. I use Google Survey Forms in my Spanish classes, both small and large, to help me teach this ethno-relative viewpoint.

Making it Work

Here's what I do. When learning about greetings, attitudes toward work, eating habits or any culturally relevant behavior, I want my students to reflect upon their own culture and practices first before talking about what other cultures do. Google (www.google.com) has a great, free, survey template that allows students to assess their own attitudes about a given cultural topic and allows me to gather information from my students quickly and creatively. First, I have to have a Google account (free and easy) and then I go to Google Docs and create a new form. I choose from a selection of six types of questions: multiple choice, short answer, long

answer, scale, check from a list, or grid. I can use the same type of question or mix and match. After I have written my questions, I send the survey directly to my students' email accounts. When they open the email, they are taken straight to the survey; they can then answer immediately and send the data right away with just a few clicks.

Future Implications

All the data are then tabulated and sent to me in a pie graph or bar chart. I can easily access this information in the classroom (or print it in my office and make copies) and show students the results to open discussion. In addition, I get immediate feedback on what students know or what opinions they have about a given topic and can plan my lesson accordingly. Typically, I then assign a reading about the same topic in the target culture and we compare and contrast. Students are willing to take the survey because it does not require more than a few steps and they are curious to see and talk about the results… in Spanish. I can also assess learning, particularly affective. For example, my survey can include pre- and post- questions on where students see their own listening or speaking skills, or cultural knowledge. It is a great way to collect data that I can use to evaluate my own teaching and improve student learning. This Google-Doc has added efficiency, variety and creativity to my Spanish lessons. True love.

A CLASS WIKI FOR THE PHYSICAL SCIENCES

Paul Cooper
George Mason University

Keywords: wiki, physical science, student writing

Framework

This article describes a wiki-based project I developed in Fall 2009. The goal was to have students in an upper-level Physical Chemistry course prepare class lecture notes for the semester. The aims of this project were: 1) to determine if a wiki is a suitable technology for student-written lecture notes in a physical science lecture course; and 2) gauge student feedback for a preliminary determination of effectiveness as a learning tool. Wikis are an excellent tool for collaborative writing projects, however in physical science

courses, there is often a need to insert figures, tables and many equations.

Making it Work

The wiki for this project was hosted by PBworks (www. pbworks.com), although any provider can be used. Free accounts through such providers can often meet the needs for a class website, however, paid account features are often a welcome addition and provide the instructor with more options. GMU has a license agreement with

PBworks to host wikis for GMU faculty, and other institutions may have similar agreements. The PBworks interface allowed for the uploading of images, the creation of tables, and the insertion of complex mathematical equations using LaTeX. Students found it easy to create well-presented lecture notes.

Setting up the wiki is not a difficult or lengthy process. An hour or two of exploring the intuitive interface, and an instructor should be sufficiently skilled to manage such a project as described above.

During the first lecture, the project was thoroughly explained to the class. Students were assigned to groups, and groups were assigned to a particular lecture for which they were responsible for note taking. Students from a group were allowed to negotiate how to divide up the work amongst the group members. Authorship tracking built in to the wiki quickly showed what each student wrote, so that grades could be assigned individually rather than on a group basis. At the completion of a student's set of lecture notes, I returned prompt editorial feedback. Students received a grade for their work that counted towards their final course grade. Additionally, editing by students outside of that lecture's group was encouraged and extra credit was given to those who participated in the editing.

Future Implications

Students were anonymously polled at the end of semester. Some key statistics follow: 84% of students strongly agree/agree that the wiki helped them understand the lecture material; 9% of students felt the project was a negative experience; the overall rating for the course was 4.70/5.00 (up from 4.37/5.00 in the previous year). Other questions revealed ~55% of the class was positive towards the educational aspects of the wiki, ~30% was neutral, and ~15% was negative.

The ease with which students successfully created the wiki-based notes shows that the technology is quite capable of lecture note taking (and other projects) for even equation-orientated physical science courses.

Program-wide implementation of this, or similar writing projects, could provide a unique way to both improve students' understanding of lecture content, and through increased writing (with editorial feedback), improve student writing in physical science programs.

||||||||||||||||||||||||||||||||||||||||||||||||||||||||||||||||||||||||||||||||||||||||||||||||||||||||||||||||||||||||||||||||||||||||||||||||||||||||||||

Using multiple-response clicker questions to identify student misunderstanding

Daniel King
Drexel University

Keywords: personal response system, clickers, student feedback, multiple choice questions, question types

Framework

Personal response devices (or clickers) facilitate rapid student feedback to questions asked by an instructor during class. While they are most commonly used in large classrooms (more than 100 students) as a way to create an active learning environment, they can be effective in small classes (less than 30 students) as well.

Making it Work

This technology consists of four components: a clicker (that the student uses to answer a multiple choice question), a receiver to collect the responses, software to process the votes and a computer/data projector to display the voting results, usually as a histogram. The size, shape, functionality and cost of the clickers vary by manufacturer (e.g., e-Instruction, www.einstruction.com; i-clicker, www.iclicker.com; Turning Technologies, Inc., www.turningtechnologies.com). Turning Technologies (the brand that I use) sells their basic devices for $30 each, plus $100 for the receiver (one receiver can handle up to 1000 devices). In most cases, students purchase their own clicker (separately or bundled with the textbook), and often can sell them back to the bookstore if they are not used in other classes. I purchased my own set that students use in my classes. Each company has their own software, which is usually available for free. The questions can be incorporated into PowerPoint slides and/or appear in a separate program, depending on the clicker software. Most devices only allow students to answer multiple choice or true-false questions, although some newer devices and/or software allow students to submit numeric and text responses. The anonymous nature of these devices (student answers are reported in aggregate) promotes participation by all students. While individual student answers are not seen by their peers, the answers are collected by the software and can be viewed later by the faculty member to determine how each student is performing.

After using clickers for several years I began to think about the limitations of using multiple choice questions. I became concerned that correct answers represented students' ability to eliminate wrong answers, rather than their understanding of the content (Wood, 2003). To address this, I modified many of my clicker questions to allow students to submit more than one correct answer. With the Turning Point software, this required only a setting change to adjust the number of answers that could be submitted for each question. Some of the questions were reworded to include more than one correct answer, while other questions were unchanged (i.e., still only one correct answer). For faculty who are already using clickers, it would be very simple to change existing clicker questions to multiple-response questions. Below I will describe the benefits of three types of multiple-response questions.

First, I took a standard single-answer, multiple-choice question and simply allowed students to submit more than one correct answer. In previous years, most students might have identified the correct answer, and I would have then moved on to the next topic. However, given the option to choose more than one correct answer, students who might have been able to identify the "best" answer, now might choose two correct answers. This lets me and the students know that there is confusion about the topic, and I can address the misunderstanding in real time.

Second, I can eliminate the need for artificial, and awkward, formats that are often used in multiple-choice questions, where students are asked to choose correct statements from a list. When students had to choose only one correct answer, I was forced to create a series of groupings (e.g., statements 1 and 2 are correct, statements 1 and 3 are correct, all of the above statements are correct) as answers to the question. The list of choices for the student rarely incorporated all of the possible groupings, which meant that students were able to eliminate some of the groupings based on information about only one of the items. If students can choose more than one correct answer, then each item in the list becomes an answer choice. So, if the correct answer had been "statements 1 and 3 are correct", the new question would just require students to choose answers 1 and 3. This means that

each item is voted on independently (without using any groupings), and the students must evaluate each statement on its own merits. Each answer represents the student's understanding of that concept/statement.

The third example involves the conversion of a problem-solving question into two clicker questions. When students incorrectly answer a clicker question involving a calculation, it is difficult to determine if the students had trouble setting up the calculation or doing the math. So, I now add an additional clicker question before the calculation in which students either have to identify which equations/constants they need to use or have to determine what information in the question will (or will not) be used in the calculation. This helps students think through the set-up of the calculation and identify any values that are extraneous, such as a mass or temperature that might not be used in the calculation, which improves their problem-solving skills. This helps me identify where students are making their mistakes. Once I know where they are getting stuck, I can more effectively help them.

Future Implications

I have used this technique for the past two years in general chemistry classes. Students receive all of the standard benefits of using clickers (e.g., active engagement, anonymity), with more effective feedback. I have observed improved performance on exam questions related to topics that were included in multiple-response clicker questions relative to previous years when those topics were included in single-answer clicker questions. I attribute this to the fact that I am now able to identify and address misconceptions that I was unaware of in previous years.

Reference

Wood, E. J. (2003). What are extended matching sets questions? *BEE-j*, *1* (1), 1-8.

GRADING DISCUSSION FORUMS IN THE ONLINE ENVIRONMENT

MARCIA D. DIXSON
INDIANA UNIVERSITY PURDUE UNIVERSITY FORT WAYNE

Keywords: online discussion forums, assessment, evaluation, grading

Framework

Many of us use small group discussions in online courses to get students engaged with the content and each other. However, in a class of thirty students, I typically have 120 to 300 individual posts per discussion plus the group posts. If I use a follow-up whole class discussion, there are another

100–150 messages. Instructors new to online teaching feel they must read, comment, and grade every post. Don't!

Making it Work

Consider the regular classroom. When students work in groups, we do not try to grade (or even hear) every comment they make. We should not do so online either. What gets graded depends on the learning goals for the assignment. My goals for most forums are: 1) students participating and engaging in the class; 2) students reading and talking about the content; 3) students critically thinking about the concepts.

What I do to evaluate each of these goals is:
To evaluate participation: I simply count posts. Are they present in the forum and doing more than reading?

To evaluate reading and talking about content: I read enough of a post to know it is meaningful and content related, that the student is stating why he/she agrees with an idea or what he/she would add, change or delete and why.

To evaluate critical thinking of concepts: I read the groups' final answers, in detail, and comment on them. Note, this is the only place that an indepth reading and commentary are necessary or valuable. If I were to comment on each individual posting, students might become afraid of "saying the wrong thing" which could actually defeat the goal of getting them to participate.

Grading/commenting/facilitating goes like this:
Shortly after the discussion begins: check in to see how the groups are doing. Comment about each group's progress.

Check in sporadically after that in the same manner we circulate to groups in a classroom. The first couple of discussions, send individual emails to students who are not participating or not participating successfully.

At the end of the discussion: grade the final group post/answer according to the objectives of the assignment. Then read enough of each individual's posts to know if they have met the requirements for number of content (meaningful) posts for that forum and whether they started "on time." For instance, I require an initial substantive post of each group member by the first day of the discussion.

The follow-up whole class discussion is a "debate" to see which group best defends their own answer and critically analyzes the answers of other groups. This is done so all of the students can benefit from the other groups' discussions. These posts are skimmed to find a "winning group." Then one email is sent to the class announcing who won and why.

Future Implications

Students in the last two semesters have rated the discussions a 4.3/5.0 scale for being engaging and applicable to their lives. They do not seem to need more feedback. I manage the discussion, keep students engaged, have them critically consider the concepts, and still stay sane!

Sometimes less is more

Marianne Niedzlek-Feaver and Betty L. Black
North Carolina State University

Keywords: online review, online quizzing, feedback and online review, customizing feedback, customizable review

Framework

Metabolism is a difficult topic for students. Instructors struggle with the problem of attempting to focus on intangible concepts such as energy conversion or necessity of converting nutrients into chemical forms useful to cells. To begin to appreciate cell structure and organization, students need also to learn metabolic reactions and associate important steps in the process with appropriate cell organelles.

Making it Work

We have developed a program for review of cellular respiration that utilizes a diagram of cell organelles with questions (blanks) at appropriate points on the diagram. Each blank has a pull-down menu of 10 potential answers to be chosen by the student (Figure 1). We utilized 12 questions about products and reactions associated with steps of the process or locations where specific steps of cellular respiration

occurred. The only feedback provided was the number of answers that were correct when students had filled in the blanks and checked their score.

Future Implications

We were somewhat surprised at student reactions to this type of review. There were several unsolicited comments praising it as "wonderful" and the "perfect" learning device. Since students' final scores on the review were recorded, they regarded it as a quiz and accused us of devising a cheat-proof test. They seemed to understand that guessing (with 12 blanks and 10 potential answers for each) would end in frustration and failure. We suddenly realized that by providing little feedback we were motivating students to go back and review the material until they could score 100% on the review. Some students asked for more reviews of this type, exercises that would tell them if they were on the right track, but also force them to learn the material if they wanted a good score. We were so delighted with the response to our "less feedback is sometimes best" approach that we changed our future plans, which had involved adding detailed feedback for each wrong answer.

Now we will concentrate on the same type of tool that can be modified for other reviews and is customizable by faculty. The new program will feature 40 potential locations for menus on the page background; we anticipate that instructors will pick 15 or less of these locations for menu placement. Instructors can utilize their own diagram or photograph for the background and can customize each menu with their own terms (up to 12) for answers. Upon completion of an attempt, the review program will also deliver to the student not only the number of correct answers, but also a unique receipt number as proof that the work is his or her own. The program will also feature a reordering of terms within the menus after each attempt and an optional

timer for use by instructors who wish to use the program as a timed quiz. Funds for these revisions have been secured through a NCSU in-house grant for improving summer school education and the program should be available for testing in July 2011. This program will be available free of charge to any interested educator. All we ask is for feedback from recipients so that we can continue to improve our product. Please contact the authors for more information.

Thus, our message is that sometimes less feedback can be more beneficial to students, especially for difficult material that requires repeated attempts to master. This type of feedback discourages guessing, yet provides students a way to estimate their progress in mastering the topic. Is this a program for constructing the "perfect" quiz? No, unfortunately, but this program may prove a good tool for producing quizzes that motivate students to continue reviewing until the material is thoroughly understood.

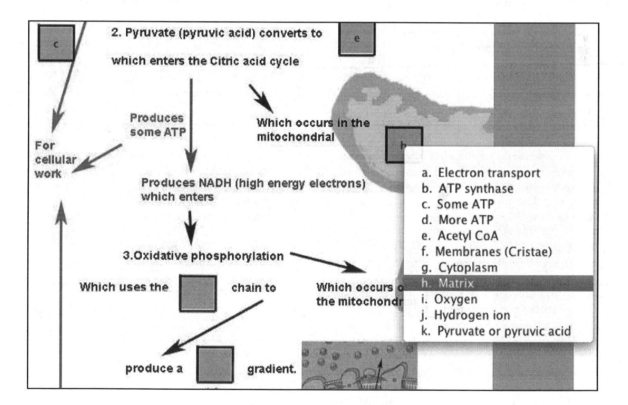

Figure 3.1. Part of the review on aerobic respiration showing the pull down menu that provides a list of answers to the questions. Note that this student has already chosen answers to some questions as indicated by letters in the boxes. The student is attempting to choose the correct answer for the next question (the cellular location of the citric acid cycle reactions) by choosing mitochondrial matrix from the list of possible answers. Students can change answers until the quiz is submitted. Answers in the menu list are reordered for each attempt of the quiz.

Using Prezi to produce creative critical thinking assessments

Frank Wray
Raymond Walters College, University of Cincinnati

Keywords: critical thinking, assessment, presentation technology

Framework

Creating assessments in the classroom that involve critical/creative thinking rely on the creative nature of the instructor that produces them. While we now know that there are several ways to develop critical thinking assessments in the classroom (see Combs, Cennambo, and Newbill, 2009 for an exhaustive list), very few of us allow our students to be involved in the creative process to actually demonstrate critical thinking.

Prezi (http:// Prezi.com) is a web-based presentation portal that allows the user to create rich and visually appealing presentations. While the primary use is for presentations, I posit a side benefit of creating the presentations is that the creator must connect a logical flow of ideas on a single canvas (e.g. http://Prezi.com/hgjm18z36h75/why-should-you-move-beyond-slides/). These ideas can be words, pictures, audio files, videos, YouTube videos, or even documents. Essentially, the user is creating a concept map (i.e., a diagram showing the relationships among concepts) of the topic of interest!

Making it Work

Creating a Prezi presentation is very simple. The instructor can use 30 minutes in a computer lab to orient the students to the technology and the students can start creating Prezi presentations 15 minutes after their initial exposure. Best of all is that they have fun with it and they can easily create work outside of the classroom. The use of this technology can be used in conjunction with any topic or class size. In addition, students can be productive in producing Prezi presentations in groups or individually. Once more, Prezi is especially valuable as an evaluative tool to gauge whether or not the student(s) is/are understanding particular content. In addition, the presentations provide a reflection tool for the instructor to see if they are addressing the student learning outcomes.

The following steps provide a good way to introduce the students to the technology and provide them with the tools to create assignments that can be viewed and assessed.

1. Have students create a Prezi account (It's a free account).
2. Show the students the basic tutorial video (http://Prezi.com/learn/)
3. Provide students with a sample topic that was previously covered in class. Included with this topic is a list of relevant and associated words to that topic (e.g. Topic: "Glucose and Insulin Interaction". Words: Glucose, blood, pancreas, insulin, body cells, etc.).
4. Stress to the students that the words are there only for guidance and that they can use different media to represent the words and/or concepts (e.g. for glucose, they could use a picture of a glucose molecule, or use audio to describe the effect of negative feedback on the process, or use a YouTube video to show how glucose enters a cell).
5. Demonstrate how to double-click anywhere on the canvas to write text.
6. Show the students how to use the editing tool called the "zebra." The "zebra" allows the student to resize, rotate, scale, and create hierarchy to the text. Regardless of the size, the orientation, or the position of the visual element, it will come into perfect view during the presentation. (e.g. http://Prezi.com/uvuptd6tvouc/peer-learning/)
7. Show how images and movies can be easily inserted onto the canvas. Using the "zebra", the images and movies can be resized and rotated as well.
8. Finally, show how to connect the storyline or path. The canvas can be zoomed out so that all elements can be shown. Next, the students are shown how to create the paths between the visual elements by clicking on the "Path" button. The students simply click on the topic elements in the best logical order. This order can easily be edited and changed if desired.
9. When finished, the student simply clicks on "Show" and use the arrow buttons to proceed through the presentation. (A student example is at http://Prezi.com/otum7wunvbim/glucose-homeostasis/)

> the Prezi presentations become a simple, yet powerful and fun, evaluative tool for both the student and instructor.

Future Implications

It should be noted that with each Prezi assessment there is an associated grading rubric so the students know exactly what the expectations are for a grade. It is also recommended that the instructor provide a "Presentation Code of Ethics" where it is explicitly stated what is or what is not appropriate material that can be used (an example of this "Code of Ethics" can be obtained by emailing the author). With these rules in place, the Prezi presentations become a simple, yet powerful and fun, evaluative tool for both the student and instructor. In addition, the student is given more ownership of their learning because of their ability to create this work on their own and rely on their own creativity.

References

Combs, L. B., Cennamo, K. S. & Newbill, P. L. (2009). Developing Critical and Creative Thinkers. *Educational Technology. September/October*, 3-14.

‖‖‖

INFORMATION LITERACY: BUILDING CRITICAL SKILLS FOR LEARNING AND COMMUNICATING ABOUT RESEARCH ON THE WEB

KAREN CICCONE, CHARLIE MORRIS, AND ERIN SILLS
NORTH CAROLINA STATE UNIVERSITY

Keywords: website evaluation, information literacy, web publishing, website design

Framework

Information literacy is a necessity for today's digital native who relies heavily on the internet as an information source. Additionally, basic knowledge of web publishing is a useful skill and an asset in the job market. Students in our introductory lecture course on World Forestry build these competencies by evaluating and creating webpages. Students are taught to critically evaluate information found on the web and then use those skills to find high quality websites to link from their own research webpages. Creating web pages demystifies the web and reinforces the need for critical evaluation of information found on the web. We have employed a range of technologies for these assignments, including online forms and wikis, and both desktop and online website development tools.

Making it Work

Students develop website evaluation skills through in-class practice and discussion, reinforced by an out-of-class assignment. In class, students evaluate instructor-selected websites on a controversial topic. We select websites that at first glance seem authoritative and objective, but that are funded by and represent various private interests. Metzger (2007) stresses the importance of motivation in determining the amount of effort students put into critically evaluating information they find online. We select websites that are designed to persuade (and sometimes deceive) in order to illuminate the range of stakeholders and strategies operating on the web, thereby motivating students to assess the credibility of websites before citing them for class assignments.

Students first work in small groups to answer key questions, and then report back and discuss their answers with the whole class. The key questions focus on credibility of the websites:

1. Who made this website?
2. What is the agenda of the person or organization that made this website (e.g., who funds it)?
3. What is the purpose of this website? Who is the intended audience?
4. How authoritative is this source to address this topic (e.g., does author have relevant credentials)?
5. In what situations and how might you cite this source in a research paper?

Future Implications

To assess their understanding, we have students select a website related to international forestry and write an evaluation of the site on our course wiki. Other types of technology that could be used for this assignment include discussion forums and web forms. The web form option has the advantage of simplifying formatting and prompting students to address each evaluation criterion. In addition to answering the questions above, we ask students to describe the content and coverage of their chosen website, note the currency of the information provided, and comment on the design of the site itself. The annotated list of websites becomes an online resource for students in the course.

After these evaluations are posted, students begin work on their final project for the course: a one-page website on a current topic in World Forestry, selected by the students in consultation with the instructor. The assignment is to create a webpage that serves as a guide and gateway to research on the selected topic and that demonstrates good website design skills. This assignment teaches basic web publishing skills while reinforcing students' critical evaluation skills, as well as underscoring the need for those skills.

Before digging into the assignment, some technical details need to be established. The most critical decision is which website development tool to support. For example, in some years we have opted for Dreamweaver, which students use in conjunction with their personal space on the university web server. We allow students to use any website development tool, but we only provide technical support for the selected tool. At the beginning of the semester, we also assess students' prior experience constructing websites to determine how much training and technical support they will require. We have found that our students can learn the basics of web publishing in one in-class tutorial supplemented by documentation. If further help is required we sometimes offer help sessions outside of class and answer questions via online discussion forums and email.

Regardless of software, students should get some exposure to HTML and good design practices. We introduce students to design issues by having them create their webpage through a series of incremental steps. The first assignment is simply to post the proposed title of their webpage and their name, followed by posting an annotated bibliography including both references from the scientific literature and hyperlinked websites. The first full draft of the webpage is required to include at least one image, with the source appropriately cited and alternative text that meets Section 508 accessibility standards (Section 508 of the Rehabilitation Act, 1998). Other requirements for the draft are a revised title, key question(s) investigated, a table of contents, an outline of the main sections, the annotated bibliography, and a final section that describes the purpose and author (the student) of the webpage. These draft webpages are peer reviewed, using the same evaluation skills that the students developed in the website evaluation assignment.

As with any class project, the quality of research webpages submitted by students varies from 'beautifully formatted and information rich' to 'barely meeting the minimum criteria'. All students at least learn that anyone — from fellow students with limited expertise, to private interests with a particular agenda to promote — can post information on the web. Most students report that by the end of the course, they are confident about creating other webpages, that they learned a great deal about their selected topic, and that they learned more from the webpage assignment than they would have from a traditional term paper. (In response to questions on each of these, more than two-thirds of the students selected positively a 4 or 5 on a 5-point Likert scale.) Student comments included "I really enjoyed this assignment. It was a nice break from writing papers," and student recommendations for how to improve the assignment included "more peer review!"

We expect that the research webpage assignment will continue to evolve, especially in terms of the actual technological platform used for creating the pages. The main purpose of this assignment is to equip students with information literacy skills, but an important secondary skill learned is how websites work and are put together from a "basic" technical perspective. However, the meaning of "basic" is changing as WYSIWYG tools (e.g., Google Sites, Blogger, WordPress, and many others) become more widespread, more effective, and more likely to be what students will use in their future jobs. Thus, we are shifting towards these web service platforms, while still providing explanations of web standards, HTML source, best practices in design, and search engine optimization.

References

Metzger, M.J. (2007). Making sense of credibility on the web: Models for evaluating online information and recommendations for future research. *Journal of the American Society for Information Science and Technology,* 58(13), 2078–2091.

Section 508 of the Rehabilitation Act, 29 U.S.C. §794d (1998). Retrieved from Section 508 website: http://www.section508.gov/

ENHANCING TEACHING AND LEARNING THROUGH TECHNOLOGY

RICHARD B. SCHULTZ
ELMHURST COLLEGE

Keywords: active learning, hybrid-based, online course, discussion forums

Framework

This brief Quick Hit concerns the engagement of higher education students for the purpose of promoting active learning in a relatively small classroom, usually less than 30 students. It is most appropriate for a hybrid-based or online course format, although it can be used effectively in any classroom situation as well.

The use of discussion forums has long been used by faculty members to promote student engagement and learning. However, students who do not engage but, rather, "lurk" in discussion forums may or may not be effectively contributing to the discussion and collaborative learning process. This Brief Quick Hit offers a suggested format and recommended tool for invoking student learning, participation in an engaging discussion, promoting collaborative learning, and assisting students with proper citation techniques. In addition, this technique provides students with a variety of access modes, assists with assessment, and decreases faculty time allocated to grading.

Making it Work:

The technique begins with a "critical thinking question," referred to hereafter as a "CTQ." The faculty member assigns s tudent partners (usually two to a learning team) an open-ended question regarding a specific topic of discussion germane to the weekly lesson. Students have 72 hours to research the question and each student prepares their own individual 300-word response to the CTQ. They must use proper citation styles and include a minimum of five (5) reference sources (promoting information literacy) to support their response. One of the student partners is selected to post the collection of two responses to the Discussion Board in a single thread. Once the responses are posted, other students in the course are encouraged to read and respond to the post. The original authors of the response are charged with fielding questions and comments from other students in that discussion thread. Additionally, those students who were assigned the CTQ are required to post on a Voicethread site as to the summary of the discussion from their perspective at the conclusion of the discussion forum (usually after one week of discussion). Voicethread is a collaborative, multimedia slide show that may include images, documents, and/or videos and allows students to navigate slides and leave comments using their mobile devices in 5 ways — using voice (with a microphone or telephone), entering text, attaching an audio file, or video (via a webcam). This makes the entire threaded discussion available to be archived and accessible to students to have a broader view of the content presented in the CTQ. The only software necessary is a course management system and access to a Voicethread site(free access and use) . The costs are generally absorbed by the institution as part of their alternative delivery or distance learning technology budgets.

It is recommended that students work on a weekly modular schedule of which discussion of the CTQs can be discussed. It is also recommended that original posts be accomplished in the first 72 hours of the weekly module such that subsequent discussion can take place over the remainder of the weekly module.

A detailed grading rubric is furnished to students at the start of the course thus setting the tone for expectations and engagement level on the part of student participants. Faculty members will find that the grading of the CTQ discussions can be accomplished in two parts: 1) the grading of the original CTQ partner posts after 72 hours and 2) subsequent posts, all according to grading rubrics provided to students at the onset of the course. Again, the grading rubric sets the tone for the expectations and quality of posts as well as all included elements. The discussion board format allows faculty to easily discourage plagiarism while effectively applying "teaching moments" to instruct students on the correct use of citation techniques. Voicethread discussions can be graded in an identical manner with the added benefit of recreating the chronological order of contributions on the Voicethread site. Proactive instructors should provide weekly feedback to students via a completed rubric (illustrating areas of strength and potential weaknesses) which helps students to improve their future responses and weekly participation.

> The discussion board format allows faculty to easily discourage plagiarism while effectively applying "teaching moments" to instruct students

Future Implications:

While the technique of the CTQs and the subsequent active discussion has been very successful over the past six years in which it has been employed, the future plan is to require further participation in the Voicethread by implementing requirements for various modes of participation as mentioned above. This introduces students to various modes of participation and familiarizes them with mobile computing activities.

Proactive instructors should provide weekly feedback to students via a completed rubric (illustrating areas of strength and potential weaknesses) which helps students to improve their future responses and weekly participation.

"Guest Cam" in the classroom — Making speeches real

Tatiana Kolovou
Indiana University

Keywords: Adobe Encoder, Skype, presentations, audience, audience analysis, camera, speeches

Framework

The idea of the "Guest Cam" is to bring more authenticity into the classroom, by using two technology tools, Adobe Encoder and Skype.

Making it Work

Any class size that benefits from an outside guest observing an in-class activity (team or individual presentations) would be appropriate. Students need opportunities to practice speaking to audiences composed of people other than their instructor and peers. In the Business Presentation courses in the Kelley School of Business at Indiana University, we attempt to simulate different audiences by asking the class to "pretend" to be a potential investor, the board of a company, etc. However, the questions the "pretend" audience can ask can't replicate that of a real potential investor or board member. The student presenting doesn't experience the same stress level when performing in front of peers for the eighth or ninth time during the semester. And the student doesn't have a "REAL" audience to think about during the research and preparation stages (a fundamental course objective.) However, arranging for travel to bring in actual guests for 800+ students proves a logistical impossibility and limits the topics that students can address to areas of expertise of only the handful of guests invited. The idea of the "Guest Cam" and the emergence of Skype and Adobe Acrobat allows us to reach out to hundreds of guests without the logistical problems.

OUTCOMES

1. **Audience Analysis** — instead of analyzing a "fictional audience," students research who will be watching them that day and learn to study and anticipate real questions this audience may bring to them.
2. **Comfort with Technology** — students will have to present in front of a camera numerous times in their career. This experience will allow them to become more comfortable and to learn how to interact with a remote audience.

3. **Q&A Rigor** — this section of the presentation is much more rigorous compared to the student audience coming up with their own questions.
4. **Business Community Exposure** — students are exposed to a particular business outside of a Kelley School roundtable or a networking event.

TIMELINE

A camcorder and external microphone can be purchased in the beginning of the semester. Adobe Connect is a one-hour download. Skype is a 5-minute download on a laptop or desktop.

Future Implications

Adobe Connect is an easy tool to use for virtual office hours and remote speech practices with the instructor.

Skype maybe limited in some workplaces so it might be limited in use. Adobe Connect only requires a URL connection and has a more stable connection and at times audio on sessions with international guests.

TOOLS

Webcam attached to classroom computer and external microphone.
(approx. $25 each)

PROGRAMS

Skype
http://www.skype.com
This program is free on the internet. Skype can be programmed onto classroom computer by the IT department. If not, an external lap top works as well.

Adobe Connect
http://www.adobe.com/products/acrobatconnectpro/

An image of what Adobe Connect looks like when the camera is pointing to our classroom during a speech is available at www.quickhitstech.com

The idea of the "Guest Cam" and the emergence of Skype and Adobe Acrobat allows us to reach out to hundreds of guests without the logistical problems.

USING PERSONAL RESPONSE DEVICES (CLICKERS) IN HUMANITIES CLASSES

CHAD ROHRBACHER
NORTH CAROLINA STATE UNIVERSITY

Keywords: clickers, personal response devices, significant learning, learning with technology, teaching and learning, assessment, composition and rhetoric, writing

Framework

By using clickers, personal response systems, in an English composition class, instructors can engage students in high order thinking skills like evaluation and low order skills like memorization in creative and entertaining ways.

Clickers are relatively inexpensive and easy to implement. We use Turning Point Technology (TPT). The basic package includes a receiver, 30 clickers, and carrying case and runs about $950.00 (but may be cheaper depending on adoption). After this initial package, students could be required to purchase their own clickers at around $40–50.00.

Clickers integrate with PowerPoint or can be utilized as stand-alone software. When we purchased our package, TPT facilitated a one-hour training session that gave us the basics. Once familiar with Clickers, preparing a typical slide takes less than a minute to create.

Clickers are often advertised for large lecture courses; however, many of the same reasons it's successful in those contexts is why it's successful in composition. My composition classes are typically capped at 24 students a sentence describing the size and setting of the class Clickers help facilitate a learner-centered, active-learning environments which promote comprehension of material during class, and increase student learning.

Generally exercises take about 40 minutes, though they can easily be altered to instructor's needs by modifying the number of questions asked.

Making it Work

This in-class exercise is similar to Family Feud. Students are randomly grouped into small teams of 3 and each team is given one clicker. Students are asked a question via PowerPoint. They discuss the question within their team for an allotted time, and click an answer. If they are correct, they earn a point for their team.

If students are incorrect, the question goes to the next team that selected the correct answer. That team has an opportunity to "steal" the point by explaining why their answer is correct. Before the team answers they can discuss the rationale. By requiring the rationale along with their answer, teams are deterred from merely guessing. If that team is incorrect the question goes to the next team and so on until the rationale can be given.

Questions are based on low order concerns like grammar and mechanic issues, correct citation techniques, requirements of a summary, using a research database correctly, etc. High order questions include argument analysis and rhetorical appeal identification, evaluating concepts (for example if a thesis or topic sentence is "good" or not), what the "best/most appropriate" piece of evidence for a particular topic sentence is, etc.

Questions can also be based on visual texts like advertisements, flyers, or movie clips.

Each point a team earns is a "bonus" point added to homework. In this way, students are not adversely affected for not performing well but still motivated to earn as many points as possible and thus engage with the material.

> This exercise allows students to see their weaknesses (real-time formative feedback) while instructors can use the statistics to refine the curriculum to address class difficulties in a timely manner.

After analyzing the data, I review the questions students did most poorly on. I give all students Clickers and ask the questions again, retesting, to see if students improved their understanding or if a more thorough discussion is needed.

Future Implications

This exercise allows students to see their weaknesses (real-time formative feedback) while instructors can use the statistics to refine the curriculum to address class difficulties in a timely manner. Clicker software is easy to navigate and offers instructors access to valuable data that assists them in assessing and enhancing curriculums for student learning.

I believe this format can be developed for other humanities courses to improve critical thinking, critical reading, and understanding of important disciplinary concepts.

Let students design the test

James M. VanderVeen
Indiana University South Bend

Keywords: collaboration, examinations, Google Docs

Framework

Every semester, when the exam is quickly approaching, students always ask for a study guide. In one instance, the course was an introductory general education class with a lot of terminology being introduced. I decided to have the students work together to make their own study guide. That guide would ultimately form the basis for their exam.

Making it Work

Because the class enrollment was large (50–75 students) and the classroom was not designed for group work, I used the collaborative functionality of a spreadsheet from Google Docs (found at docs.google.com). The students were provided with a link to a document a couple of weeks before the test was to be given. I explained that I wanted a total of 75 terms by a certain date. They were responsible for posting three concepts from the textbook and providing a definition or explanation for each in their own words. These words could be added to the list or replace those already present. In this way, the students could influence what was on the test. Since there were more than 50 students in the class, there was a lot of shuffling of terms going on. To encourage participation from all, I told them that if I did not get the prescribed number of terms, I would add the hardest and most confusing concepts to the list myself. I need not have worried; the number was reached more quickly than I predicted. Words were added and dropped, only to be put back on. I could see from tracking the revision history that most of the class was involved in these "negotiations," suggesting an engagement not seen in other courses.

The advantage to a spreadsheet from Google Docs is that students have access to the file on any computer and at any time. The program allows concurrent edits, so if more than one student is accessing the file at the same time, they will see a different colored cursor adding text even as they do so themselves. There is a "revision history" button that can help undo any accidental deletions. By setting the access of the file so that anyone with the link could edit, the students did not need an account. The program is free and does not require installation on a machine to use.

A week before the exam, I halted their editing privileges. They could still see the file, but they could no longer make changes. This list of terms and definitions that they thought were the most important to know became their study guide. It also formed a significant portion of their test. After checking the spelling of the terms and the accuracy of the definitions, I copied the file into a word processing document, hid the definitions from the terms I wanted to use, added numbers and additional open-ended questions, and had an exam that was more than a fair evaluation of student knowledge.

Future Implications

In the end, the students learned more from creating the guide than they ever would have if I made it for them, and they were engaged in the process of studying. In one evaluation of the course, a student wrote, "The exams were very fair and covered the right material … Loved that they were student directed." Another said, "I'm not a big fan of rote memorization, but I liked how the exams were set up and how we got to basically make the tests." They became stakeholders in their education, deciding as a whole what was important to learn and then using what they made to document their understanding of the material.

They became stakeholders in their education, deciding as a whole what was important to learn and then using what they made to document their understanding of the material.

PERSONAL SALES PITCH: VIDEO ASSIGNMENT

MICHELLE GACIO HARROLLE
NORTH CAROLINA STATE UNIVERSITY

Keywords: video assignment, resume, sales

Framework

Within these difficult economic times, job markets are becoming increasingly more competitive. Many employers are inundated with hundreds of applicants, have limited time to review them, and spend on average 20–30 seconds on each applicant's resume. Additionally as technology continually adapts, employers are using websites such as YouTube and Facebook to recruit candidates. Some employers want to see short video clips of potential employees illustrating why one candidate should be interviewed/hired over the next candidate. Therefore, for this technology based assignment, students create a 20 second personal video that sells/shows their value as a potential employee. The two goals of the videos are to teach students about selling value and self-worth in a short period of time and to provide students a technology tool that places them at the top of the resume (video) pile.

Making it Work

Students can produce any type of video including PowerPoint slides with voice over, photos with music background, or streaming videos. The only qualification is that the format of the final video must be either Windows Media Video (.wmv) or QuickTime file (.mov).

Within college/university systems (e.g., university libraries), students usually have access to simple video making hardware (i.e., flip video cameras, smart phones, etc.) and software (i.e., PowerPoint, Windows Movie Maker, iMovie, etc.). Within our university, students are able to download Windows Movie Maker for free and are quickly taught the simple to use Windows Movie Maker program in class in approximately 20 minutes. Students are able to use any program they feel comfortable using.

In my experience, students have no problems with creating the videos. However, they have a difficult time expressing their true value and tend to generalize their skills and traits. For example, students will state, "I am hard working, enthusiastic, and an excellent leader." Students must be able to explain value with specific, detailed, and concrete examples. For example, "I am a proven leader and have successfully supervised 10 interns while generating a 20% increase in sales in the past six months." To help students create quality sales pitches, I post examples of previously made videos on the online course management system (e.g., Moodle, Vista).

When grading the videos, I base the overall grade on value (level of confidence in the applicant), personal appearance, and level of creativity within the video. As my course is not a video editing course, grades are focused on the content in the video and not the quality of the picture (i.e., poor video due to shaking). Students who I would consider as a potential candidate for an interview receive the highest marks. Additionally, students are deducted points if they exceed the 20-second time limit.

Future Implications

This assignment has been very helpful to the seniors in the class. Recently, two students were given interviews at top sport businesses based on their videos. These videos are also included in senior e-portfolios. As technology changes and becomes easier to use, assignments should also adapt.

USING DISCUSSION FORUMS AS A LEARNING TOOL

LINDA CHRISTIANSEN
INDIANA UNIVERSITY SOUTHEAST

Keywords: discussion forums, online learning, active learning, essay practice, assignment practice

Framework

For my business law and ethics course, I needed a way to offer students considerable practice on a particular learning activity, but the grading of multiple individual submissions is too burdensome. The main learning goal for ethics requires mastery of an ethical analysis process, in which students analyze an ethical dilemma using tools and techniques learned in the class and come to a supported conclusion. It demands critical thinking, systemic reasoning, and knowledge of the course material; a fairly demanding process to learn and master.

To help with this process, I developed a set of assignments using technology to offer both repeated practice for student learning and reasonable amounts of instructor grading. Use of this model — in whole or in part — would be appropriate for any exercise in which an instructor who wishes to use repeated practice of a concept, or who requires multiple drafts so students can improve their writing. It would be easy to adopt some or all of these ideas to fit many assignments in an online, hybrid, or face-to-face course.

Making it Work

I have integrated the use of discussion forums as a way to increase practice opportunities and feedback for the analysis that is a required component of my course. Students post their work on class discussion forums, critique each others' work, and review all of the instructor feedback on others' work in the class. This process accomplishes the following: holds students accountable to complete the assigned work; helps them learn through critiquing others' work; and allows them to benefit from my grading of all group submissions, all accomplished with a reasonable and efficient use of instructor time.

1. Establish groups of students in a size you feel is appropriate for the assignment. I use 4–6 students and have 6–10 groups. Craft the assignment, assign a case study, or have each group of students select a topic.
2. Each student writes an analysis draft individually for this first round of practice. Each student posts the individual drafts under his/her group's forum.
3. Each member of the group critiques the work of the other group members according to the instructor's grading rubric and/or directions in order to learn the process better individually and also to provide feedback to each other.
4. Each group writes an improved draft together, taking advantage of the progress in learning from each other. This work is to be done as a group, rather than merely a blending of the writings of each person. The group draft is posted under the appropriate thread in a forum named "Group Drafts." Students submit a peer review of each group member directly to the instructor.
    a. This is the only part of the process performed by groups. It leverages feedback opportunities by requiring feedback from one another, as well as allowing the instructor to invest more time in grading fewer, and presumably better, submissions. With fewer analyses to grade, and the greater quality from the group analysis building on the individual work, the instructor can devote more time to each submission and provide the entire class more in-depth feedback.
5. Each student in the class reads and critiques the work of some or all of the other groups, posting comments in that submission's thread. Students learn from seeing what is done well and what problems to avoid.
6. The instructor grades each group's work by typing comments and feedback (I use capital letters and insert comments throughout the text) and posts it under a forum named "Professor Feedback." Because these critiques are posted, every student in the class is able to benefit from additional guidance and direction from the instructor.
7. Because my exercise is tested on the final exam, I require students to hold back one of the other groups' drafts to use as a final practice exam. Each student practices the process one more time and posts the final project under a forum called "Last Individual Practice." (Note: students can practice many times by analyzing all of the case studies before posting the critiques required in step 5 above.) The students can 'self-grade' their work by reviewing the group's submission, student comments, and the instructor's feedback for that case study or topic.

Future Implications

This use of technology benefits all involved. Research and my experiences show that student learning and performance increases, without a tremendous work and time commitment by the instructor (Andresen, 2009; Kirk, 2003).

In my classes, student performance on the ethics exam has improved. Previously, students generally preformed much better on the law exam (a more traditional essay exam format) than on the ethics exam. Since implementation of this technology, most students perform as well on the ethics exam as on the law exam, with about a third of the class earning higher grades on the ethics exam.

In the two years I have used this method, students have reported positive feedback on teaching evaluations, with no negative comments. Students report that this is the most interesting group work in which they have participated because of the level of preparation of their classmates.

This technology offers an efficient use of instructor time by using the online forums to leverage feedback opportunities. Without it, an instructor's choices include either little practice and feedback for students or an intense amount of grading for the instructor. This technology facilitates the repetition sometimes needed for the learning process, with a reasonable amount of work by the instructor.

References

Andersen, M.A. (2009). Asynchronous discussion forums: Success factors, outcomes, assessments, and limitation. *Educational Technology & Society, 12* (1), 249-257.

Kirk, J.J., & Orr, R. (2003). A primer on the effective use of threaded discussion forums. (ED472738).

USING CLICKERS TO PROMOTE PARTICIPATION

PATRICK J. ASHTON
INDIANA UNIVERSITY PURDUE UNIVERSITY FORT WAYNE

Keywords: clickers, electronic participation, engagement, classroom polling

Framework

"Clickers," or electronic handheld response devices, have received quite a bit of attention recently, both in academic journals (e.g., Martyn, 2007; Caldwell, 2007) and in the popular press (e.g., Sternberg, 2010). Are they a means to promote student engagement in the classroom, or just another gimmick? In my experience these devices can serve a variety of pedagogical purposes while increasing student interest and engagement. The necessary equipment includes software running on a classroom computer, a radio frequency (rf) receiver that plugs into a USB port on the computer, and an individual clicker for each student. Students generally purchase their clickers at the bookstore, where they run $20–$30. (Students can often sell them back to the bookstore, or to subsequent students through the usual informal channels.) Clicker packages are available from a number of companies. Some textbook publishers are promoting them as part of a learning package, and some universities have signed contracts to provide the software and receivers campuswide. Each student in a class must have their own unique clicker, which they register for that class through a link provided by the instructor. When a student registers their clicker for a given class, they are assigned a pad number for that class (arbitrarily in the order in which they register). The software, which runs concurrent with, or over top of PowerPoint, provides a screen with a visual representation of the pad numbers for that class. When a student presses a key on their clicker and hits "Send," the box containing their pad number changes color. The student then knows that their response has been recorded. Clickers have a combined numeric/alphabetic keyboard of nine keys that allows for a wide range of responses. (For implementation FAQs and suggestions see, e.g., Ohio State and Wisconsin-Milwaukee websites.)

Making it Work

I use clickers to take attendance. When students come into class, the attendance screen is up on the projector. The software provides an attendance option such that, when the students hit any key and press "Send," their pad number changes color and their attendance is registered in a database that can be downloaded to an Excel spreadsheet or a grading program. This also helps ensure that students are motivated to bring their clickers to class and have them out and ready to go at the beginning of class. I leave the attendance screen up while I make announcements and answer questions, to give latecomers a chance to register.

How else can you use clickers? Some instructors use them for Just-In-Time Teaching. You can prepare short quizzes in advance and then give them in class. When you close each question, a bar graph of the answer distribution appears almost instantly on the screen. This not only gives the instructor feedback on the students' background knowledge and preparation, but the data can be a discussion starter itself — e.g, why do you think most people answered this way? Why did no one pick a particular answer? Some instructors also give quizzes that count for a grade using the clickers. Like attendance, the responses go automatically into a database that can be downloaded.

I also use the clickers for classroom polling. I find relevant public opinion polls on the web (there is a vast amount of data available), and generate (or copy) graphs of the outcome of selected questions. In class, I ask students the identical questions. The clicker software provides a bar graph of their responses which I then compare with the survey data. I then ask for hypotheses about why their responses do or don't match the broader data. It never fails to be an interesting discussion.

I also use the clickers for confidential polling in the classroom. The software provides the opportunity to dissociate the act of response from its content. I assure students that I can track whether they respond, but not how they respond. Since their responses are only reported in the aggregate, there is no way (if the class is not too small) to surmise how each student responded. I use this technique for discovering student opinions about controversial issues (which many of them may be unwilling to express openly) and to generate information about sensitive issues and experiences. For instance, I can instantly feed back to students their opinions on current events — nationally, locally, or on campus — and I can rivet their attention and personalize issues by showing that there are students sitting in their very classroom who have had experiences we are reading about or discussing. For example: Have you or someone close to you struggled with an eating

> It brings the issue home to students when they have evidence that people in the room with them have these experiences.
> • • • • • • • • • • •

disorder? addiction? been the victim of a hate crime, child abuse, or a sexual assault? been homeless? Have you ever cheated on an exam or plagiarized a paper? It brings the issue home to students when they have evidence that people in the room with them have these experiences, but it doesn't put those people on the spot because of the anonymity and confidentiality. I also ask the students to generate questions about which to poll their fellow classmates. Frequently they come up with more than I have time to get to in a semester. But it does give them a sense of ownership of the process and another way to display their learning.

Future Implications

I ask the students to evaluate their usage of the clickers on the course evaluation. Eighty-five percent of the students strongly agree or agree that they enjoyed using the clickers to take attendance and that they thought it was an efficient way to do so. Eighty-nine percent strongly agree or agree that finding out the results of the clicker surveys increased their interest in the class. Sixty percent strongly agree that they pay more attention when using the clickers in class, and 91 percent recommend using them in the future. So clickers serve a number of valuable pedagogical purposes, and students like them, too.

References

Caldwell, J.E. (2007) Clickers in the large classroom: Current research and best-practice tips. *CBE Life Sci Educ,* 6(1), 9-20. Retrieved from http://www.lifescied.org/cgi/content/full/6/1/9

Martyn, M. (2007). Clickers in the classroom: An active learning approach. *Educause Quarterly, 30,* 2. Retrieved from http://www.educause.edu/EDUCAUSE+Quarterly/EDUCAUSEQuarterlyMagazineVolum/ClickersintheClassroomAnActive/157458

The Ohio State University Learning Technology Site: Clickers. Retrieved from http://lt.osu.edu/resources-clickers/

Steinberg, J. (2010, November 16). "More professors give out hand-held devices to monitor students and engage them" *The New York Times.* Retrieved from http://www.nytimes.com/2010/11/16/education/16clickers.html

University of Wisconsin Milwaukee Student Response Systems. Retrieved from http://www4.uwm.edu/ltc/clickers/

Technology-mediated feedback

Kathryn Lee
Texas State University - San Marcos

Keywords: engagement, social participation, shared construction of knowledge, Web 2.0

Framework

The Internet has changed from being mostly a read-only environment focusing on the delivery of information (Web 1.0) to a read-write environment (Web 2.0) promoting user engagement, social participation, and shared construction of knowledge (Collis & Moonen, 2008; Harrison & Barthel, 2009; Rosen & Nelson, 2008). The use of Web 2.0 tools is widespread and has far reaching implications (Harrison & Barthel, 2009; Bos & Lee, 2010).

I use a Web 2.0 tool to provide quality and individual feedback on student work with literally a few clicks of a button. Technology-mediated feedback allows me to provide timely feedback to my students on electronically submitted assignments. Screencast software, such as Jing, captures (electronically records) the computer screen and records audio feedback (via computer microphone) as I critique student work, highlighting specific parts of the document under examination. This free software is extremely easy to download and use. One click begins the screencast (five-minute limit) with audio. Another click uploads the recording into a screencast format, and the output is a web link that can then be copied and pasted into email correspondence or other electronic means. The receiver of the hyperlink has to only click on it to view the screencast via Flash, which is routinely used on both Mac and PC computers and can easily be downloaded for viewing.

One important benefit of using technology-mediated feedback software, such as Jing, is that it provides students a way to literally see and hear the instructor's feedback as s/he reviews the learning artifact. Many of my online graduate students in teacher education have reported high levels of satisfaction with the feedback tool and often report they feel a strong sense of

Many of my online graduate students... have reported high levels of satisfaction with the feedback tool and often report they feel a strong sense of immediacy and personalization with me.

• • • • • • • • • • •

immediacy and personalization with me, even though the course is entirely online. A screencast tool may be used to provide feedback on any electronically submitted assignment in any type of class, including face-to-face, online, and hybrid.

Making it Work

I use the screencast tool to provide feedback to my online graduate secondary education students in "Evaluative Techniques for Classroom Teachers." In this online course, approximately twenty graduate students create an instructional unit in their content area and then develop a variety of assessments for their unit. Initially, the students create a detailed test blueprint of their instructional unit, comprised of (a) at least six learning objectives aligned with state and national standards, (b) identification of Bloom's cognitive levels inherent in the objective, (c) knowledge dimensions that will be assessed, and (d) prior knowledge and skills required by the students to complete each objective. Below is an example of one objective within the blueprint, which illustrates the level of detail required for the task.

Future Implications

The screencast and audio feature allows me to provide detailed feedback to the students so that they are able to make effective revisions to their blueprints. The quality and quantity of feedback I am able to provide via screencast, instead of text only, has improved the quality of the students performance and decreased the number of student iterations required to perform the learning task.

Screencast software, such as Jing, offers many affordances. Jing (a) is easy to use (point and click), (b) is free, and (c) allows for quality feedback. It has the added benefit of providing a sense of immediacy between the instructor and students.

Web 2.0 tools are continuously emerging and improving. They provide individuals a variety of educational tools to enhance learning and instruction. These Web 2.0 tools allow unsophisticated users of technology to develop and create sophisticated multimedia artifacts. Clearly technology will continue to change the way we live and work in our modern world.

References

Bos, B., & Lee, K. (2010). Problem-based instruction and web 2.0: Meeting the needs of the 21st century learner. In C. Maddux (Ed.), *Research highlights in information technology and teacher education 2010* (pp. 71-78). Chesapeake, VA: Society for Information Technology and Teacher Education (SITE).

Colllis, B., & Moonen, J. (2008). Web 2.0 tools and processes in higher education: Quality perspectives. *Educational Media International, 45*(2), 93-106.

Harrison, T. M., & Barthel, B. (2009). Wielding new media in Web 2.0: Exploring the history of engagement with the collaborative construction of media products. *New Media & Society, 11*(1/2), 155-178.

Rosen, D., & Nelson, C. (2008). Web 2.0: A new generation of learners and education. *Computers in the Schools, 25*(3), 211-225.

TechSmith (1995). *Jing*. Retrieved January 15, 2011: http://www.techsmith.com/jing/

Unit Objectives	State Standards	National Standards	Bloom's Cognitive Levels	Knowledge Dimensions	Prior Knowledge	Pre-Assessment	Formative Assessment
1 The student will define Contemporary Art and the formal elements and principles that exist in Contemporary Art by analyzing illustrations and formulating his/her own idea of what Contemporary Art is.	(1) **Perception:** The student develops and organizes ideas from the environment. The student is expected to: (B) Analyze visual qualities to express the meaning of images and symbols, using precise art vocabulary. (3) **Historical/cultural heritage:** The student demonstrates an understanding of art history and culture as records of human achievement. The student is expected to: (A) study a selected period, style, or movement in art (B) trace influence of various cultures on contemporary artworks.	**Content Standard: 2:** Using knowledge of structures and functions **Content Standard: 3:** Choosing and evaluating a range of subject matter, symbols, and ideas.	Knowledge Comprehension	**Factual Knowledge** **Conceptual Knowledge**	Factual – knowledge of the principles and elements of art. **Conceptual** – knowledge of how to formally assess works of art.	Focused Listing	1. What formal elements and principles do you see in the illustrations that were presented? 2. What is your definition of Contemporary Art?

Figure 3.2. Contemporary Art - 6 weeks Art & Art History - 11th &12th grade.

WebQuests: A gateway activity for online teaching and learning

Robin Lightner
University of Cincinnati, Raymond Walters College

Keywords: webquests, online videos, learning objects

Framework

Students spend a significant amount of time playing around online. "Among 18–24 year old students, one-third (33%) say they have increased their consumption user-generated videos over the past year," (Watershed Publishing, 2009). WebQuests take advantage of students' comfort playing around online in service of the course's learning outcomes.

"A WebQuest is an inquiry-oriented lesson format in which most or all the information that learners work with comes from the web," (Dodge, 2007). WebQuests package learning objects (e.g., from MERLOT) that the instructor organizes to meet the course's learning outcomes. For example, in a WebQuest about criminal sentencing, students answered a variety of questions about trends from the U.S. Sentencing Commission's website (Ritchey, 2010). They found their own web sources about corporate crime, and then analyzed a recent article about whistle-blowers. In my classes, I frequently link to YouTube videos that illustrate psychology content or NPR audio content (stories or interviews) about recent development in the field. After exploring this type of content, students answer higher level critical thinking questions. These questions link the content of the story to material that has been covered in class or assigned reading. For example, students watch a video about an infomercial and describe the problems in the experiment and make an evaluation of the usefulness of this type of evidence.

WebQuests are useful for important pedagogical reasons including: 1) they introduce very current research or relevant popular media in the field, 2) they offer practice in the critical thinking skills of application, analysis and evaluation, 3) They add variety to the course material coverage, 4) they ensure that content has been covered outside of class so that class time can be spent on active learning, and 5) most importantly, they build the habit of transfer of learning. The instructor hopes that these types of connections from content to new online information will be made automatically by students who have learned our course material. If we want students to transfer, we must design activities for students to practice transferring course content to a variety of real world contexts (Halpern & Hakel, 2003), for example where they play and socialize online.

Making it Work

For faculty, building WebQuests are an easy entry to online instruction. WebQuests can range from a somewhat complicated website to simply a linked Word document. To design a WebQuest, follow these steps.

1. Identify the student learning outcome. These action-oriented statements describe what a student will be able to do resulting from the course, e.g., apply theories of cognitive development to explain children's behavior.
2. Collect media examples. This step is the most time consuming. Many faculty collect these sources and organize them by key word in an ongoing basis, for example by using Evernote.
3. Write higher-level critical thinking questions about the media. Explicitly tell students to use content from the course as they respond to questions, for example by having them underline key vocabulary words. This list of critical thinking verbs is helpful for question design.
4. Post your WebQuest in a course management system. Students submit answers in a discussion board, or privately to the instructor in a Word document. If possible, use an anti-plagiarism tool like SafeAssign.
5. Prepare your students to be successful. Inform students about your expectations about using references and paraphrasing. Provide students with a rubric that describes your criteria (e.g., Hazari, 2005). Before you assign a WebQuest, distribute a good and a poor sample assignment. Have students use your rubric to evaluate and discuss the differences.

Future Implications

Rubrics are particularly helpful to communicate standards. Figure 3.3 is an example of a rubric that I use regularly for my WebQuests.

Over the last three years of using WebQuests, my students' performance shows that initially, they score lower on connections and explaining content. This improves over time as I give them feedback on their work. The good and poor paper comparison has improved the quality of the content of responses.

The best hybrid courses do not have isolated content separate from what happens in-class (Kaleta et al., 2005). WebQuests can effectively integrate students' online, independent work with reading and in-class discussions. To be successful, the instructor must invest time and energy finding the links and ensuring the links are working each time the course is administered. The instructor must provide adequate, timely feedback and take the steps to prepare students to be successful including assigning reading, doing

Connecting material from class	1 missing or irrelevant	2 needs improvement	3 good	4 excellent
	The wrong concepts are applied to the example or there is no explanation of the connection.	Some of the key concepts are not included, or thee connection is unclear.	Concepts are mentioned but how they are connected is not entirely clear. May have missed some concepts.	All of the relevant concepts are included. The connection between the material and the concepts is clear.
Explaining concepts/ Adding ideas	1 missing or irrelevant	2 needs improvement	3 good	4 excellent
	No explanations are given.	The terms are not described accurately or they are not paraphrased.	The terms are described accurately but some aspect is missing.	The terms are described accurately in the author's own words.
Organization	1 missing or irrelevant	2 needs improvement	3 good	4 excellent
	The organization is confusing to the reader.	At time the organization is confusing. The paper needs transitions or explanations.	The organization is mostly logical with transitions, but may have an area or two where the reader gets lost.	The organization is logical with an introductory paragraph, transitions, and a conclusion.
Grammar	1 missing or irrelevant	2 needs improvement	3 good	4 excellent
	The grammatical errors make the paper difficult to understand.	There are several grammatical errors.	There are only a few errors.	The paper is free from grammatical errors.
Tone/Professionalism	1 missing or irrelevant	2 needs improvement	3 good	4 excellent
	The tone is inappropriate for science writing.	There are frequent lapses in tone.	There are a few lapses in tone.	The paper is clear, concise, and free from slang, first and second person pronouns, cliché's and rhetorical questions.

Figure 3.3. Rubric for WebQuests.

preparatory activities, and explaining any resulting confusion. Sometimes the technology tools that are the simplest can revitalize a course and turn wasted surfing sessions into deep reflection about the relevance of course content.

References

Dodge, B. (2007). WebQuest.org. Retrieved from http://webquest.org/index.php.

Halpern, D. F. & Hakel, M. D. (2003, July/August). Teaching for long-term retention and transfer. *Change*, 37-41.

Hazari, S. (2005). Strategy for assessment of online course discussions. *Journal of Information Systems Education*, 15(4), 349 – 355.

Kaleta, R., Garnham, C., & Aycock. A. (2005). Hybrid courses: Obstacles and solutions for faculty and students. *The Annual Conference on Distance Teaching and Learning*. Retrieved from: http://www.uwex.edu/disted/conference/Resource_library/proceedings/03_72.pdf

MERLOT: Multimedia Educational Resource for Online Learning and Teaching. Retrieved from: http://www.merlot.org/merlot/index.htm

Ritchey, L. (2010). Socio-QUESTS. Retrieved from: http://sites.google.com/site/socioquesthighered/home

Schuster, B. (2010). Understanding experimentation in psychology: A WebQuest designed for Psychology 101. Retrieved from: http://psychexperiment.tripod.com/

Watershed Publishing (2009, November 30). College students spend 12 hours/day with media, gadgets. Retrieved from http://www.marketingcharts.com/television/college-students-spend-12-hoursday-with-media-gadgets-11195/.

…we must design activities for students to practice transferring course content to a variety of real world contexts (Halpern & Hakel, 2003), for example where they play and socialize online.

Use of SoftChalk Software to create interactive content

Karen Banks
Indiana University Bloomington

Keywords: self-assessment, interactive, free, web pages, learning management systems, online, mastery learning

Framework

SoftChalk is an easy-to-use software that will bring interactivity to your course content whether you teach a small class or a large lecture, or teach in a traditional classroom or online. You may not have the technology skills or the time to create web pages and interactive content for your students. The SoftChalk software completes these tasks for you. Faculty simply type in content and in minutes the SoftChalk software creates multiple web pages that are linked together. Faculty can simply upload an image and a SoftChalk template will guide you through adding pop-up text annotations to the image. Video and audio can also be added. Faculty can easily create interactive games and quizzes in minutes by typing in the content into a template. These games and quizzes add to student motivation and provide self-assessment. SoftChalk works with most Learning Management Systems like Oncourse and Blackboard. It can also be placed on the Internet or on a CD-ROM. You can track student results so you know where students are having problems. SoftChalk complies with accessibility standards. You can download a free trial version at www.softchalk.com or purchase the software for $595.

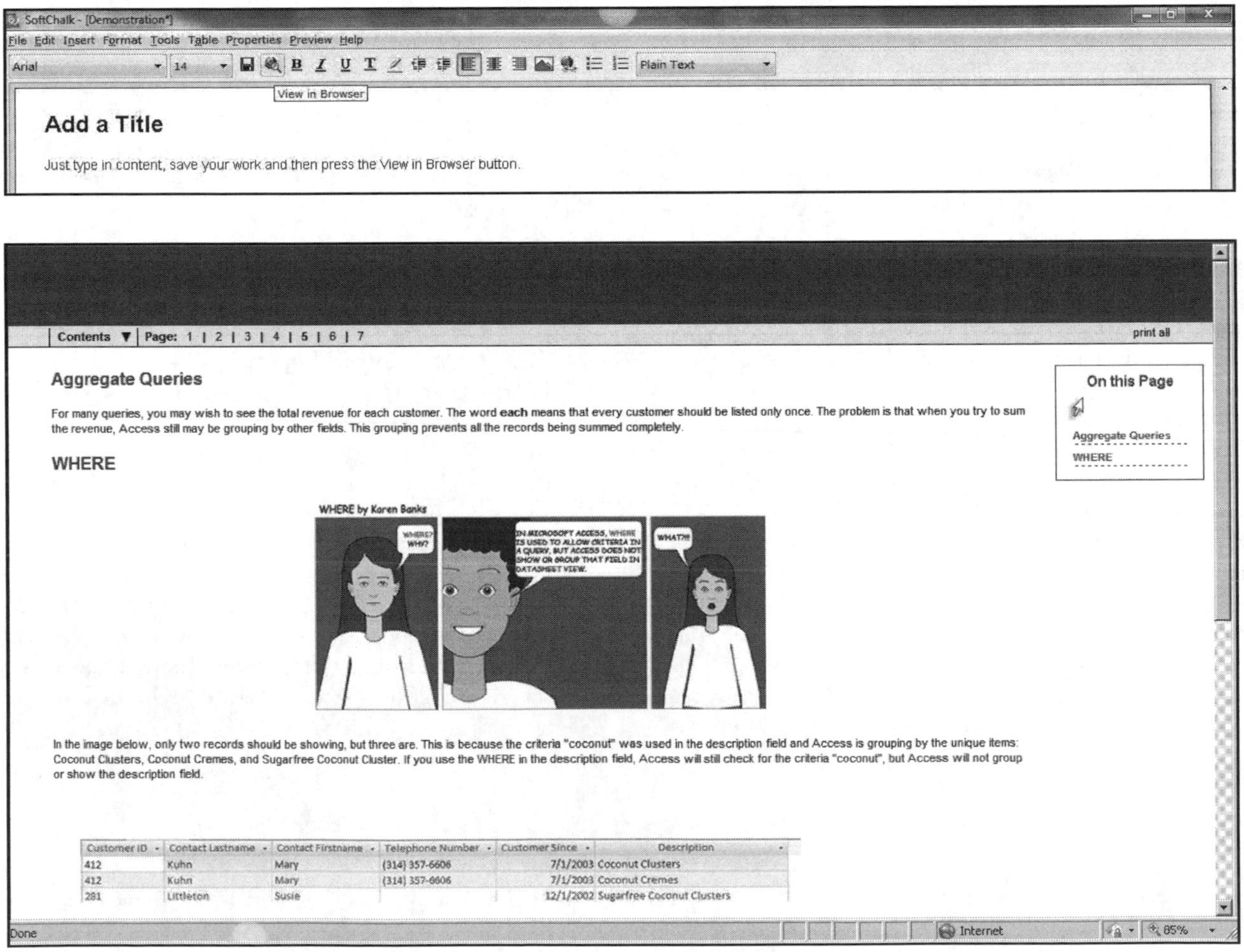

Figure 3.4. SoftChalk interface examples.

Making it Work

Implementation

1. Type in the content for your course into SoftChalk. It is that simple.
2. Save your work, click the Publish button and SoftChalk creates a web page.
3. Add a page break for a second web page. SoftChalk creates the links.

There are more advanced features that allow you to customize the look of the page. I matched the red in Oncourse so that it looks like it is a part of Oncourse. Students can access the content through a link in the Modules tool in Oncourse. Students do not realize that they are seeing a page created by SoftChalk. Students believe that they are using Oncourse. Figure 3.4.

Images are easy to add and if students place their cursor on a certain part of the images, you can have informative text appear.

Students can check their knowledge with interactive games and quizzes. The interactive games and quizzes are easy for faculty to create. For example, to create a crossword puzzle you just need to type in the word and the clue.

The SoftChalk web site provides sample lessons, case studies, and contests to encourage instructors showcase their best work.

Future Implications

Outcomes/Assessment

SoftChalk provides formative evaluation for students with quizzes and games and provides a fun method for learning class content. Students know immediately if they have not mastered the content and can work through the content until they gain mastery. Instructors can track student results so problem areas are identified.

> Students know immediately if they have not mastered the content and can work through the content until they gain mastery.

Future Directions/ Modifications/ Hybrid context

The use of the SoftChalk software helps to move the responsibility for learning the class content to the student outside of the regular class period. This allows for class time to be more efficiently used by the instructor.

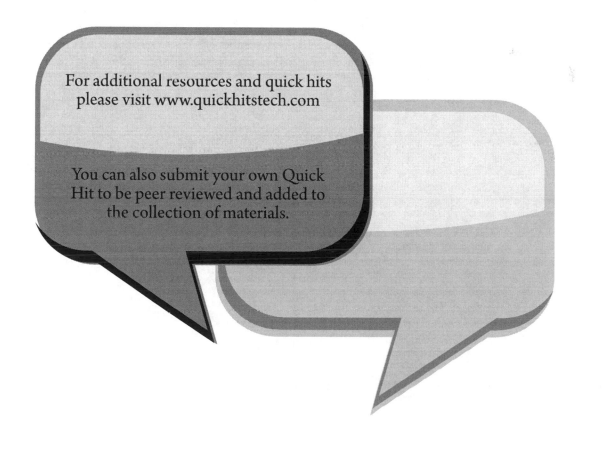

For additional resources and quick hits please visit www.quickhitstech.com

You can also submit your own Quick Hit to be peer reviewed and added to the collection of materials.

BECOMING MORE EFFICIENT

BECOMING MORE EFFICIENT: BEST PRACTICES THAT MAXIMIZE LEARNING

MARCIA D. DIXSON
INDIANA UNIVERSITY PURDUE UNIVERSITY FORT WAYNE

One of the most lauded aspects of using technology is more efficient use of resources. Administrators, faculty and students seem to believe that technology can make better use of student time, better use of faculty time, and better use of resources (i.e., classroom space). Why, then, do we frequently hear faculty complain, "I have so much more to do! More email to read, more discussion posts to grade!" And students lament that now they have discussions during and beyond class time because we have extended their classrooms into cyberspace (without cutting anything else). The motto when using technology should be, "Because you can do something, does not mean you should do something." Technology is a set of tools. The important thing is to choose the most appropriate tool and do not overuse it (i.e., if you only need to put in one nail, use a hammer - don't buy a nail gun!)

This chapter offers ideas and suggestions about how to be sure we are using technology in ways that maximize opportunities to learn but minimize extra work for students and faculty. For instance, if a quick check of students' understanding of vocabulary is needed, why create a worksheet they turn in to be graded, when a classroom management system will grade a quiz automatically and provide them with instant feedback? We can make the most use of time in class and still cut down on the amount of that time for students by meaningfully extending discussions and assignments into cyberspace, creating a hybrid course. If we provide the links, students can find resources without having to spend hours searching on the Internet. Our students can also having engaging and enriched discussions and build community with their peers if we structure assignments keeping certain things in mind (including not grading every post which, while conscientious, can stifle discussion).

The quick hits in this chapter include ways to help students come to class more prepared and engaged, to use class time more productively, and to provide more effective feedback. For instance, quick hits include several ways to help students be more prepared using SoftChalk software for interactive games and quizzes or Articulate Presenter to move presentation of material outside the classroom. Students may be come to class ready to engage when they have experienced google.docs for quick surveys (similar to clickers but occurring before class so the class can begin with the results students have generated) or created spreadsheets where they "negotiate" which concepts are most important and, therefore, testable. Once they are in the classroom, students can use Prezi to help build a visual image of the relationship between ideas and schools of thought or clickers for quick checks of what they know and do not know. The chapter also introduces the reader to the use of Wiki to help students build better lecture notes from content rich courses. After students have accomplished assignments, several ways of sharing feedback are offered including embedding comments in the video of student presentations or having students critique each other's work in a discussion forum.

The quick hits offered here focus on enriching learning environments while keeping in mind that students and faculty have very real time constraints. They can help instructors finds the best tool for the job.

JUVENILE JUSTICE WIKI PROJECT – CONSTRUCTIVISM THROUGH TECHNOLOGY

SCOTT WM. BOWMAN
TEXAS STATE UNIVERSITY – SAN MARCOS

Keywords: wiki, constructivism, technology integration

Framework

Having taught a face-to-face Juvenile Justice course several times previously, there were three student misconceptions that consistently challenged their understanding of the juvenile justice system: a) juveniles commit crimes primarily of their own free will, b) criminal behavior is the product of current circumstance, with little influence from demographic or historiographic events, and c) the criminal justice function/profession acts separate from other social functions. It was further believed that, with the exception of undergraduate internship opportunities or service learning courses, criminal justice students' primary exposure to the pedagogical criminal justice system is through classroom lectures and textbooks.

After being introduced to a variety of technological integrations, the decision was made to incorporate a "wiki" into the course. A wiki is a constructivist, collaborative web-based environment that incorporates words, pictures, and hyperlinks and is created or edited by individuals that have access to it. In developing this wiki course project, the primary goal was to promote a more accurate, constructivist understanding of the factors that increase the likelihood of a juvenile entering the juvenile justice system and the pragmatic difficulties that juveniles (and their families) face when attempting to offset these factors. Additionally, the goal is to bridge the gap between theory and praxis in the juvenile justice system and "breathe life" into a largely theoretical course. With these goals in mind, a semester-long "juvenile wiki project" was established, where students take random cities and compare/contrast the textbook explanations of criminal justice and social systems with the actual practices of cites throughout the country. In addition, they create a fictional "wiki-juvenile" to determine the likelihood of their "wiki juvenile's" success or failure within the system, as well as the practical challenges they and their families face in their assigned city. Furthermore, students collaborate by examining, questioning, and critiquing, their peers' findings. Finally, students' motivation, prior knowledge, feedback, and project evaluation were considered prior to implementation and continue to be factors in the projects' evolution.

Making it Work

At the beginning of the semester, students are asked the question "what are the variables that increase the likelihood of a juvenile entering the juvenile justice system." Students provide approximately 75 different factors that are placed into the categories: "family", "socioeconomic structure", "neighborhood", "schools", and "gangs." Students are next asked to create their fictional "wiki juvenile" with at least three of the aforementioned factors and are assigned a random zip code to determine the likelihood of their "wiki juvenile" entering into the juvenile justice system.

Prior to the start of the "juvenile wiki project", classes are provided instruction on the needed requirements for effective completion. A university librarian not only provides detailed instruction to students, but also provides a "widget" within the campus technology system, allowing students to send "instant messages" throughout the semester with technological questions or concerns. Each wiki assignment is made available online with detailed expectations and a basic example of assignment expectations. Assignments include Webbased presentations of available information on criminal justice systems in their respective cities, analysis of the similarities and/or differences between the textbook explanation of a particular subject and students' findings for their particular city, and collaboration of information amongst peers.

Over the course of the semester, a traditional textbook is utilized as the primary source of presenting course theories, systems, and practices, with the "juvenile wiki project" acting as a technological, praxis-based course supplement. For example, chapters on juvenile policing, probation, treatment, and institutionalization were presented from the textbook and discussed face-to-face. Next, students would research the services and activities in their assigned zip codes to determine their strengths, limitations, and opportunities for improvement, as well as the larger relationship to their "wiki juvenile." They were responsible for technologically "contacting" various agencies in their zip code, retrieving Webbased information, and presenting/discussing it on their wiki page. Overall, the wiki project's value comes in its paradigmatic shift in teaching, while maintaining an integral interconnectedness to the course.

Future Implications

Student evaluations of the three semesters' wiki projects suggest that students overwhelmingly valued the wiki project and found it to be a constructivist, paradigm-shifting way of learning. Students' statements include: "The wiki really helped me understand the justice system and how it works and also helped me understand the differences in different state(s)", "Yes, learning specifically, all semester long, about my city has helped me understand the detailed process of it all." In addition, students indicated that they experienced "real-world" learning through the wiki project. Their comments include: "Yes, a book can only do so much and this was as close as we could get to applying material learned to the real world" and "It was eye-opening to issues within the juvenile justice system and allowed for us to make real-world connections between the textbook and today's society."

Personal evaluation suggests that technological integration through the wiki project enhanced the overall presentation of course objectives. In the previous version of this course, communication and collaboration were primarily traditional classroom interactions between instructor and student. This project enhances the overall interactions between instructor and student, as well as amongst students. Since each individual is responsible for creating a wiki page

and providing feedback to their peers' wiki pages, it enhances traditional course communication. Moreover, since the wiki page assignments correlate to the major course topics, classroom discussion was also enhanced.

The greatest challenge of technology integration was stepping away from the paradigm of a "safely" and easily prepped class into a technologically constructed, semester long project. This was not only overcome through the numerous technological resources available to instructors and students on campus, but also in the simplicity of the wiki system. Because the wiki project is constructivist, there was minimal preparation or advancement needed by the instructor.

Finally, it is noteworthy that this project was awarded the 2010 Teaching With Sakai Innovation Award. The award is an international recognition for instructors that have creatively "promoted excellent pedagogy and innovation in teaching and learning" through technology.

MITIGATING THE WORKLOAD AND INCREASING STUDENT SATISFACTION WITH ONLINE DISCUSSION THREADS

WORTH WELLER
INDIANA UNIVERSITY PURDUE UNIVERSITY FORT WAYNE

Keywords: online discussions, discussion threads, student satisfaction, retention

Framework

One of the most productive ways to replicate the best features of a face-to-face class in an online environment is to engage your students in robust topic-oriented discussions relating to the learning goals of the class. Numerous studies, in fact, show that student satisfaction with an online course easily correlates with how well classroom discussions are managed (Drouin, 2008; Shea, et al., 2006; Stein, et al., 2005).

Two related issues, though, can prevent online discussions from achieving their goal: student interaction and satisfaction can quickly wane without an adequate amount of instructor intervention (An, et al., 2009), and consequently, the task of responding in a meaningful way to a huge discussion thread can bring an instructor to his or her knees, pedagogically speaking. Technology can mitigate these problems, however.

Making it Work

Most teaching platforms have some way to track discussions in terms of their numbers. I require my students to have one initial message and three responses for each discussion topic. I give examples in the syllabus as to what a satisfactory

response looks like, and I tell them I grade both on the number of posts and on their level of engagement (thus avoiding the issue of "right" or "wrong" responses). Blackboard Vista actually counts the discussions for me, and once the thread closes I assign grades accordingly after perusing a small sample for content.

The harder task of course is responding to all those posts. My answer to that problem is simple — I don't. Instead, I review about ten posts midweek (my discussions are set up on a weekly schedule, with one or two topics per week. I make a short podcast about what I'm seeing, adding my own two cents. Podcasting is simple and free, and a three-minute audio file is easy to upload (much longer than three minutes and I'm just yakking). I use Audacity, but Mac users will find that Garage Band will do the same thing. Students only need what's already on their computer to listen to my responses, or I just tell them to Google QuickTime or iTunes or Windows Media Player for their free audio players.

There are instructions all over YouTube how to use Audacity or Garage Band to record your comments, so I don't need to go into that here. In a nutshell, though, it takes me about 30 minutes on a Wednesday morning to peruse the discussions, make an unscripted recording (I may make a few notes), and upload it to that week's topic.

Future Implications

Judging from the robust discussion threads I get in my classes (up to 90–100 posts for any given topic in a 22 student section), from the results of Qualtrics surveys I conduct at the end of the semester, and from random comments I get at final exam time, these podcasts are a big hit with my students, not to mention that they are fun for me and that they take the stress out facilitating classroom discussions. The pedagogy appears sound too, as an over-abundance of instructor intervention does not correlate with more student-to-student interaction. In fact, minimal (but adequate) instructor intervention appears to allow students "to more freely express their thoughts and opinions" (An, et al., 2009).

References

An, H., Shin, S., & Lim, K. (2009). The effects of different instructor facilitation approaches on students' interactions during asynchronous online discussions. *Computers & Education, 53*(3), 749-760.

Drouin, M. (2008). The relationship between students' perceived sense of community and satisfaction, achievement and retention in an online course. *The Quarterly Review of Distance Education, 9*(3), 267-284.

Shea, P., Li, C. S., & Pickett, A. (2006). A study of teaching presence and student sense of learning community in fully online and web-enhanced college courses. *Internet and Higher Education, 9*, 175-190.

Stein, D. S., Wanstreet, C. E., Calvin, J., Overtoom, C., & Wheaton, J. E. (2005). Bridging the transactional gap in online learning environments. *The American Journal of Distance Education, 19*, 105-118.

Techiquette: The etiquette of technology

DeDe Wohlfarth and Nate Mitchell
Spalding University

Keywords: technology, best practices

Framework

So often, we find a collision between the seemingly antiquated world of etiquette and the brashly efficient world of technology. What is acceptable in texting, friending, and skyping seems uncomfortable if not downright rude in face-to-face social exchanges. To alleviate miscommunications and misunderstandings, we always have conversations about the etiquette of technology, or "techiquette", both in our syllabus and as we begin new course. Students and professors need to be clear about the following areas:

- Can papers be emailed?
- Will feedback be electronic or handwritten?
- How many days are reasonable to expect for an email response?
- What electronics will be permitted in the classroom and for what purposes?
- Should emails utilize proper English and grammar?
- Should papers and tests utilize proper English and grammar?
- How should information be posted on Blackboard or other classroom resource technology?
- What copyright rules are relevant and how do we follow these?
- What course material should be printed and what should remain virtual?

- How will students (and professors) handle emergency phone calls during class time?
- Is texting your professor acceptable, and if so, under what conditions?
- What are the consequences when someone breaks the norms of etiquette once we have established them?

Making it Work

Although we have a tendency to think that only hybrid and online courses need to establish norms about the use of technology, we have found that early communication concerning these issues benefits all classes, including undergraduate and graduate classes and small and large classes. The only tools necessary are a well-thought-out syllabus and a forum for a discussion, whether on-line or in a classroom.

Having a techiquette conversation takes time the first day of class, but it alleviates problems and misunderstandings later in the semester as stress and stakes increase.

Future Implications

Although we have never formally measured the benefits of having such a conversation with our students, students have consistently told us that they feel relieved to understand the often unwritten and unsaid rules that guide our use of technology. And personally, we found it is easier to nudge a student to behave with technological manners when the rules of the game have been previously agreed upon.

This idea can be easily modified to suit a wide variety of classroom needs, but essentially is a transportable tool that works across disciplines and classroom levels.

PREZI AND THE DECODING OF HISTORY

DAVID PACE
INDIANA UNIVERSITY

Keywords: Prezi, history, active learning, collaborative learning

Framework

For the last five years, I and the other members of the Indiana University History Learning Project (Diaz, Middendorf, Pace, & Shopkow, 2008; Glenn, 2009) have been using the "Decoding the Disciplines" process (Pace & Middendorf, 2004) to make explicit the kinds of mental operations required for success in college history courses and to find new ways to model these skills for students. One of the central bottlenecks to learning in history that has been identified through this research is the difficulty many students have in understanding that systems of thought are not just random collections of opinions. They do not see the integral unity of worldviews such as Marxism or nineteenth century liberalism, nor do they understand the assumptions or values that underlie such ideologies.

Thus, I have been searching for new ways to help students grasp the organic nature of intellectual systems. The new presentation software, Prezi, has given me a tool to help students overcome this bottleneck to learning. It remains to be seen whether this fluid and flashy system will dislodge PowerPoint as an accompaniment to lecturing, but I have found that putting it in students' hands can greatly aid their learning.

Making it Work

I used Prezi for the first time in the fall of 2010 in an intensive writing seminar on the history of Western ideas about conflict and competition. Exploring the possibilities of the program, I began by giving students indirect control over the system. I asked the student learning teams to generate a list of concerns of two very different thinkers, the medieval philosopher Thomas Aquinas and the 18th century writer Bernard Mandeville. I wrote the names of the two writers in large print in the open field made available by Prezi and then typed in each of the issues identified by the teams onto the screen twice, once near each writer. I used Prezi to increase or decrease the size of each issue until the class was satisfied

that its magnitude appropriately represented the importance of the idea for that thinker. Salvation, for example, was expanded to giant proportions in the vicinity of Aquinas, but virtually disappeared near Mandeville. The result was a clear visual representation of the two systems of thought that had been generated by the students themselves.

Future Implications

I had hoped that this process would help more of the students grasp fully the connectedness of intellectual system, but I was completely unprepared for the almost visible burst of conceptual "light bulbs" that went off in the room as the students began to recognize both that each system of thought had its own organic unity and that each generated a very different view of reality. Therefore I decided to use the approach later in the semester in a more complex exercise designed to help the students understand the differences in four of the issues we had been studying (Marxism, 19th century liberalism, nationalism/fascism, and pacifism). During class, each team was asked to answer five questions with respect to one of the four groups of intellectuals:

- What are the most essential core beliefs of your group?
- How would your group dismiss the arguments of the other three?
- What would have drawn individuals to each of these positions?
- What groups in society do you think would be most apt to be attracted to each position?
- Are there areas of overlap between any of these groups?

I had asked students from each team to bring a laptop to class, but I had intended for them to make up lists of points that I would then combine into a single Prezi presentation with their help. I soon discovered, however, that one of the groups had already downloaded the program and was creating its own display. Other teams soon realized what was happening, joined in the process, and soon all four teams were simultaneously developing different parts of the Prezi. The level of student involvement was extraordinary, as the students debated what their team should include and how the material could be most logically organized to respond to the questions I had posed. The work continued for the rest of that class period and into the beginning of the next, with individual students spontaneously making additions between class meetings.

It was clear both that an enormous flood of creativity and enthusiasm had been released by the process, but also that the students were gaining a more thorough understanding of how ideologies function and bump up against each other. There was a great deal of play involved in the process, as students searched the web for images that made their points. One team unearthed Lego action figures of Marx and Engels, and the group focusing on nationalism and fascism arranged its materials in the shape of a swastika. But to the extent that the biological function of play is to practice new ways of dealing with the world, this seemed all to the good. Moreover, the exercise gave the class a new burst of energy in mid-November when morale is usually at its lowest, and that enthusiasm lasted through the finals period, when two of the teams presented Prezis that summed up the material in the course.

At least one of the students actually incorporated the software into the process of paper writing. In a videotaped interview at the end of the semester, she commented: "Professor Pace introduced this … software online called Prezi to us this semester … it's really great. I actually used that to help me try and figure out a thesis too … Power Point … is really linear, but Prezi, you can, like write — I wrote the question in the middle and just brainstormed, but with typing, instead of writing, and you can make things bigger, and make things smaller as it pertains to your thought process. So I used that to help me develop my arguments."

It is clear from my experiences that, if Prezi is put into the hands of students and they are given a clear task, it can create a great sense of ownership and involvement in learning, and help them break out of narrow, linear ways of conceptualizing complex phenomenon.

More information about the Decoding the Disciplines and the History Learning Project may be found at http://www.iub.edu/~hlp/. Examples of student Prezis may be found at:
1. http://prezi.com/idrsfkhgambr/copy-of-the-struggle/
2. http://prezi.com/7lk9lcltgrjl/j300-final-presentation/
3. http://prezi.com/fbmfwg9y5zrh/copy-of-final/

(It is important to remember that these visual presentations were originally accompanied by extended verbal explanations.)

References

Diaz, A., Middendorf, J., Pace, D., & Shopkow, L. (2008). The History Learning Project: A department "decodes" its students. *Journal of American History, 94* (4), 1211-1224.

Diaz, A., Middendorf, J., Pace, D., & Shopkow, L. (2007). Making thinking explicit: A history department decodes its discipline. *National Teaching and Learning Forum, 16,* 2.

Glenn, D. (November 16, 2009). A teaching experiment shows students how to grasp big concepts. *Chronicle of Higher Education.*

Middendorf, J., & Pace, D. (2009). Just in time teaching in History. In S. Simkins and M. Maier, (Eds.) *Just in Time Teaching Across the Disciplines.* Sterling, VA: Stylus Publishing.

Pace, D., & Middendorf, J. (2004) *Decoding the disciplines: Helping students learn disciplinary ways of thinking: New Directions in Teaching and Learning, 98,* New York: Jossey-Bass.

If Prezi is put into the hands of students and they are given a clear task,
it can create a great sense of ownership and involvement in learning,
and help them break out of narrow,
linear ways of conceptualizing complex phenomenon.

IMAGES FOR EDUCATION—CRIME FREE!

ANDY GAVRIN
INDIANA UNIVERSITY PURDUE UNIVERSITY INDIANAPOLIS

Keywords: images, online courses, hybrid courses, fair use, public domain

Framework

Whether you are teaching online, in a hybrid setting, or authoring curricular materials for your class, you will occasionally want or need to incorporate images. These may be drawings, photographs, paintings, graphs, charts, or other types of still images, or they may be videos, animations, etc. The purposes also range widely: images may provide visual interest, help students understand the application of the material to their lives, reach students who are primarily visual learners, or be the primary focus of the lesson.

Making it Work

Whatever the purpose, instructors have many ways to obtain images.

One method is stealing, a.k.a. violating someone's copyright. The ease with which this can be done online makes it incredibly tempting, especially if you need it today, but don't do it! There are too many reasons to list, but the worst in my book is the lost opportunity to take credit for the rest of your work. One stolen image makes it impossible to publish all of the adjacent material you wrote on your own!

In fact, there are many "crime free" methods for getting great images. Here are some of the methods I have used over the last 15 years.

1. You can create your own images. Digital cameras are ubiquitous and easy to use. Excel and other mathematical programs can generate charts, graphs, and other graphics. Most faculty members have some experience with these technologies, so I will not dwell on this.
2. You can "borrow" images under a few circumstances under the fair use doctrine. This is a slippery area of law, and educational purposes DO NOT make all uses "fair" but there are a few simple guidelines. Relevant information may be found at
    *   http://citl.indiana.edu/services/instructionalTechnology/fairuse.php or
    *   http://copyright.columbia.edu/copyright/fair-use/fair-use-checklist/.
    For those who want the source, see US Copyright Law, Title 17 at http://www.copyright.gov/title17/
    If you familiarize yourself with these rules, you can use many "found" images, at least temporarily.
3. You can use images that are in the public domain.
    *   Works created by employees of the US government.
    *   Works that the author has placed in the public domain
    *   Works to which the copyright has expired.
    This last point is tricky. There are many ways a copyright can expire. See http://copyright.cornell.edu/resources/publicdomain.cfm for details. There is one easy rule, though. Anything published before 1923 is in the public domain.

There are many sources for such images. I list a few here, but Google can bring you to many more.

US Government sources (also a test of your acronym knowledge)
NASA: http://nix.nasa.gov/, http://grin.hq.nasa.gov/center.html, http://nssdc.gsfc.nasa.gov/photo_gallery/
Library of Congress: http://www.loc.gov/rr/print/
NOAA: http://www.photolib.noaa.gov/index.html
NIH: http://www.media.nih.gov/imagebank/index.aspx
US Air Force: http://www.af.mil/photos/
NFWS: http://digitalmedia.fws.gov/
National Gallery of Art: http://www.nga.gov/
Many agencies: http://www.usa.gov/Topics/Graphics.shtml

Other sources, including pages that aggregate many sources
http://digitalgallery.nypl.org/nypldigital/index.cfm
http://people.uwec.edu/koroghcm/public_domain.htm
http://srufaculty.sru.edu/david.dailey/public/public_domain.htm
http://copyrightfriendly.wikispaces.com/
http://opg.cias.rit.edu/library/public-domain-resources

Happy hunting!

Chats: A mess or a must?

David S. Stein and Constance E. Wanstreet
The Ohio State University

Keywords: synchronous chats, online discussion, electronic coaching

Framework

We think discussion that leads to shared understanding is a must in our online courses and we use learner-led, text-based chats to take advantage of the spontaneity that comes with real-time communication. But when we review chat transcripts, we see that learners are sharing their opinions about the issues, generally unsupported by the readings. Their small-group discussions are shallow. They're not integrating perspectives from others and are not always coming to a group decision about how to respond to the issue under discussion. The task of making sense of the mess and turning it into a summary is often left to the student moderator to accomplish. The summary addresses the issues and is shared with the larger class and the instructor. As the course instructors, we wonder who is learning—everyone in the group or only the student moderator?

Making it Work

We no longer assume that college students in an online course have the necessary skills to integrate information and resolve issues under discussion. To help our learners develop those skills and efficiently get to shared understanding, we provide e-mail coaching before their chats. Here are common coaching tips we share with our learners during the course of the term to facilitate higher-order learning:

1. Refer to one another by name. Greet one another and engage in some social communication to build cohesiveness.
2. Confirm who the moderator and summarizer are at the very beginning of the chat and decide on the next week's moderator and summarizer at that time.
3. Consistently follow a convention that will signal where you are in your response. For example, use ellipses (…) to signal when you aren't finished. When you are finished, you might try using "end" or some other convention. It cuts down on five people talking at once.
4. Summarize where you are before moving on to the next discussion question and check for everyone's understanding.
5. Get input on every question.
6. Include examples from the readings to support your positions.
7. Offer reasons why you agree or disagree with a comment.
8. Moderator, give everyone a chance to participate in the discussion. By that we mean that if you haven't heard from someone in awhile, ask if s/he has anything to add.

Future Implications

We examined chat transcripts from groups that received e-mail coaching and those that did not. The group that received coaching before each chat showed more evidence of higher-order thinking when compared to groups that received intermittent coaching or no coaching at all. In light of those results, a future direction is to provide continuous coaching for all learner-led groups.

Using audience response systems for classroom post-test reviews

Marjorie Vogt and Barbara Schaffner
Otterbein College

Keywords: audience response systems, clickers, post-examination reviews

Framework

Post-test reviews are a traditional way of assessing student summative knowledge through examination. Post-test reviews in the face-to-face classroom include reviewing the test and correct answers at the end of the examination period, in order to provide rationale directly to the learners to improve knowledge acquisition and critical thinking skills (Twigg, 2009). Post-test reviews, however, can be somewhat time consuming, and occasionally evolve into a discussion about individual student's points or answers.

Making it Work

One way to enhance post-test reviews is through the use of the audience response system or clickers. Although there has been some information in the literature about the use of clickers in formative assessment, such as testing students' understanding during a didactic lecture, and some information about using clickers for graded tests, there is little information about the use of clickers in a post-test review (Fies & Marhall, 2006; Kay & LeSage, 2009).

Clickers have been successfully used in an undergraduate nursing class post-test review. At the completion of the test and collection of answer sheets, faculty conducted a post-test review of the test using clickers. Each question was viewed on the overhead screen, and students used the clickers to indicate the correct answer. If the question was difficult and students were unable to discriminate the correct answer, faculty promoted student-student interaction to discuss the answers, and then re-polled the class. Faculty were also able to discuss test-taking strategies based on the immediate feedback of the student's clicker responses.

Future Implications

Students were positive about the experience, stating they appreciated the immediate feedback, the interpersonal interactions with each other and the test-taking strategies shared. The clickers allowed them to anonymously respond to the question and anticipate their grade for the exam. Further exploration of the use of clickers in a post-test review is indicated.

References

Twigg, P. (2009). Developing and using classroom tests. In Billings, D. & Halstead, J. *Teaching in nursing: A guide for faculty (3rd ed)*. Saunders Elsevier: St. Louis.

Fies, C., & Marshall, J. (2006). Classroom response systems: A review of the literature. *Journal Of Science Education and Technology, 15*(1), 109.

Kay, R., & LeSage, A. (2009). A strategic assessment of audience response systems used in higher education. *Australasian Journal of Educational Technology, 25*(2), 235-249.

FOSTERING E-LEARNING DISCOURSE AMONG PROFESSIONAL NETWORKING GROUPS

STEPHEN C. BISHOP AND DANIEL T. HICKEY
INDIANA UNIVERSITY BLOOMINGTON

Keywords: discourse, networking, graduate-level courses, learning theory, course management system

Framework

Many instructors struggle to foster worthwhile discussions in on-line courses. We have refined a strategy that fosters extended discourse around the big ideas of a course while maintaining a reasonable workload for faculty and students. We refined this method in graduate-level courses on Learning Theory and on Educational Assessment with class sizes ranging from 15 to 40 students. The method does not use a discussion forum. Rather, the discussion takes place as comments placed directly on student-generated wikifolios. The method is structured to discourage initial discussion of concepts in the abstract. Instead, students discuss how course concepts take on different meaning in different contexts. This strategy should work in any e-learning setting where students are able to post wikis and make comments directly on those posts. This feature is available in the Sakai open-source course management system and in many commercial e-learning platforms.

Making it Work

First, each student posts an entry to their wikifolio that defines a personally meaningful context for applying big ideas of the course. The context needs to be specific enough to reveal differences in the relevance of specific course concepts, but general enough to consider most (but not all) course concepts. In our courses, this is an instructional goal. Our students are also asked to describe their institutional status (e.g., pre-service vs. in-service, teacher, administrator, or researcher).

As students are posting their entries, the instructor sets the tone for the discussion with comments pointing out how contexts and roles might intersect with course content. For example, in the learning class, primary teachers are warned that metacognition does not emerge until the later grades; students in the assessment class are warned that portfolio assessment is easier in some domains (English) than others (math). During this time, the instructor also introduces a strategy that builds community and saves time. Rather than posting similar detailed comments across multiple wikifolios, the instructor encourages students to read and comment on more detailed comments posted previously on other students' wikifolios that will be relevant.

Next, the instructor uses the wiki posts to organize the class into networking groups of a manageable size (i.e., 3–6). In our case, students are assigned to a primary networking group based on their educational domain (literacy, comprehension, writing, math, or science) and a secondary networking group based on their current or future role (teacher, administrator, or researcher).

The weekly routine is based on a strategy that follows from contemporary situative theories of learning. Students post a weekly page to their wikifolio that articulates which of the "big ideas" and "specifics" of the textbook chapter are more relevant and less relevant to their instructional problems and roles. Like most textbooks, ours include summaries of the key implications of each chapter. The process of identifying the most relevant and least relevant topics of a chapter for a personally relevant goal provides a good functional context for reading the chapter. It also provides a good framework for helping students discuss that chapter. Somewhat surprising, asking students to articulate the single big idea of the chapter that is least relevant to them is very helpful for getting students to read and discuss all of the big ideas in a given chapter. Classmates quite naturally come up with ways that the "least relevant" implication is relevant. We know that the method fosters learning, because we sometimes see students change their ranking based on comments; we encourage more of this disciplined discourse by adding comments to the discussion threads that acknowledge both the comment and the modification.

The assignments and instructor comments continually encourage each student to practice projecting a unique professional identity in their wikifolios, comments, and threaded discussions. This scaffolds increasingly sophisticated engagement around their own problem while fostering participation in discourse beyond their problem and their domain. Assignments include specific steps that encourage students to find similarities within their group, and to contrast differences across groups.

In order for this strategy to work, it is important to not directly grade student comments. Our strategy is inspired by the user-generated content in typical digital social networks. "Lurking" is actively encouraged in the syllabus, the assignments, and the course grading structure. The wikifolio contents and comments are never directly graded; rather points towards the course grade are assigned to brief reflections on each wikifolio entry asking the students to summarize three types of engagement. Consequential engagement concerns the consequences of the big ideas for specific instructional contexts and educational roles; critical engagement considers which contexts and roles are best for considering the big ideas of the week; collaborative engagement concerns the discussions they engaged in during the week.

As the course progresses, one or two students typically emerge as discussion leaders within each group. The leaders typically represent the group when interacting with the other groups and the instructor uses their wikifolios strategically to advance the level of discourse within each group. Relatively extensive instructor commentary on the leaders' wikifolios provides highly contextualized guidance that is immediately useful for the entire group. This avoids exhausting and repetitive individualized feedback, and provides a safe space for all students to engage in the discourse at whatever level they find comfortable. This structure has made it possible to bring in challenging assignments that previously could only be managed in the advanced face-to-face class. The structure works because less-experienced students are able to view the posts and instructor comments of the more-experienced students.

Future Implications

So far, the results are quite promising. In the most recent classes, all of the students successfully completed all of the assignments, including the aforementioned challenging ones. In the most recent learning class, weekly wikifolios averaged 1,580 words. The sixteen students posted 997 comments, while the instructor only posted 50. The average student comment length was 120 words, ranging as long as 730 words. Over half were part of threaded discussions, and very few were isolated comments made merely for the sake of commenting. Out of sixteen students, all but one collaborated across professional networking groups at least once.

Accountability for broader course coverage is assessed with formal examination using multiple choice and short answer items from the textbook item bank. To provide reasonable accountability in the online format, the exam was timed, and the items were randomly selected from the subset of items whose answers could not readily be looked up in the textbook. Exam scores are currently averaging around 90% with the lowest scores falling around 70%. Course evaluations are now consistently positive and much more so than are typically obtained in online courses.

We know that the method fosters learning,
because we sometimes see students change their ranking based on comments;
we encourage more of this disciplined discourse
by adding comments to the discussion threads that acknowledge
both the comment and the modification.

BLOGGING TO PROMOTE ROBUST CLASS PREPARATION

MICHAEL MORRONE
INDIANA UNIVERSITY

Keywords: blog, wiki, promoting engagement, team-based learning

Framework

Taylor (2010) suggests that interactive learning coupled with mechanisms to create accountability is necessary to facilitate learning for millennial students. One way to boost interactive learning outside of class is to have students collaborate using Web 2.0 tools, such as blogs, wikis, and other social networking technologies (Parschal, 2010). These Web 2.0 tools allow learners to read, write, create, connect, and learn in robust and personally determined ways (Moore, 2006).

Making it work

I teach an introductory Business Communication class and use team-based learning, adapted from the methods described by Larry Michaelsen (2009). Students are placed in teams on the second day of class and work in these teams every day. To assure students are ready for active application of content, the course has three "readiness assurance days." Where Michaelsen uses scantrons and multiple choice quizzes to assure students are preparing for class, I wanted my students to write course-content-oriented arguments as their readiness assurance process (RAP); I have my students comment on cases I post in a course blog or course wiki.

Steps to use blogs or wikis for readiness assurance

Step 1: I post business communication cases in a course wiki, using the course management system's wiki tool, or a course blog, created with blogger a free tool available through Google. The cases include embedded multi-media resources, such as flash files, pictures, video, and audio files. The posts also include links to course content.

Step 2: Before each readiness assurance day, the students respond to the blog or wiki post. I vary the location of the posts between a course blog and course wiki, because my students will benefit from learning different communication channels that are becoming more common in business. I make the course blog, Communication Skills for Success (www.kelleybuscomm.blogspot.com), accessible through the course management system's web content links. I ask students to respond by:

1. Identifying concepts from the reading that they consider most important for analyzing the case
2. Applying the identified concepts to the case, and
3. Comparing or contrasting the individual student's analysis with a classmate's

Step 3: Students bring copies of their comments to class for review by their team. The review process works as follows:

1. Each team determines the comment that is "most helpful for learning course concepts."
2. I collect the "most helpful" comments and redistribute them, so that each team receives a copy of every team's "most helpful" responses.
3. Each team then ranks the other teams' responses from most to least helpful. Readiness assurance grades are based on these rankings. This mechanism creates an incentive to write and select strong comments. As part of the ranking process, team discussions lead to debate within the teams as they work toward consensus about application of course concepts. After readiness is assured, subsequent class meetings build on the case presented in the RAP.

One example of this process's impact on learning

In Business Communication we expect students to learn to contextualize intercultural messages. I, therefore, created a blog post that asks the students to consider inter-cultural-non-verbal communication. The post describes non-verbal communication then leads to an embedded video scene from a documentary called Well-Founded Fear (Camerini, 2000). In the scene a government official interviews a refugee applicant. These interviews, under US law, are to be conducted in a non-adversarial manner. However, the refugee applicant and the interviewing officer both have aggressive communication styles, resulting in a power grab by the asylum officer.

Typically, when I've facilitated in class discussion of this case as opposed to online, a majority of students begin discussion by thinking the applicant is lying. But as the discussion develops their eyes tend to open and see the richness of non-verbal communication ... which, of course, is a substantial part of the expected learning outcome.

When I switched the process to a pre-class discussion on the course blog, I noticed that students who saw the problematic non-verbal cues of the asylum officer spoke up more forcefully and quickly in their blog comments. This was unexpected; however, it was extremely beneficial to student learning, as the students discovered the complexities of non-verbal communication without my influence. In the past, in class, I often had to make the points about how the asylum officer's behavior impacted the interview; in other words, I led the students to a key learning outcome. I was thrilled that the students made this leap without me.

Future Implications

The activities create accountability in several ways. First, the RAP makes students accountable to me that they have learned course concepts at the lowest level of Bloom's taxonomy, so that they are ready for in-class activities that emphasize application and learning at higher levels of the taxonomy. Second, the students are accountable to all students, as the process requires that each comment include reaction to other students' comments. Third, the ranking process generates team accountability. Fourth, the blog and wiki become the source of follow up in-class activities and assignments.

The process emphasizes several forms of evaluation:

1. The blog comments compare and contrast differing views and applications of course concepts.
2. The teams discuss the individual comments to determine which one is most valuable for learning course concepts. This conversation requires critical evaluation of the individual comments.
3. Students receive two grades, an individual grades on their comments and a grade for the team's choice of best comment. To deemphasize the competitive element in the process, an alternative is to use class time to have each team review the team members' individual comments and to collaborate to write a comment for the team grade.

4. After completing the ranking process, the teams debrief on their effectiveness. In this process each team member completes a team-evaluation rubric. Then the teams compare and discuss the responses in the rubric
5. After the RAP, the class discusses characteristics of effective comments, including effective writing style, considerations of audience, and depth and breadth of coverage of course content.

References

Camerini, M., & Robertson, S. (2000). *Well-Founded Fear.* United States: New Video.

Michaelsen, L.K. (2009). *Getting started with team-based learning.* Retrieved July 26, 2011: http://serc.carleton.edu/files/cismi/broadaccess/teamworkshop/getting_started_team-based_lea.pdf

Moore, M. G. (2006). Using new technologies in open and distance learning. *Open Education Research, 12*(6), 16–20.

Parschal, T. (2010). Web 2.0: Read, write, create, connect, and learn—Opportunities for online learning. *Journal of Psychological Issues in Organizational Culture, 1*(2), 80-89.

Taylor, M. (2010). Teaching generation NeXt: A pedagogy for today's learners. In *2010 Higher Learning Commission Collection of Papers.* Retrieved July 26, 2011: http://taylorprograms.org/images/Teaching_Gen_NeXt.pdf

---

Spreadsheet modeling optimization problems

Morteza Shafii-Mousavi
Indiana University South Bend

Keywords: linear programming, optimization, Excel spreadsheet, simplex method, Excel solver

Framework

A key concept students learn in the freshman course, M118 Finite Mathematics, is modeling and solving constrained optimization problems. We teach the mathematics behind optimization with various capacity constraints as well as how to solve the linear programming model by the Simplex Method. This algorithm is a tedious method which is tiresome for large problems. To enhance the students' learning, and their appreciation of these powerful mathematics, we model such problems using Excel spreadsheets and use the Excel solver module to solve the problem.

Making it Work

For example, we use problems from our course textbook (Barnett & Ziegler, 2008). One such problem is given below:

Construction-resource allocation. A contractor is planning to build a new housing development consisting of colonial, split-level, and ranch-style houses. A colonial house requires ½ acre of land, $60,000 capital, and 4,000 labor-hours to construct, and returns a profit of $20,000. A split-level house requires ½ acre of land, $60,000 capital, and 3,000 labor-hour to construct, and returns a profit of $18,000. A ranch house requires 1 acre of land, $80,000 capital, and 4,000 labor-hours to construct, and returns a profit of $24,000. The contractor has available 30 acres of land, $3,200,000 capital, and 180,000 labor-hours.

a. How many houses of each type should be constructed to maximize the contractor's profit? What is the maximum profit?

b. A decrease in demand for colonial houses causes the profit on a colonial house to drop from $20,000 to $17,000. Discuss the effect of this change on the number of houses built and on the maximum profit.

c. An increase in demand for colonial houses causes the profit on a colonial house to rise from $20,000 to $25,000. Discuss the effect of this change on the number of houses built and maximum profit.

Prior to solving the problem, students are shown how to model the problem in an Excel spreadsheet. Table 4.1 displays the organizational spreadsheet for part B of the problem.

This spreadsheet includes formulas that sum up the products of the decision variables and per unit resource usage amounts as well as total profits. For example, the total usage of land is computed using the Excel formula SUMPRODUCT(F6:H6,$E$16:$G$16); where F6:H6 are cells containing per unit land resources for colonial, split-level, and ranch homes, respectively, and where E16:G16 represent the numbers of each type of produced house. This model allows us to discuss trial and error approaches to solving the feasible and optimal mix of houses. For example, the spreadsheet in Table 4.2 shows the profits and resource utilization for producing 20 of each type of house. Although total profits are high, the solution is not feasible since all of the capacity constraints are violated. The spreadsheet

model makes it very easy to test numerous combinations of the three types of houses and to discuss whether or not they are feasible. Even when feasible outcomes are obtained there is no insurance that these outcomes are optimal.

Students quickly learn that a trial and error approach which could conceivably list every possible outcome is not only time consuming but very inefficient. Besides exploring the solution to this problem using the Simplex Method and graphical techniques, we teach students how to use the Excel solver to find the optimal solution.

Numerous other examples have been used (Shafii-Mousavi and Kochanowski, 2010) dealing with manufacturers, nutrition, portfolio allocation, and the like.

References

Barnett, R. A., & Ziegler, M. E. (2008). *Finite Mathematics for Business, Life Sciences, and Social Sciences*, 11th Edition. Upper Saddle River, NJ: Pearson/Prentice Hall.

Shafii-Mousavi, M., & Kochanowski, P. (2010). The use of spreadsheets and service-learning projects in mathematics courses. *The Journal of Computational Science Education*, 1 (1), 13 – 27.

Table 4.1. Excel spreadsheets for Modeling Linear Programming Problem.

	C	S	R	USEAGE		CAPACITY
LAND PER HOUSE (ACRES)	0.5	0.5	1	0	<=	30
LABOR PER HOUSE(HOURS)	4000	3000	4000	0	<=	180000
CAPITAL PER HOUSE($)	60000	60000	80000	0	<=	$3,200,000
PROFITS PER HOUSE	$17,000	$18,000	$24,000	TOTAL PROFIT $0		
ACTIVITIES	NO. C	NO. S	NO. R			
DECISION VARIABLES	0	0	0			

C=COLONIAL, S=SPLIT-LEVEL, R=RANCH

Table 4.2. Excel Trial and Error Demonstration of the Construction Problem.

	C	S	R	USEAGE		CAPACITY
LAND PER HOUSE (ACRES)	0.5	0.5	1	40	<=	30
LABOR PER HOUSE(HOURS)	4000	3000	4000	220000	<=	180000
CAPITAL PER HOUSE($)	60000	60000	80000	4000000	<=	$3,200,000
PROFITS PER HOUSE	$17,000	$18,000	$24,000	TOTAL PROFIT $1,180,000		
ACTIVITIES	NO. C	NO. S	NO. R			
DECISION VARIABLES	20	20	20			

C=COLONIAL, S=SPLIT-LEVEL, R=RANCH

Using podcasts for added instructional effectiveness

Bruce Spitzer
Indiana University South Bend

Keywords: podcasts, instructional review, instructional effectiveness

Framework

This quick hit describes how I use podcasts syndicated through a course management system to help students review the day's lesson, preview the next class session, and remember what tasks must be completed prior to the next class meeting.

Making it Work

These follow-up podcasts are appropriate for classes of any size and any format. They are especially useful for classes that meet just once weekly: they allow the instructor an opportunity to interact, albeit asynchronously, with a group of students more than just the single weekly class meeting.

I've found them especially helpful for undergraduate students who sometimes have trouble managing the large workload that often results from once-weekly class meetings.

Tools:

For many, the hardware and software to create acceptable-quality podcasts are already available. For those seeking very low-cost options, I'd suggest Audacity, an open-source audio recording software package (audacity.sourceforge.net; available for both Mac and PC) and an inexpensive USB or 3.5mm plug microphone available from any big-box electronics store.

For a higher-quality recording, investment in a Blue Snowflake or Snowball USB microphone (www.bluemic.com) ensures a more robust audio recording.

Mac users have access to Garageband for recording and editing audio. Garageband is included in the iLife suite of applications resident on all Macs shipped in recent years.

There is no cost to students associated with listening to podcasts. One misnomer that must quickly be squelched is that an Apple iPod is necessary to listen to a podcast. Software such as iTunes or Windows Media Player are available free and will play nearly all common audio files. In addition, .mp3 files will play on many portable digital audio players readily available on the market.

Once the instructor has learned the processes for recording, editing, and exporting audio to useable formats, the timeline for implementation is nearly nil.

There are a myriad of resources available to help instructors learn the processes around digital audio recording and editing.

Once the recording is exported in a useable final format (.mp3 is nearly universal), syndication/publication through various course management systems is often as easy as uploading any digital resource to Blackboard, WebCT, Sakai, or other online course management system. In lieu of such course management system syndication, distribution may be achieved as easily as attaching the finished digital audio file to an email message sent to every member of the class.

I would suggest that instructors develop a "format" for each session's podcast. For example, I've been successful with a format that follows this outline:
1. Welcome
2. Review of the class session
3. Preview of the next class session
4. List of tasks to complete before next class session
5. Some value-added component that is related to the course content, but not specifically covered in class. (I provide students a "tech tip of the week.")

If instructors script the content, the content then becomes easily available to student with hearing disabilities simply by sending them the text of the podcast.

Future Implications

Students have remarked that the follow-up podcasts provided each week serve their intended purpose: as a review and reminder of the course content being studied and an audio checklist to help students ensure they've completed the necessary work for the upcoming class.

I've been able to entice reticent students to listen to the podcasts by offering several extra-credit opportunities throughout the semester, and describing the opportunity only in the podcast. Students invariably mention the extra-credit opportunities to others in the class and those who have not listened in the past quickly learn the value of listening to the podcasts.

Once instructors become adept at recording audio-only podcasts, they may be less fearful of venturing into creating richer podcasts that include digital images synchronized to the audio portion. While Garageband can do this easily, Audacity does not. However, inexpensive applications such as ProfCast (www.profcast.com), which marries audio and PowerPoint slides, are available for both the Mac and PC platforms.

Brown and Green (2007) have written about podcasting in general and specifically video podcasting including history, technical aspects, and education applications of podcasts.

Reference

Brown, A., & Green, T. (2007). Video podcasting in perspective: The history, technology, aesthetics, and instructional uses of a new medium. *Journal of Educational Technology Systems, 36*(1), 3-17.

IMPLEMENTATION OF AND FEEDBACK ON THE USE OF A WEB-BASED HOMEWORK MANAGEMENT SYSTEM

ELLEN D. BARTLEY
ST. JOSEPH'S COLLEGE

Keywords: web-based homework management

Framework

Students often enter required introductory quantitative courses with little interest in the subject and/or concerns about their ability to succeed in the course. Problem-solving is typically an essential component of learning in this type of course. Connect TM is a web-based homework management system, linked to the student textbook. It has been used in an introductory accounting course for three semesters. Instructor and student feedback both indicate that this tool has positively impacted student engagement, learning, and performance. There is no cost to the instructor or institution. Students pay approximately $40 per semester for access to the system.

Making it Work

Ease of implementation for both the student and instructor is an important feature of this technology. The publisher offered a one-hour introductory webinar for the instructor. The instructor provided a brief demonstration during the first class session. Traditional aged students found the program to be quite intuitive and rarely took advantage of the tutorials provided. Non-traditional aged students also found the system to be quite user friendly.

Students found the program to be quite intuitive and rarely took advantage of the tutorials.

Initially, the instructor must perform a one-time set up to establish a unique link for each section, and provide the link to the students. Subsequently, instructors must create each assignment within the program. Instructors may use textbook problems and/or add their own assignments. There are many options for the instructor to choose from when setting up the assignment, such as the number of attempts the student is permitted, the amount of the time allowed, as well as various levels and timing of feedback provided to the student. Levels of support range from no feedback to correcting the assignment and providing links to the electronic version of the textbook.

This tool provides the opportunity for both formative and summative feedback and assessment. In this course, required homework was prepared by the students in Connect. Optional practice problems were posted for students prior to each examination.

Students must initially register for the program via the unique course link provided by instructors. They may either purchase the program directly on the publisher's website, or use an access code if one was provided with the textbook. Once established, students may bookmark the website for easier future access. Students prepare and submit assignments electronically in accordance with the parameters set up by the instructor.

In three semesters of required participation, the time spent by the instructor on grading homework was virtually eliminated. Reports are available and downloadable for the instructor. The more significant benefit has been engaged students. When using Connect TM students came to class well prepared and asked very specific questions about what they had trouble with. If a student does not perform well on a particular assignment, the instructor is able to look at the details and provide timely feedback to the students.

Anonymous student evaluations were submitted each semester regarding the students' use of and reaction to the homework management system. Results have been overwhelmingly positive; students reported that the homework management system was helpful and strongly recommend its continued use. The primary reason that students cited was the instant feedback. They did not have to wait until the next class to find out how they did. Completing questions successfully or being able to work through them with the feedback encouraged students to complete assignments. The only negative feedback reported by students report was that they had difficulty translating problems from the electronic format, which often uses drop down menus, to paper for examinations.

Future Implications

A web-based homework management system is adaptable to many types of quantitative courses. The timely feedback provides the instructor with the opportunity to focus valuable class time on the more challenging topics or nuances of particular topics. Although used in class sections of approximately 30 students, the ability to download reports makes it easily used in larger classes. The web-based product is also well suited to distance learning settings.

Group work online

James M. VanderVeen and Joshua W. Wells
Indiana University South Bend

Keywords: collaboration, presentations

Framework

When students work together on a project, it can increase their engagement in the learning process. They must know enough of the topic to teach one another and they are active participants in the creation of a product. But finding the time to meet outside of class presents a challenge to many busy students. Even an hour or two set aside during the class might be utilized inefficiently by having one student monopolize the time at a computer. By collaborating in a dynamic, real-time, cloud-based work environment, however, some of these problems are resolved.

Making it Work

We have used the Presentation software available through Google Docs to facilitate student group work in a variety of classes, from introductory courses meeting general education requirements to small senior-level seminars. The program (found, with tutorials, here: http://www.google.com/google-d-s/presentations/) is free, can be used on any computer with web access, and requires no installation. The key advantage is the ability to collaborate at any time and from any location. Students only need to go to the specific page for the presentation (which can be shared with anyone who has the link or only with specific email addresses) to begin the editing process, and any number of students can make changes simultaneously. The commands and functions associated with Google Docs Presentations should be familiar to anyone with some experience using Microsoft PowerPoint, Apple Keynote, or similar programs. The file saves automatically after any changes are made. Multiple viewers are denoted by different colored highlighted cursors, and all users present are listed on the interface. A link to the finished presentation can then be shared as widely as the students wish — to the instructor alone or publicly viewable to anyone online.

Future Implications

There are a number of ways in which the presentation activity can be integrated into a course. An instructor can select the images or titles for the slides ahead of time, and then distribute a link to the skeletal presentation to each group. The students would then organize the presentation to reflect their own ideas and add details with information gathered from the sources they have found. Alternatively, a topic can be assigned to each group, and they would be free to create the presentation to meet the requirements of the assignment. Each member of the group could have responsibility for a separate section, or they could work together on each slide at a lab on campus or over the phone. Either way, the outcome is a complete presentation that can then be delivered to the other student groups during class time or shared via the web for viewing at each student's convenience.

Our students have responded positively to this type of work, and they have thought of ways to include the utility of online collaboration in other contexts. One student explained, "Google Docs was a new media I have not used before so I appreciate that new experience." More said the projects were "fun," "enjoyable," and appreciated the break to the normal classroom experience.

TEACHING PROFESSIONAL COMMUNICATION THROUGH EMAIL

AUDREY L. DETERDING
INDIANA UNIVERSITY SOUTHEAST

Keywords: email, professional communication

Framework

I like Facebook, Twitter, and texting. My students do, too. And therein lies the problem I've experienced with communication between faculty and students: the consistent informality that arises when one begins to think "going to take a nap" is standard for quality communication. The line between social media acceptability and professional communication acceptability is often one that students fail to realize even exists. Although I inform my students that any emails I send are considered "official course communication" most students really do not understand what that means, especially from a formal/informal standpoint.

As technology becomes increasingly more common, I see a corresponding increase in the informality of correspondence from my students. It is not uncommon to receive an email which is not signed and full of shorthand ("R u around today?"). Another issue is accessibility. Students assume that I am available around the clock, and they find nothing odd about asking me at an 8am class if I received the email sent around 3am. Telling them I have not yet checked email that morning often comes across as shocking.

As an assistant professor in Communication Studies, many students incorrectly assume that all I care about is oral communication, especially since many of them meet me in a Public Speaking classroom. However, my focus, and my discipline's, is on communication-both written and oral. Because of these issues with emails, and a desire to uphold the values of my discipline for excellence in all forms of communication, I developed a policy for email which I include in all my syllabi.

Note: Oncourse is my university's online teaching and learning environment.

Making it Work

Communicating with me
1. I check email only during the week: from about 9 am–7pm. Do not expect me to reply to email on the weekends.
2. It is your responsibility to regularly check your email and Oncourse to stay apprised of classroom happenings.
3. You are required to use Oncourse for email. It helps ensure the emails don't get lost and keeps things organized. I will not reply to emails sent outside of Oncourse while you are my student.
4. Check the syllabus and Oncourse first. Can you answer your question from these resources? If you can and you email me, I will simply refer you to these resources.
5. Subject lines should clearly indicate the nature of the email (e.g. "Appointment this week", "Question about journal entry 6", etc.).
6. Greet me. That's right. Don't jump into your message; actually take the time to address me.
7. Sign it. Not your signature that just attaches it to the mail, but a genuine signature.
8. No IM abbreviations.
9. Take the time to check spelling and clarity — I dislike trying to figure out stuff that should be straightforward.
10. Use the appropriate channel of communication. Email is great for easy questions that require only short responses but lousy for continued guidance. If you have a complex question, come and see me rather than emailing me!
11. If these rules are not followed, the first time I will send an email back asking you to follow email guidelines and resend the email. After the first time, I simply won't reply.

I initially only included these guidelines in my lower level classes, thinking that my upper level students wouldn't need such reminding. I have since realized how wrong I was, and I now include this policy in all my syllabi. These rules are pretty static except for the first which I tweak each semester to correspond to my teaching schedule. I had one semester in which I taught late afternoon and night classes, and then I started checking emails around 11am and continued until 9pm.

Future Implications

Since I incorporated these rules, I have been pleased with the results. In any given class, I send replies asking the student to check the syllabus on how to construct an email to perhaps 10%–15% of the class. Very rarely does a student not resend the email; most are sent beginning with an apology. When replying, I always thank the student for resending the email because his or her question was an important one, and I was glad I had the chance to answer. I want students to follow appropriate guidelines; I don't want them to feel too intimidated to send an email.

In many facets of higher education we strive to model the real world environment we are preparing our students to enter. By adding this policy to my syllabus, I'm reinforcing the real world model in another channel of communication.

COUPLING VISUAL METAPHORS WITH DISCUSSION FORUMS TO ENHANCE REFLECTION AND INQUIRY

FREDRICKA F. JOYNER
INDIANA UNIVERSITY PURDUE UNIVERSITY INDIANAPOLIS

Keywords: critical thinking, instructional technology, online teaching/learning

Framework

In an online teaching and learning environment, one of the core challenges is to provide opportunities, structures, and formats that increase MEANINGFUL interaction and give students the opportunity to practice and demonstrate higher order thinking skills. This Quick Hit describes a small teaching intervention that integrates a simple technology tool (Wordle™) into the discussion forum format resulting in deeper levels of student engagement and the development and use of higher order thinking skills. While the specific example is focused on online discussion forums, the approach could be applied across disciplines and learning environments.

Four different threads weave together to provide the context and purpose for this Quick Hit:

- There are increasing opportunities to leverage technology tools (in both online and face-to-face learning environments) to facilitate deeper levels of student engagement and the development and use of higher order thinking skills.
- In the undergraduate online learning environment, discussion forums are a frequently used approach for getting student interaction and participation. It has been my experience that the interaction that takes place is often superficial and that typical applications of the discussion forum tool fail to stimulate higher order thinking skills (critical and creative thinking), active inquiry, and meaningful interaction. Most of the postings are simple recall and I am frequently disappointed by what I have come to call the "what he said syndrome" in which each student simply rephrases previous postings.
- It has been my experience that creating and reflecting upon visual metaphors can be an effective tool for encouraging deeper thinking about a subject. Visual metaphors can help reveal patterns and themes, connections, and finer nuance. They can also create an "AHA!" experience.
- Working together to create, and then reflect upon, a collective artifact provides an opportunity to learn about both content and one's self in the context of the larger whole.

A *Quick Hit* Summary of Theoretical Underpinnings

This Quick Hit is designed to enhance meaningful interaction and stimulate higher order critical and creative thinking skills by using a collective visual metaphor based on prior experience to fuel a discussion forum organized around Kolb's 4-Stage Cycle of Learning (1984). It is based on the following theoretical foundations:

Critical and Creative Thinking

One of the purposes of this Quick Hit is to stimulate higher order critical and creative thinking. Generally speaking, the critical thinking domain includes logical thinking and reasoning while the creative thinking domain encompasses putting things together in new ways and developing alternate ways of approaching or framing an issue. There are many useful frameworks, taxonomies, and rubrics that organize levels and types of thinking (e.g., Huitt, 2009; Fink, 2003) and you might consider working with one of these to assess the demonstration of higher order thinking skills in this project.

Visual Metaphors

Carroll (2001) describes a visual metaphor as a tool for inspiring insights. That is, with visual metaphors, the image is essentially 'food for thought.' It becomes the task of the viewer to use the image for his or her own insight. A visual metaphor can be a powerful teaching tool, encouraging deeper thinking and tapping into related emotional content.

Making it Work

Kolb's 4-Stage Cycle of Learning provides the framework for this teaching intervention.

1. Develop a focus question(s) for the activity that requires students to respond with a list of words. The question(s) should be focused on concrete experience (Stage 1 of Kolb's Model – Concrete Experience) and, in this example, designed to allow students to reflect upon, organize, and pull forward prior knowledge/experience. This prior knowledge/experience provides the starting point for the meaning making associated with deeper levels of reflection and inquiry.

   Example: What five words would you use to describe aspects of your "best" work experience? What five words would you use to describe aspects of your "worst" work experience?

2. Use Wordle™ (www.wordle.net) to create a "word cloud(s)" of the words (figure 4.3). The word cloud becomes a collective artifact that synthesizes individual experiences into one image that suggests broader patterns and themes. (Tip: If the students all post their words in a Wiki it simplifies the amount of cutting and pasting required.)

Figure 4.3. Example of aspects of best work experiences word cloud.

3. Post the word cloud in the discussion forum with prompt(s) that encourage reflection and inquiry. (Stage 2 of Kolb's Model — Reflective Observation)
Example: Spend some time looking at and thinking about the word cloud(s). What do you notice about our collective experience with work? If you were a manager, what would you pay attention to in order to create a positive work experience? What surprised you? What did you expect? What else?

4. If your experience is anything like mine, in the ensuing discussion you will notice many examples of higher order thinking skills, both in terms of critical thinking — depth, breadth, and context — and creative thinking — new patterns and alternate approaches. Many of the posts will begin to explore new implications for action (Stage 3 of Kolb's Model — Abstract Conceptualization) and some of the posts will move toward ideas for application (Stage 4 of Kolb's Model — Active Experimentation).

5. Apply a critical/creative thinking rubric to assess the demonstration of higher order thinking skills.

References

Carroll, N. (2001). Visual metaphors. In *Beyond aesthetics: Philosophical essays* (pp. 347 – 368). Cambridge, UK: Cambridge University Press.

Huitt, W. (2009). Bloom et al.'s taxonomy of the cognitive domain. Educational Psychology Interactive. Valdosta, GA: Valdosta State University. Retrieved December 4, 2010, from http://www.edpsycinteractive.org/topics/cogsys/bloom.html

Kolb, D. (1984). Experiential learning: Experience as the source of learning and development. Englewood Cliffs, NJ: Prentice Hall.

Fink, D.L. (2003). Creating significant learning experiences: An integrated approach to designing college courses. San Francisco: Jossey-Bass.

Wordle™ www.wordle.net

the discussion forum format resulting in deeper levels
of student engagement and the development
and use of higher order thinking skills.

USING TECHNOLOGY TO IMPROVE EMPIRICALLY BASED CLINICAL PRACTICE

NATHANAEL G. MITCHELL AND DEDE WOHLFARTH
SPALDING UNIVERSITY

Keywords: technology, clinical practice, empirically based practice

Framework

One of the primary goals in the training of professional psychologists is to instruct students in the critical thinking skills to make an empirically based clinical decision. This is also a necessary skill for a variety of disciplines including nursing, physical therapy, social work, occupational therapy, etc. In practice, the information needed to make these determinations is primarily technology based. Following is a description of one such technique in training developing psychologists in the proper use of technology to aid in empirically based clinical decisions.

Making it Work

First, students read journal articles concerning the theory and application of empirically based decision making. The articles include web resources for finding recent research on the treatment of different disorders and discuss the importance of integrating information including client characteristics and realistic challenges in making clinical decisions.

Second, during the following class students bring their laptops and receive a clinical vignette that is complex regarding client/patient characteristics (e.g., multiple diagnoses, minority status, complex barriers to treatment, etc.). These patient characteristics are strategically chosen to represent populations that are often excluded from research on psychological treatments (e.g., randomized clinical trials) making this a realistic problem-based learning strategy.

Third, students are placed into groups and instructed to use their laptop computers or the university's computer lab to search for empirically based psychological treatments of the client's particular disorders utilizing the web resources from the articles. Additionally, the students are required to find web resources to assist in making clinical decisions with regards to other specific client/patient characteristics provided (e.g., strategies working with Asian American clients).

Finally, the groups come back to class to discuss the resources they found and the clinical decisions that were made based upon those resources. The discussion that ensues is lively as students excitedly share their "best" resources and ideas. This allows for critical thinking about the quality of the resources used as well as the final conclusions reached by the various student groups.

Future Implications

This activity would be appropriate in any clinical disciplines that utilizes research and critical thinking in clinical decision making (e.g., psychology, pharmacy, social work, nursing, education, medicine, dentistry, etc.). The only implementation issues are providing the articles, the clinical vignette, and computer lab availability.

Students don't wait for semester course evaluations to tell us how useful this activity is for their learning. Instead they report using the strategies they learned in class immediately with their clients.

This assignment could easily be modified for large classes or online classes by having online discussions about evidenced based practice and posting the clinical vignette online for students to do as an out-of-class activity.

They report using the strategies they learned
in class immediately with their clients.

EMBEDDED FEEDBACK IN VIDEO RECORDED STUDENT ASSIGNMENTS

BRENDA BAILEY-HUGHES
INDIANA UNIVERSITY

Keywords: Adobe Pro, embedded feedback, video assignments

Framework

As Tyler returns to his dorm, his roommate Scott asks, "Soooo? How did your speech go?" Tyler sighs and says, "Who knows." A week later, Tyler returns to class and is handed a paper with nearly illegible comments from his professor. He stares at the comments but can't figure out what anything means. He checks his grade, crumples the page, and then drops the feedback sheet in the trash can.

Tyler's experience is neither unusual nor hypothetical. Instructors in many disciplines have long recognized the value of videotaping performance as a means of student evaluation and feedback. Education majors watch themselves teach. Public speaking students watch themselves present. Psychology students watch themselves counsel, etc. However, videotaping alone is not a useful learning tool and in fact may actually be counterproductive to learning objectives

if students view the video without any accompanying constructive feedback (McCroskey & Lashbrook, 1970; Diehl, Breen, & Larson, 1970). Imagine a different scenario:

Tyler puts his book bag down and says to Scott, "I think I did better! I can't wait to see what my prof said. Want to watch?" "Sure," Scott responds, as Tyler's recorded speech begins to play on the computer. Soon, the instructor's feedback pops onto the screen: "Good eye contact!" Sure enough, Tyler is looking right at his audience. While watching, Tyler makes a list of things to improve.

Making it Work

Following the instructions below you can embed your comments into recordings of student performances. Your comments will appear at the very moment the related behavior occurs. For example, the student might see, "That was a good transition," at the exact place in the speech that the

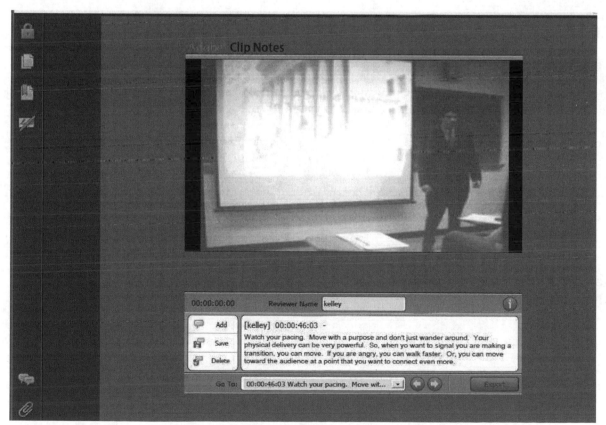

Figure 4.4. Example of feedback on video assignment.

transition occurred. "Good evidence," will now be a more meaningful comment because your student will recognize exactly what you are referencing.

1. Install Adobe Pro, Creative Suite 4, Production Premium (Version 5.5 now available)
2. Open Media Encoder CS4
3. Convert video files to PDF format
4. Drag all video files into the box
5. Select Format>Clip Notes Windows Media and Preset>NTSC Source to 512KBPS
6. Change output file to where you want to save converted files
7. Select "Start Que"
8. Open and play the PDF file
9. Select "ADD" which will pause the video. Add your comment.
10. Save your work!

Future Implications

In a small study comparing the performance of public speaking students who received embedded feedback on three speeches to the performance of those who received traditional paper feedback, no statistically significant findings were present. However, the comments from students who received the embedded feedback indicate tremendous preference for the method. The latest version of Adobe Pro, Creative Suite 5.5, Production Premium retails for $1,699 but educational discounts are available and many institutions have licensing agreements so there is no cost to the instructor to load and use the software. The Creative Suite is a powerful tool with many features and functionality but can be mastered for the Embedded Feedback purposes in a couple of hours. Students need no special software to view the embedded feedback video recording as it opens with a standard pdf viewer.

References

Diehl, E., Breen, M., & Larson, C. (1970). The effects of teacher comments and television video tape playback on the frequency of nonfluency in beginning speech students. *Speech Teacher, 19,* 185-189.

McCroskey, J., & Lashbrook, W. (1970). The effect of various methods of employing video-tape television playback in a course in public speaking. *Speech Teacher, 19*(3), 199-205.

Using cartoons or short movies to engage students

Karen Banks
Indiana University Bloomington

Keywords: motivation, engaging, collaboration

Framework

I use cartoons or animated short movies to reinforce key concepts and to help keep student motivation and interest high in a large or small class. Cartoons and animated short movies are even more effective when students create their own and provide constructive criticism for other students. Student created cartoons or animated short movies force students to explain difficult concepts in their own words. Students benefit by seeing the different explanations of their classmates and they have a great time creating them.

Videotaping alone is not a useful learning tool and in fact may actually be counterproductive to learning objectives.

The software that I have found on the Internet tends to be easy to use.

There are many different free web sites. Google the Internet to find a site that best reflects your class, your skill level, and time commitment. I have listed some of the sites I have found in the next section.

Making it Work

Instructors or students can spend a few minutes or a few days working on a cartoon or an animation. Some web sites are easier to use then others, but the easier ones tend to be more restrictive in the choice of materials for creation.

To start out you might try these sites
- http://www.pixton.com/
- http://www.makebeliefscomix.com/
- http://www.toondoo.com/
- http://stripgenerator.com/strip/create/
- http://superherosquad.marvel.com/create_your_own_comic

I created the cartoon above for a difficult concept in database development (see figure 4.5). The cartoon helped to start a discussion about the concept.

I also created an animated short movie to remind students about a common mistake in database development (this can be viewed on at www.quickhitstech.com). I used software at http://www.xtranormal.com/. The web site provides a template. I choose the characters and typed in the text for the characters to say. This software is no longer free to use, but the owners will send educators free credits to use. For an animated short movie, I type the text of the conversation to the right of the animation so that foreign students or students with hearing problems can easily follow along.

I select a template that I wish to use and then I select the number of actors. I choose the sets, actors, sounds (see figures 4.6 and 4.7).

Then, I type in the words for each character to say. I can even set camera angles and motions. I save and publish the movie and I am done. I can go back and edit the movie if needed.

Figure 4.5. Cartoon illustration of challenging concept.

Figure 4.6. Xtranormal.com example.

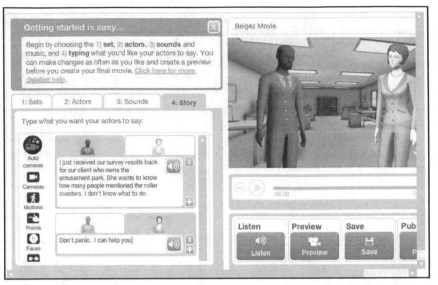

Figure 4.7. Xtranormal.com movie options.

Future Implications

Outcomes/Assessment

Whenever I show a cartoon or animated short movie, the classroom instantly becomes quiet. Students ask me about the content and want to know how I created it. Students are quite creative and become competitive in trying to create the best cartoon or animated short movie. Students gain a deeper understanding of concepts when they can see cartoons or an animated short movie created by other students and then provide constructive criticism in a guided discussion.

Future Directions/ Modifications/ Hybrid context

With the permission of each student, you can easily collect multiple methods for explaining difficult concepts to show future classes. Suddenly students are in charge of the content and enjoy explaining and criticizing each other's work.

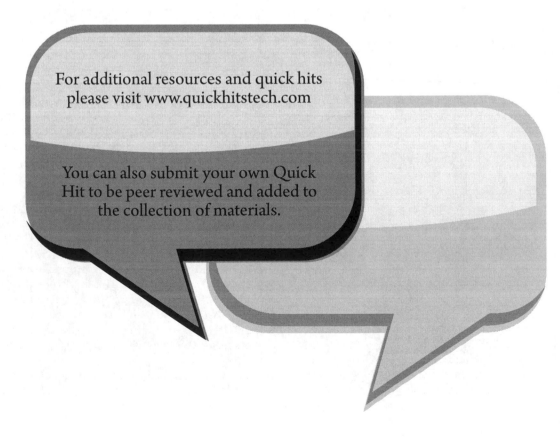

For additional resources and quick hits please visit www.quickhitstech.com

You can also submit your own Quick Hit to be peer reviewed and added to the collection of materials.

ANNOTATED BIBLIOGRAPHY

Anderson, T. (2004). Teaching in an online learning context. In T. Anderson and F. Elloumi (eds.) *Theory and practice of online learning*. Athabasca, Canada: Athabasca University Press. Retrieved June 22, 2011: http://cde.athabascau.ca/online_book/ch11.html#one.

This chapter outlines principles of effective online teaching from a model based on three principles: cognitive presence, social presence, and teaching presence. This chapter would be an excellent choice for those who are new to teaching online as well as those who have been teaching online for some time.

Bonk, C.J., & Graham, C.R. (2006). *The handbook of blended learning: Global perspectives, local designs*. San Francisco, CA: John Wiley & Sons.

The Handbook of Blended Learning is a comprehensive resource that highlights the most recent practices and trends in blended learning and provides targeted information for specific blended learning situations. The book provides examples of learning options that combine face-to-face instruction with online learning in both the workplace as well as more formal academic settings.

Bonk, C. J. (2009). *The world is open: How web technology is revolutionizing education*. San Francisco, CA: Jossey-Bass, a Wiley imprint. Jossey-Bass.

This book describes how web-based technology has opened up education around the world to the point where anyone can learn anything from anyone else at any time. It is especially useful in helping educators understand what's possible. The author presents his "WE-ALL-LEARN" model to outline ten key technology and learning trends, demonstrating how technology has transformed educational opportunities for learners of every age in every corner of the globe. Using inspiring stories of ordinary learners as well as interviews with technology and education leaders, he reveals the power of this new way of learning.

Chickering, A.W., & Ehrmann, S.C. (1996, October). Implementing the seven principles: Technology as a Lever. *AAHE Bulletin*, 3-6. Retrieved October 7, 2007 from Teaching, Learning and Technology Group Website: http://www.tltgroup.org/programs/seven.html.

This is a short but useful article about using technology to implement the seven principles of good practice in undergraduate education. It includes a description of each principle as well as specific ideas and examples of how they can be accomplished using technology.

The Digital Campus: The Mobile Revolution. Retrieved June 22, 2011 from Chronicle of Higher Education Website: http://chronicle.com/section/The-Digital-Campus/529/

This Special Edition from the Chronicle of Higher Education (available in print format) outlines new and evolving technologies on college campuses. Articles are varied and several directly address the issue of the use of technology without the concomitant attention to whether that technology is pedagogically appropriate or enhances student learning.

Conceição, S.C.O., & Lehman, R.M. (2011). *Managing online instructor workload: Strategies for finding balance and success*. San Francisco: John Wiley & Sons, Inc.

For those inexperienced in teaching in an online environment, teaching a course online can quickly lead to more time and effort than teaching the same course in a traditional, face-to-face environment. In this workbook, the authors help the reader sort through the many institutional and instructional issues and challenges in developing effective online instruction.

Conrad, R., & Donaldson, J.A. (2011). *Engaging the online learner: Activities and resources for creative instruction*, Revised. San Francisco: John Wiley & Sons, Inc. (Marcia)

Engaging the Online Learner provides a framework explaining the process of moving students through the phases of becoming an engaged student. The first three chapters explain this framework, how to design an online course within the engaged student perspective, and how to assess engagement. The rest of the chapters each contain a very brief explanation of a type of activity such icebreakers, learner led activities, group activities and simulations followed by several examples. The book is a solid resource for activity ideas.

Coombs, N. (2010). *Making online teaching accessible: Inclusive course design for students with disabilities*. San Francisco: John Wiley & Sons, Inc.

This book provides a great review of assistive (or adaptive) technology, laws and guidelines relevant to online instruction, and the principles of universal design. The practical advice contained in this book may help readers to avoid making mistakes that inadvertently create barriers for students with disabilities or violate federal guidelines.

Dykman, C.A. & Davis, C.K. (2008). Online education forum--Part three: A quality online educational experience. *Journal of Information Systems Education, 19*(3), 281-290.

This article focuses on techniques such as mastering one's course management system, standardizing course design, creating consistency in interactions with learners, and controlling class size. Another aspect of success considered is developing a well-honed and consistent philosophy toward teaching online that will help learners understand what is expected of them and guide the teacher when unusual situations arise. The issues and insights discussed in this Forum will provide educators with important tools and the understanding needed to embrace the world of online education.

Grant, L. K. (2004). Teaching positive reinforcement on the Internet. *Teaching of Psychology, 31,* 69–71.

The journal, Teaching of Psychology, is filled with useful ideas about teaching. In this article, an empirically supported online tutorial on positive reinforcement for an undergraduate course is described.

Hanover Research Council (2009). Best practices in online teaching. Retrieved June 22, 2011:   http://www.hanoverresearch.com/library/assets/libPdfs/Best%20Practices%20in%20Online%20Teaching%20Strategies%20-%20Membership.pdf

This comprehensive summary is split into three sections: Overview of the Principles, Guidelines, and Benchmarks for Online Education; Best Practices in Online Teaching Strategies; and An Exemplary Program and Examples of Effective Practices.

Johnson, K., & Magusin, E. (2005). *Exploring the digital library: A guide for online teaching and learning.* San Francisco: John Wiley & Sons, Inc.

This volume in The Jossey-Bass Online Teaching and Learning series, explains how faculty can effectively use digital libraries to enhance their scholarship and their teaching, especially in the design of electronic courses. This book is especially helpful in suggesting methods for integrating digital libraries into teaching and course development, outlining the skills and knowledge required in digital library use and providing a framework for faculty and librarians to collaborate in the online educational environment.

Johnson, L., Smith, R., Willis, H., Levine, A., & Haywood, K., (2011). *The 2011 Horizon Report.* Austin, Texas: The New Media Consortium. Retrieved July 8, 2011: http://net.educause.edu/ir/library/pdf/HR2011

The annual Horizon Report looks at emerging technologies' likely to impact education in three time horizons, one year or less, two to three years, and four to five years. The report identifies key trends, technologies to watch, relevance for Higher Education, and practical examples of potential uses of the technologies.

Jukes, I., McCain, T., & Crockett, L. (2010). *Understanding the digital generation: Teaching and learning in the new digital landscape.* Thousand Oaks, CA: Corwin Press.

In the first part of this book, the authors describe the differences between the experiences of students born in the past generation – the digital generation - and those of us born prior to 1980. These students, it is argued, interact with technology in a different way and are bored in traditional classrooms. The second part of the book provides suggestions for instructors in dealing with this digital generation.

Lehman, R.M., & Conceição, S.C.O. (2010). *Creating a sense of presence in online teaching: How to "be there" for distance learners.* San Francisco: John Wiley & Sons, Inc.

This book focuses on helping instructors to become aware of and understand the differences between face-to-face and online interactions in an effort to create a stronger 'presence' in online environments. The authors not only provide a map for creating presence but, also, a framework for understanding how presence influences the success of online learning.

Lewis, C.C., & Abdul-Hamid, H. (2006). Implementing effective online teaching practices: Voices of exemplary faculty. *Innovative Higher Education, 31* (2), 83-98. doi: 10.1007/s10755-006-9010-z

These authors interviewed thirty exemplary instructors of online courses at University of Maryland University College to determine practices of online teaching that are particularly effective. Their findings present specific strategies in four areas: fostering interaction, providing feedback, facilitating learning, and maintaining enthusiasm and organization.

Manning, S., & Johnson, K. (2011). *The technology toolbelt for teaching.* San Francisco: John Wiley & Sons, Inc.

Although the newest technology may be exciting, the difficulty for instructors is knowing how to choose the appropriate technology for enhancing learning. The authors of this book help instructors by providing a simple matrix that can be utilized in making these decisions.

Oberlin College and Conservatory (2010). *iPad pilot program @ Oberlin College.* Retrieved June 22, 2011: https://sites.google.com/a/oberlin.edu/ipad-pilot-program/home

This site details the efforts of faculty at Oberlin College and Conservatory in developing the use of iPads in their courses. The site includes examples, a 'dynamic' bibliography, and short videos highlighting their work.

Ortiz-Rodríguez, M., Telg, R. W., Irani, T., Roberts, T. G., & Rhoades, E. (2005). College students' perceptions of quality in distance education: The importance of communication. *Quarterly Review of Distance Education, 6* (2), 97-105.

This study used a random sample of 214 students enrolled in summer distance courses. The researchers asked the students one question: ""List as many factors as you can that you personally believe could potentially affect the quality of a distance education course in any way. Please be as specific as possible." Communication was the factor identified most often, including feedback from the instructor and effective use of communication tools.

Palloff, R.M., & Pratt, K. (2007). *Building online learning communities: Effective strategies for the virtual classroom* (2nd ed.). San Francisco: John Wiley & Sons, Inc.

This is an excellent resource for the instructor first teaching in the online environment as well as a great refresher for those who are experienced teaching online. The authors provide practical advice, including sample syllabi, as well as helping instructors conceptualize their online teaching in the broader context of excellent teaching.

Palloff, R.M., & Pratt, K. (2009). *Assessing the online learner: Resources and strategies for faculty.* San Francisco: John Wiley & Sons, Inc.

One of the most common complaints my peers who are not teaching in an online environment have is that it is impossible to accurately assess whether students have learned anything in an online class. The authors of this text provide a convincing rationale and examples of authentic methods of assessing students — tied directly to course objectives — in an online environment.

Palloff, R.M., & Pratt, K. (2010). *Collaborating online: Learning together in community.* San Francisco: John Wiley & Sons, Inc.

The authors distinguish between student interaction (student-to-student as well as student-to-instructor) and interactivity (the inclusion of material that creates active learning in an online environment). Developing collaborative activities online may lead to deeper levels of learning and is the focus of this book; the authors include practical suggestions as well as numerous examples.

Pew Social Trends Staff (2010). *Millennials: Confident. Connected.* Open to Change. Pew Internet & American Life Project. Retrieved July 8, 2011: http://pewsocialtrends.org/2010/02/24/millennials-confident-connected-open-to-change/

The Pew Social Trends Staff uses survey and census data to compare and contrast the Millennial generation to previous generations. It looks across Millennial demographics and provides an introduction to the Millennials' preferences regarding digital and social media, as well as education.

Russo, T. C., & Campbell, S. W. (2004). Perceptions of mediated presence in an asynchronous online course: Interplay of communication behaviors and medium. *Distance Education, 25* (2), 215-232. doi: 10.1080/0158791042000262139

Thirty-one students enrolled in two communication technology courses were both interviewed and surveyed about their perceptions of mediated presence of the instructor, other students, and themselves in their online course. Students report that frequency of interaction, responsiveness, message style and instructor's use of nonverbal channels (i.e., pictures, audio of the instructor) affected mediated presence.

Salmon, G. (2005). Flying not flapping: A strategic framework for e-learning and pedagogical innovation in higher education institution. *Research in Learning Technology, 13*(3), 201-218.

This paper shows how to capture and model complex strategic processes that will help universities move the potential of e-learning to a new stage of development. It offers the example of a four-quadrant model created as a framework for an e-learning strategy.

Smith, R.M. (2008). *Conquering the content: A step-by-step guide to online course design.* San Francisco: John Wiley & Sons, Inc.

This text provides a practical, step-by-step guide to developing an online course or converting a course from a face-to-face environment to an online environment, including templates, learning guides, and sample files. Using this approach will allow instructors to avoid many of the costly mistakes that are commonly made.

Song, L., & Singleton, E. S. (2004). Improving online learning: Student perceptions of useful and challenging characteristics. *Internet & Higher Education, 7* (1), 59-70. doi:10.1016/j.iheduc.2003.11.003

Two broad research questions are explored in this study: "What are the components of online learning environments that learners recognize as helpful in the learning process? and What are the components of online learning environments that learners identify as challenging?" They surveyed 76 graduate students who had taken online courses and did follow-up interviews with 14. Their findings included some general trends that students find helpful in the online learning environment such as course design, ability to use the technology, and time management. Challenges to learning in the online environment included a lack of community, difficulty understanding instructional goals, and technical problems.

Stavredes, T. (2011). *Effective online teaching: Foundations and strategies for student success*. San Francisco: John Wiley & Sons, Inc.

This book, offering an understanding of how cognitive theory applies to an online learning environment, is data and theory rich. The author outlines characteristics, key learning attributes, and challenges that impact a learner's persistence. This profile of the online learner is followed by cognitive strategies — procedural and metacognitive scaffolding — that may be used to facilitate student learning in an online environment.

West, J.A., & West, M.L. (2008). *Using Wikis for online collaboration: The power of the read-write web*. San Francisco: John Wiley & Sons, Inc.

For many, the difference between Web 1.0 and 2.0 is the ability to not only read but express yourself or write with Web 2.0. The use of Wikis in the classroom setting allows students to collaborate in creating assignments. This book guides instructors in selecting wiki services and software, preparing online students for success using wikis, thinking about pedagogical issues when creating wikis, planning and designing the wiki project framework, managing the collaborative writing process, creating projects that support cognitive processing and knowledge construction, and developing complex activities that highlight critical thinking and analysis.

CONTRIBUTORS

Annie Abbott
Assistant Professor and Director of the
    Spanish and Illinois Program
Department of Spanish, Italian and Portuguese
University of Illinois at Urbana-Champaign
arabbott@illinois.edu

Michael Abernethy
Lecturer
Communication Studies
IU Southeast
mabernet@ius.edu

Raquel Meyer Alexander
Assistant Professor
Accounting and Information Systems
University of Kansas
raquela@ku.edu

Sean Anderson PhD
Assistant Professor
Environmental Science and Resource
    Management Program
California State University Channel Islands
sean.anderson@csuci.edu

Scott P. Anstadt PhD, LSCSW, IABMCP
Assistant Professor - Division of Social Work
College of Professional Studies
Florida Gulf Coast University
sanstadt@fgcu.edu

Patrick J. Ashton
Associate Professor of Sociology
Director of the Peace and Conflict Studies Program
Sociology
IPFW
ashton@ipfw.edu

Paige Averett PhD
Assistant Professor
School of Social Work
East Carolina University
averettp@ecu.edu

Brenda Bailey-Hughes
Senior Lecturer
Business Communications; Kelley School of Business
Indiana University Bloomington
bbaileyh@indiana.edu

Maggie W. Baker
Coordinator, Service Learning
Center for Experiential Learning
Loras College
maggie.baker@loras.edu

Sharon M. Ballard PhD, CFLE, CFCS
Associate Professor
Child Development and Family Relations
East Carolina University
ballards@ecu.edu

Karen Banks
Senior Lecturer
Operations and Decision Technologies
Indiana University
ksbanks@indiana.edu

Elizabeth Anne Barber PhD
Associate Professor
Leadership Studies, School of Education
North Carolina Agricultural and Technical State University
eabarber@ncat.edu

Ellen Bartley
Assistant Professor
Business and Accounting Department
St. Joseph's College
cbartley@sjcny.edu

Clara H. Becerra PhD
Assistant Professor of Spanish
Mount Union College
BECERRCH@mountunion.edu

Mario Belloni
Associate Professor of Physics
Davidson College
mabelloni@davidson.edu

CJ Gerda Bender PhD
Faculty of Education
Manager, Curricular and Research Community
Engagement (CRCE)
Education
University of Pretoria
gerda.bender@up.ac.za

Lynne Bercaw
Department of Education
California State University
lbercaw@csuchico.edu

Stephen C. Bishop
Education
Indiana University
scbishop@indiana.edu

Betty L. Black
Professor
Biology
North Carolina State University
betty_black@ncsu.edu

Robert E. Bleicher
Associate Professor
School of Education
California State University Channel Islands
bob.bleicher@csuci.edu

Julia Blitz
Faculty of Health Sciences
Health Sciences
University of Pretoria
julia.blitz@up.ac.za

Barbara T. Bontempo PhD
Professor
English Department
Buffalo State College
bontembt@buffalostate.edu

Scott Wm. Bowman PhD
Assistant Professor
Department of Criminal Justice
Texas State University - San Marcos
scott.bowman@txstate.edu

Merilyn C. Buchanan
Associate Professor
School of Education
California State University Channel Islands
merilyn.buchanan@csuci.edu

Sheryl Burgstahler
University of Washington
sherylb@uw.edu

David B. Byrd PhD
Professor, School of Accountancy
Director, Masters of Accountancy
Accounting
Missouri State University
DavidByrd@missouristate.edu

Sandra D. Byrd CPA, PhD
Professor, School of Accountancy
Director, Low Income Tax Clinic; Public Affairs Professor
School of Accountancy
Missouri State University
sandrabyrd@missouristate.edu

Chris Liska Carger PhD
Professor, Department of Literacy Education
Department of Literacy Education
Northern Illinois University
ccarger@niu.edu

Teena A. M. Carnegie
Associate Professor
Department of English: Technical Communication
Eastern Washington University
tamc4320@yahoo.com

Russell Carson
Assistant Professor
Department of Kinesiology
Louisiana State University
rlcarson@lsu.edu

Linnie S. Carter Ph.D., APR
Assistant Professor of Public Relations
Public Relations Concentration Coordinator
Department of Journalism and Mass Communication
North Carolina A&T State University
lscarter@ncat.edu

Johannah Casey-Doecke PhD
Lecturer
I.U. School of Physical Education
IUPUI
jdoecke@iupui.edu

Joanna J. Cemore PhD
Associate Professor
Childhood Education and Family Studies
Missouri State University
joannacemore@missouristate.edu

Wolfgang Christian
Professor of Physics
Davidson College
wochristian@davidson.edu

Linda Christiansen JD MBA
Associate Professor of Business
Business
IU Southeast
lchristi@ius.edu

Karen Ciccone
Director, Natural Resources Library
NCSU Libraries
North Carolina State University
karen_ciccone@ncsu.edu

Ann Marie Clark
Associate Professor
Curriculum and Instruction
Appalachian State University
clarkam@appstate.edu

Janice Clark Young EdD, CHES
Associate Professor
Health and Exercise Sciences Department
Truman State University
jcyoung@truman.edu

Jon M. Clausen
Director of Educational Technology Programs
Educational Studies
Ball State University
jmclaus@bsu.edu

Susan Colby
Appalachian State University
colbysa@appstate.edu

Paul D. Cooper
Assistant Professor
Department of Chemistry
George Mason University
pcooper6@gmu.edu

Manuel G. Correia
Assistant Professor
School of Education
California State University Channel Islands
manuel.correia@csuci.edu

Marcie Coulter-Kern
Associate Professor
Chair
Psychology
Manchester College
mlcoulter-kern@manchester.edu

Lisa E. Cox PhD, LCSW, MSW
Associate Professor of Social Work and Gerontology
School of Social and Behavioral Sciences; Social work and
Gerontology Programs
The Richard Stockton College of New Jersey
lisa.cox@stockton.edu

Mo Cuevas
Social Work Program Director
West Texas A&M University
mcuevas@wtamu.edu

Joshua A. Danish Ph.D.
Assistant Professor
School of Education; Department of Counseling and
Educational Psychology
Indiana University
jdanish@indiana.edu

David O. DeFouw
Department of Cell Bio and Molecular Med
UMDNJ - New Jersey Medical School
defouw@umdnj.edu

Karin deJonge-Kannan PhD
Senior Lecturer of Linguistics
Co-Director, Master of Second Langue Teaching Program
Department of Languages, Philosophy, and Speech
Communication
Utah State University
karin.dejongekan@usu.edu

Audrey L. Deterding PhD
Department of Communication Studies
IU Southeast
auldeter@ius.edu

Marcia D. Dixson PhD
Associate Professor and Chair of Communications
Communications
IPFW
dixson@ipfw.edu

Timothy D. Dolan MS, RID, NCIDQ, NCIDQ Certified #
016868, IIDA, IDEC
Assistant Professor
Department of Technology
Appalachian State University
dolantd@appstate.edu

Judy Donovan
Assistant Professor
College of Education
Minnesota State University, Mankato
judy.donovan@mnsu.edu

Marion Eppler PhD
Associate Professor
Department of Psychology
East Carolina University
epplerm@ecu.edu

Amanda L. Espenschied-Reilly MS, MA
Director of Service-Learning and Community Service
Service-Learning and Community Service
University of Mount Union
espensal@mountunion.edu

Tammy Faux MSSW, PhD, LISW (MN)
Assistant Professor of Social Work
Social Work
Wartburg College
tammy.faux@wartburg.edu

Linda Felver
Associate Professor
School of Nursing, Portland Campus
Oregon Health and Science University
felverl@ohsu.edu

Patrick Feng Ph.D.
Department of Communication and Culture
The University of Calgary
pfeng@ucalgary.ca

Eugenia Fernandez
Associate Professor, CILT
Computer, Information, & Leadership Technology
IUPUI
efernand@iupui.edu

Nancy Zachar Fett LMSW
Associate Professor
Director of Social Work
Social Work
Loras College
nancy.fett@loras.edu

Lisa M Fiedor
Web Accessibility, Usability & Design Specialist
Instructional Support Services
North Carolina State University
lisa_fiedor@ncsu.edu

Billie J.A. Follensbee
Professor
Department of Art and Design, College of Arts and Letters
Missouri State
billiefollensbee@missouristate.edu

Connie M. Fossen MSSW, Ed D
Associate Professor
Field Director
Social Work Program
Viterbo University
cmfossen@viterbo.edu

Jacquelyn Frank
Assistant Professor/Coordinator,
    Gerontology Master's Program
School of Family and consumer Sciences
Eastern Illinois University
jbfrank@eiu.edu

Marilyn D. Frank MSW, PhD, LISW
Associate Professor
Department of Social Work
Minnesota State University, Mankato
marilyn.frank@mnsu.edu

Bobbi Gagne
Executive Director
Sexual Assault Crisis Team, Washington County, Vermont
sactwc@aol.com

Shari Galiardi
Appalachian State University
galiardisl@appstate.edu

Sharyn Gallagher
Adjunct Instructor
Department of Continuing Studies
University of Massachusetts Lowell
Sharyn_Gallagher@uml.edu

Andy Gavrin
Chair and Associate Professor
Department of Physics
IUPUI
agavrin@iupui.edu

Ralph A. Gillies PhD
Associate Professor
Department of Family Medicine
Georgia Health Sciences University
rgillies@georgiahealth.edu

Michael Glasser PhD
Assistant Dean
National Center for Rural Health Professions
University of Illinois College of Medicine
michaelg@uic.edu

Beth Goering
Associate Professor of Communication Studies
Communication Studies
IUPUI
bgoering@iupui.edu

Joseph Goetz PhD, AFC
Assistant Professor
Department of Housing and Consumer Economics
University of Georgia
goetz@uga.edu

Brenda Goodwin MS, Ed
Assistant Professor
Department of Health, Physical Education, and Recreation
Missouri State University
BrendaGoodwin@missouristate.edu

Judith I. Gray
Associate Professor
Social Work
Ball State University
jgray2@bsu.edu

Cynthia Green Libby DMA
Professor of Music
Department of Music
Missouri State University
cynthialibby@missouristate.edu

Lisa R. Grinde
Associate Professor
Psychology
Loras College
Lisa.Grinde@loras.edu

Laura Guertin
Associate Professor of Earth Sciences
Earth Sciences
Penn State Brandywine
guertin@psu.edu

Ann Gustad-Leiker MA, LBSW
Executive Director
Center for Life Experiences
First Presbyterian Church
cfle@ruraltel.net

Ruthanne Hackman PhD, MSW, LSW
School of Social Work
University of Pittsburgh
rhackman@att.net

Aileen Hale PhD
English Department
Boise State University
aileenhale@boisestate.edu

Jeanette Harder PhD, CMSW
Associate Professor
Program Chair
School of Social Work
University of Nebraska at Omaha
jharder@unomaha.edu

Jason Harris-Boundy PhD
Management Department
San Francisco State University
jchb@sfsu.edu

Michelle Gacio Harrolle PhD
Assistant Professor
Parks, Recreation & Tourism Management
College of Natural Resources, NCSU
michelle_harrolle@ncsu.edu

Elizabeth Hartung PhD
Professor
Sociology and Anthropology Programs
California State University Channel Islands
elizabeth.hartung@csuci.edu

Robin Hasslen PhD
Professor of Education
Education
Bethel University
r-hasslen@bethel.edu

Daniel T. Hickey
Associate Professor
Learning Science Program
Indiana University
dthickey@indiana.edu

Fred T. Hofstetter PhD
Professor
School of Education
University of Delaware
fth@udel.edu

Veronica House
Instructor and Service-Learning Coordinator
Program for Writing and Rhetoric
University of Colorado at Boulder
veronica.house@colorado.edu

Jane Hoyt-Oliver LISW-S, PhD
Director, General Education
Professor of Social Work
General Education Program
Malone University
jholiver@malone.edu

Sharron Hunter-Rainey PhD
Assistant Professor
School of Business
North Carolina Central University
srainey@nccu.edu

Jenny Huq
Director, APPLES Service-Learning Program
Associate Director, Carolina Center for Public Service
APPLES Service Learning Program
The University of North Carolina, Chapel Hill
huq@email.unc.edu

Janet E. Hurn
Senior Instructor
Physics Department
Miami University, Middletown
hurnje@muohio.edu

Marsha Ironsmith PhD
Associate Professor
Department of Psychology
East Carolina University
ironsmithe@ecu.edu

Rick Isaacson PhD
Associate Professor
Internship and Service-Learning Director
Department of Communication Studies
San Francisco State University
isaacson@sfsu.edu or Risaac123@aol.com

Nicole L. Johnson
Assistant Professor
Department of Philosophy and Religious Studies
University of Mount Union
johnsonl@mountunion.edu

Jennifer Jones
Associate Professor
School of Teacher Education & Leadership, Literacy
Education
Radford University
jjones292@radford.edu

Elizabeth H. Jones
Visiting Assistant Professor
Department of Management and International Business
Loyola University Maryland
ehjones@loyola.edu

Fredricka F. Joyner Ph.D.
Associate Professor of Business Administration and
Organizational Behavior
School of Business and Economics
Indiana University East
fjoyner@iue.edu

Linda M. Kalbach PhD
Assistant Professor
Education
Doane College
linda.kalbach@doane.edu

Ronald E. Kates PhD
Professor of English
English
Middle Tennessee State University
rkates@mtsu.edu

Patricia Proudfoot Kelly EdD
Professor Emerita
Center for Research and Development
     in International Education
Virginia Polytechnic Institute and State University
kellyp@vt.edu

Laura J. Khoury
Associate Professor
Arab Studies Quarterly B.R Editor
Sociology and Anthropology Department
University of Wisconsin-Parkside
khoury@uwp.edu

Daniel B. King
Department of Chemistry
Drexel University
daniel.king@drexel.edu

Nancy King PhD
Professor Emeritus
University Honors Program
University of Delaware
Nancy@NancyKingStories.com

Tatiana A. Kolovou
Senior Lecturer, Business Communications
Kelley School of Business
Indiana University Bloomington
tatianak@indiana.edu

Paul Kriese PhD
Associate Professor
Politics
IU East
pkriese@indiana.edu

Joan Lafuze
Biology
IU East
jlafuze@indiana.edu

Angela Lamson PhD, LMFT, CLFE
Associate Professor
Child Development and Family Relations
East Carolina University
lamsona@ecu.edu

Darcy Lear
Lecturer and Coordinator of the minor
     program in Spanish for the Professions
Department of Romance Languages
University of North Carolina - Chapel Hill
lear@email.unc.edu

Kathryn S. Lee Ph.D.
Associate Professor
Curriculum & Instruction
Texas State University - San Marcos
KL10@txstate.edu

Robin Lightner Ph.D.
Associate Professor of Psychology
Director of Learning and Teaching Center
Raymond Walters College
University of Cincinnati
Robin.lightner@uc.edu

Melody Aye Loya MSSW, PhD
Assistant Professor of Social Work
Field Coordinator
Department of Psychology, Sociology, and Social Work
West Texas A&M University
mloya@mail.wtamu.edu

Emma T. Lucas-Darby PhD, MSW, LSW, NCGC
Professor, Department of Social Work
Department of Social Work
Carlow University
etlucas-darby@carlow.edu

Johnelle Luciani RSM, MSW, PhD
Chair and Professor of Social Work
Social Work
Salve Regina University
lucianij@salve.edu

Elaine M. Maccio PhD, LCSW
Assistant Professor
School of Social Work
Louisiana State University
emaccio@lsu.edu

Martin MacDowell DrPH
National Center for Rural Health Professions
University of Illinois College of Medicine
mmacd@uic.edu

Mary Mahan-Deatherage
Director of Public Relations
Marketing and Public Relations
Katherine Shaw Bethea Hospital
mdeatherage@ksbhospital.com

Elizabeth Maier Ph.D.
Assistant Professor
Department of Justice Studies and Sociology
Norwich University
emaier@norwich.edu

Mark Malaby
Assistant Professor of Social Foundations of Education/
Multicultural Education
Education
Ball State University
mmalaby@bsu.edu

David J. Malik, PhD
Chancellor's Professor of Chemistry
Indiana University Purdue University Indianapolis
Executive Vice Chancellor of Academic Affairs
Indiana University Northwest
dmalik@iupui.edu

Dina Mansour-Cole PhD
Associate Professor of Organizational Leadership
Organizational Leadership
Indiana University Purdue University Fort Wayne
mansour@ipfw.edu

Nancy B. Marthakis D.O.
Assistant Professor
Biology
Purdue University North Central
nmarthakis@pnc.edu

E. Angeles Martinez-Mier D.D.S., M.S.D., Ph.D.
Associate Professor
Director, OHRI Fluoride Research Program
Indiana University School of Dentistry; Department of
Preventive and Community Dentistry
IUPUI
esmartin@iupui.edu

Kevin L. McElmurry
Indiana University Northwest
kmcelmur@iun.edu

Donna McIntosh MSW
Social Work Program
Siena College
McIntosh@siena.edu

Corinna McLeod Ph.D.
Associate Professor of English
English
Grand Valley State University
mcleodc@gvsu.edu

Gwendolyn Mettetal PhD
Professor of Psychology and Education
Psychology and Education
IU South Bend
gmetteta@iusb.edu

Monique Mironesco
Assistant Professor, Political Science
Social Sciences Division
University of Hawai'i, West O'ahu
mironesc@hawaii.edu

Jean Mistele
Mathematics and Statistics Instructor
Department of Mathematics and Statistics
Radford University
jmistele@radford.edu

Nate Mitchell
Assistant Professor
Director of Health Psychology Emphasis Area
Psychology
Spalding University
nmitchell01@spalding.edu

Verona Mitchell-Agbemadi
Director
Bethel University/Frogtown-Summit
    U. Community Partnership
v-mitchell-agbemadi@bethel.edu

Catherine Mobley
Associate Professor
Department of Sociology and Anthropology
Clemson University
camoble@exchange.clemson.edu

Brenda Moore
Assistant Professor and Department Head
Department of Social Work
Texas A&M - Commerce
Brenda_Moore@tamu-commerce.edu

Dave Morgan Ph.D.
Professor
Director, Undergraduate Psychology
Psychology
Spalding University
DMorgan@spalding.edu

Robin K. Morgan, PhD
Professor of Psychology
Department of Psychology
Indiana University Southeast
rmorgan@ius.edu

Charlie Morris
Distance Education and Web Coordinator
CNR Dean's Office
Information and Instructional Technology Services
North Carolina State University
charlie_morris@ncsu.edu

Michael Morrone
Kelley School of Business
IU Bloomington
mmorrone@indiana.edu

Earl F. Mulderink III, PhD
Professor of History
SUU Faculty Coordinator of Civic Engagement
History
Southern Utah University
mulderink@suu.edu

Roger Munger Ph.D.
Professor of English
English
Boise State University
rmunger@boisestate.edu

Nancy J. Nelson PhD
Director, Africana Education Program
Africana Education Program
Eastern Washington University
ayonelson@gmail.com

Marianne Niedzlek-Feaver
Associate Professor
Biology
North Carolina State University
mnfeaver@ncsu.edu

Gregor Novak, PhD
Professor Emeritus
Department of Physics
Indiana University Purdue University Indianapolis
gnovak@iupui.edu

Randall E. Osborne PhD
Professor
Psychology
Texas State University - San Marcos
ro10@txstate.edu

Jacqueline K. Owens PhD, RN, COHN-S
Dwight Schar College of Nursing
Ashland University
jowens2@ashland.edu

David Pace
Professor
History Department
IU Bloomington
dpace@indiana.edu

Pilar Pacheco
Assistant Director
Center for Community Engagement
California State University Channel Islands
pilar.pacheco@csuci.edu

Lance Palmer
Assistant Professor
Houseing and Consumer Economics
University of Georgia
lpalmer@fcs.uga.edu

Ju Park Ph.D.
Assistant Professor of Instructional Technology
School of Education
Indiana University Northwest
park49@iun.edu

Alan Penczek
Adjunct Professor of Philosophy
Department of Philosophy
Stevenson University
apenczek@stevenson.edu

Laurie F. Peters Ph.D., RN
Professor/Dean, School of Health Sciences
Health Sciences
Ivy Tech Community College, Kokomo
lpeters@ivytech.edu

Grace Pinhal-Enfield Ph.D.
Adjunct Instructor
Department of Cell Bio and Molecular Med
UMDNJ - New Jersey Medical School
pinhalgr@umdnj.edu

Gary Pinkston
Professor of Eduational Technology
School of Education
IU Southeast
gpinksto@ius.edu

Claudia M. Reder PhD
Lecturer
English
California State University Channel Islands
claudia.reder@csuci.edu

Barbara Rich
Associate Professor
BSW Program Coordinator
School of Social Work
University of Southern Maine
rich@usm.maine.edu

Julie Richards MSW, LICSW
Undergraduate Program Coordinator and Senior Lecturer
Department of Social Work
University of Vermont
julie.richards@uvm.edu

Susan R. Ridout
Professor of Literacy Education
School of Education
IU Southeast
sridout@ius.edu

Jane Riehl
Coordinator of Field Placements
School of Education
IU Southeast
jriehl@ius.edu

Janice G. Rienerth PhD
Professor of Sociology
Department of Sociology and Social Work
Appalachian State University
rienerthjg@appstate.edu

Kathy Ritchie PhD
Associate Professor
Department of Psychology
IU South Bend
kritchie@iusb.edu

Diane Robinson BS, BA
Community Health Educator
Piedmont Health Services and Sickle Cell Agency
drobinson@piedmonthealthservices.org

Donald A. Rodriguez PhD
Associate Professor and Program Chair
Environmental Science and Resource Management
California State University Channel Islands
donald.rodriguez@csuci.edu

Ingrid Rogers PhD
Emerita Professor of Modern Languages
Department of Modern Languages
Manchester College
ingridnrogers@gmail.com

Chad Rohrbacher
Assistant Professor
English
North Carolina Agriculture and
    Technology State University
cmrohrba@nat.edu or c.rohrbacher@gmail.com

Helen Rosenberg
Associate Professor
Sociology and Anthropology Department
University of Wisconsin-Parkside
Helen.Rosenberg@uwp.edu

Pete Sanderson PhD
Professor of Computer Science
Mathematical Sciences Department
Otterbein College
Psanderson@otterbein.edu

David M. Sarcone PhD
Associate Professor
International Business and Management
Dickinson College
sarconed@dickinson.edu

Barbara H. Schaffner PhD, CNP
Professor
Otterbein University
bschaffner@otterbein.edu

Carolyn Schult PhD
Associate Professor and Chair
Department of Psychology
IU South Bend
cschult@iusb.edu

R.B. Schultz Ph.D., C.P.G.
Associate Professor, Geosciences and GIS
Coordinator, GIS Certificate Program
Department of Geography and Geosciences
Elmhurst College
richs@elmhurst.edu

Jeremy Schwartz PhD
Assistant Professor
Department of Economics
Loyola University Maryland
jsschwartzl@loyola.edu

Debbie Schweitzer
School Technology Coordinator
Technology
Phoenix School of Discovery
debbie.schweitzer@jefferson.kyschools.us

Charles Scott
Professor
Department of Economics
Loyola University Maryland
cscott@loyola.edu

Scott Sernau
Sociology
IU South Bend
ssernau@iusb.edu

Morteza Shafii-Mousavi PhD
Professor of Mathematics
Mathematics
IU South Bend
mshafii@iusb.edu

Suzi Shapiro
Assistant Professor of Psychology
Humanities and Social Science
IU East
sjshapir@indiana.edu

Dustin Shell
Instructional Technology Analyst
Center for Academic Technologies &
    Educational Resources (CATER)
University of Cincinnati College of Nursing
Dustin.Shell@uc.edu

Erin Sills
Department of Forestry and Environmental Resources
North Carolina State University
sills@ncsu.edu

Julien Simon
Assistant Professor
World Languages and Cultures
Indiana University East
jjsimon@iue.edu

Thomas J. Smith PhD
Assistant Professor
Department of Curriculum and Instruction,
    School of Education
North Carolina Agricultural and Technical State University
smithtg@ncat.edu

Scott Smithson PhD
Associate Professor of Communication
Department Chair
Communication
Purdue North Central
ssmithson@pnc.edu

Armando E. Soto-Rojas
Assistant Professor
Indiana University School of Dentistry; Department
    of Preventive and Community Dentistry
IUPUI
arsoto@iupui.edu

Firat Soylu
Education
Indiana University
fsoylu@indiana.edu

Caile E. Spear
Associate Professor
Kinesiology/COE
Boise State University
cspear@boisestate.edu

Laura Jacobsen Spielman
Assistant Professor, Mathematics Education
Department of Mathematics and Statistics
Radford University
lspielman@radford.edu

Bruce Spitzer
Assistant Professor of Instructional Technology
Education
IU South Bend
baspitze@iusb.edu

David S. Stein PhD
Associate Professor
Workforce Development and Education
Ohio State University
stein.1@osu.edu

Nancy Francisco Stewart PhD
Associate Professor
Department of Sociology and Social Work
Jacksonville State University
nfstewar@jsu.edu

Kyle Andrew Sturgeon
Program Director, Instructor
Architecture
Boston Architectural College
sturgeon.kyle@gmail.com

Samantha Sturman
Senior, Writing Emphasis
Department of English
Boise State University
samanthasturman@gmail.com

Margaret-Mary Sulentic Dowell
Assistant Professor, Reading Education
Department of Educational Theory, Policy & Practice
College of Education
Louisiana State University
sdowell@lsu.edu

Barbara A. Sylvia MSW, PhD
Professor
Social Work
Salve Regina University
sylviab@salve.edu

Laura Talcott
Senior Lecturer and Psychology Laboratory Coordinator
Department of Psychology
IU South Bend
ltalcott@iusb.edu

Mark Urtel
Assistant Professor
Physical Education
IUPUI
murtel1@iupui.edu

Annemarie Vaccaro Ph.D.
Assistant Professor
College Student Personnel Program
University of Rhode Island
avaccaro@uri.edu

James M. VanderVeen PhD
Assistant Professor
Department of Sociology and Anthropology
IU South Bend
jmvander@iusb.edu

Nagaswami S. Vasan
Department of Cell Bio and Molecular Med
UMDNJ - New Jersey Medical School
vasanns@umdnj.edu

Marjorie Vogt PhD, DNP, CNP, CNE
Professor
Director of DNP/NP Programs
Otterbein University
mvogt@otterbein.edu

Ken Vollmar
Professor
Computer Science Department
Missouri State University
KenVollmar@missouristate.edu

Constance E. Wanstreet PhD
Adjunct Assistant Professor
Editor, Longaberger Alumni House
College of Education and Human Ecology
Ohio State University
wanstreet.2@osu.edu

Brian A. Warner
Applications Analyst
University of Cincinnati College of Nursing
brian.warner@uc.edu

Nataki S. Watson
Graduate Student
Counseling, School of Education
North Carolina Agricultural and Technical State University
nkwatson@ncat.edu

Madonna Weese Extension Specialist 4-H Youth
Development
State 4-H Office
University of Illinois Urbana Champaign
mweese@illinois.edu

Gretchen Wehrle PhD
Chair, Psychology and Sociology Department
Associate Director for Faculty Development,
    Dorothy Stang Center
Psychology and Sociology Department
Notre Dame de Namur University
gwehrle@ndnu.edu

Worth Weller
Continuing Lecturer
Department of English and Linguistics and
    Division of Continuing Studies
Indiana - Purdue University Fort Wayne
wellerw@ipfw.edu

Joshua W. Wells
Informatics
IU South Bend
jowells@iusb.edu

Steve Willis PhD
Associate Professor of Art Education
Department of Art and Design
Missouri State University
SteveWillis@missouristate.edu

Andi Witczak
Director
Center for Service Learning
University of Kansas
awitczak@ku.edu

DeDe Wohlfarth Psy.D.
Professor
Director, Child, Adolescent, and Family Emphasis Area
Psychology
Spalding University
dwohlfarth@spalding.edu

Liz Wolvaardt
Faculty of Health Sciences
Health Sciences
University of Pretoria
liz.wolvaardt@up.ac.za

Frank Wray Ph.D.
Professor of Biology
Biology
Raymond Walters College; University of Cincinnati
wrayfp@ucmail.uc.edu

Amy Zink
Senior Lecturer
Spanish; Department of Modern Languages
IU Southeast
azink01@ius.edu

INDEX